RECLAIMING THE *Past*

RECLAIMING THE *Past*

LANDMARKS

OF

WOMEN'S

HISTORY

Edited by Page Putnam Miller

INDIANA
UNIVERSITY
PRESS
BLOOMINGTON AND INDIANAPOLIS

The paper used in this publication meets the minimum requirements of American National Standard for Information Sciences—Permanence of Paper for Printed Library Materials, ANSI Z39.48-1984. ∞™

Manufactured in the United States of America

Library of Congress Cataloging-in-Publication Data

Reclaiming the past : landmarks of women's history / edited by Page
　　Putnam Miller.
　　　　p.　cm.
　　Includes bibliographical references and index.
　　ISBN 0-253-33842-5 (cl)
　　　　1. Historic sites—United States.　　2. Women—United States—
　　History.　　I. Miller, Page Putnam,　date.
　　E159.R42　1992
　　973'.082—dc20　　　　　　　　　　　　　　　　　　　　　　91-46604

1　2　3　4　5　　96　95　94　93　92

CONTENTS

ILLUSTRATIONS

1 ◆ Landmarks of Women's History

PAGE PUTNAM MILLER

Historic buildings can evoke powerful images, eliciting new insights and jarring old memories. Historic resources physically link us to our past, stimulating our imagination and assisting us in better understanding and appreciating the past. When tangible remains exist, they complement the written documents and offer the possibility of asking different questions and seeing the past from a new vantage point. From studying houses, schools, workplaces, and neighborhoods one can gain understanding about the probable interaction of people within the structure, about the pace, values, and activity of the inhabitants, and about the use of space. Buildings, along with their technological and domestic artifacts, reflect the behavior patterns of the lives of the people who inhabited them.

Research by the National Park Service (NPS), for example, on the thirty-six-room house built by Clara Barton helps to illuminate the complex character of this remarkable woman. Clara Barton, who worked against great odds to organize a successful medical supply operation during the Civil War and who later led the effort to establish the American Red Cross, is frequently presented as a wealthy Victorian woman who personified the traditional feminine virtue of compassion. According to Sandy Weber, a historian with the National Park Service, when the Clara Barton Historic Site in Glen Echo, Maryland, first opened, it "was furnished in a generic Victorian style, with velvet-upholstered parlor sets and knickknacks scattered about on marble-topped tables." Extensive NPS research, however, revealed that the house had never been intended as a residence but was to be a warehouse for Red Cross relief supplies. Always frugal, Barton decided in 1897 to move into the building and make it her supply center, her headquarters, and her home. With the historic structure study

Clara Barton National Historic Site, Glen Echo,
Maryland, 1970. Victorian furnishings originally
displayed when the site first opened. (Photograph
courtesy of National Park Service)

Clara Barton National Historic Site, Glen Echo, Maryland. Main Hall of the
Clara Barton House as reinterpreted by the National Park Service.
(Photograph courtesy of National Park Service)

completed, the NPS made an "abrupt shift from a cozy Victorian residence to a rather barren, barn-like structure." Barton's practicality, lack of ostentation, and inventiveness became apparent. As Weber notes, it was no longer possible to mask her eccentricities behind a genteel Victorian facade, which had done injustice to her accomplishments and her extraordinary character.[1]

The sense of place is equally as important as the research potential of these tangible resources. In preserving battlefields there is often reference to the "hallowed ground" and to the need that many people have to tread the ground, to see the past in the mind's eye, and to sense the historical moment.[2] In the tradition of the battlefields that commemorate the lives of those who died there, one site in women's history that merits this kind of recognition is the building that housed the Triangle Shirtwaist Factory in New York City. On March 25, 1911, almost one-third of the five hundred workers, mostly young women working in crowded upper floors among noisy machines dripping oil, flammable lint in the air, and locked doors, died trying to escape a fire. Public outrage over this fire was the catalyst for pioneering legislation to promote safer working conditions. Today this building, which was restored after the fire and subsequently given to New York University, has been turned into classrooms. But this is a significant place; it is "hallowed ground" for those who wish to recall women's past and particularly for members of the International Ladies Garment Workers Union who meet annually outside the building to recall that day when many young women perished in flames or died after jumping from ninth-story windows.[3]

Sarah Orne Jewett, an American author whose own home now sheds light on her writings, was a great admirer of the Bronte sisters. After visiting their home in England she wrote, "Nothing you ever read about them can make you know them until you go there." Jewett added, "Nevermind people who tell you there is nothing to see in the place where people lived who interest you. You always find something of what made them the souls they were, and at any rate you see their sky and their earth."[4]

There are, however, few historic buildings in the United States open to the public with interpretive programs that focus primarily on women's past. If Americans had to rely on existing historic sites for their understanding of women's history, a very limited and distorted picture would emerge. About fifty historic sites, mostly house museums, have as their primary mission the preservation of structures and the development of interpretive programs about women, with most specializing in the life of a particular woman.[5]

While almost one-third of the public historic sites associated primarily with women are operated by local, state, or federal agencies, the majority have evolved from the efforts of nonprofit organizations and foundations seeking to commemorate their leaders or to preserve the memory of a particular individual. For example, the Woman's Christian Temperance Union and the Girl Scouts of America support historic house museums for their founders. And foundations and associations such as the Rachel Carson Foundation, the

Louisa May Alcott Memorial Association, and the Mamie D. Eisenhower Foundation foster the preservation of a historic building associated with the life of the woman they wish to remember and to commemorate.

Among the approximately fifty women's history sites with public programming, there are a number of multiple historic museums for certain women. Six separate house museums preserve structures and provide interpretive programs about Mary Baker Eddy, the founder of the Church of Christ, Scientist. There are also two separate historic sites for Harriet Beecher Stowe, the author of *Uncle Tom's Cabin*; author Pearl Buck; Laura Ingles Wilder, the widely read author of children's books; the temperance leader Carry A. Nation; and for Gene Stratton-Porter, the Indiana naturalist, photographer, and writer.

The first unit of the National Park System associated primarily with women was the Clara Barton National Historic Site, authorized by Congress in 1974. In 1977 Congress authorized the establishment of the Eleanor Roosevelt National Historic Site at Hyde Park, New York. The Richmond, Virginia, home of Maggie L. Walker, the first woman banker, became a unit of the National Park Service in 1978. In 1980, Congress also authorized the Women's Rights National Historical Park in Seneca Falls, New York, which preserves the history of the early women's rights movement and includes the home of Elizabeth Cady Stanton and the Wesleyan Chapel where the first women's rights convention was held in 1848. Among the historic sites focusing on women, the Women's Rights National Historical Park is unique in that it brings together a cluster of houses and meeting places to interpret a major movement in American social history.

Two other sites that are not owned or administered by the National Park Service, but which are "affiliated areas," receiving technical assistance and some funding from the National Park Service, are the Mary McLeod Bethune Council House and the Sewall-Belmont House, both located in Washington, D.C. The Bethune House deals not only with the work of this important African American educator but also with the reform work of African American women's organizations. The Sewall-Belmont House was the headquarters for the National Woman's Party, which played a key role in the decade preceding the passage of the suffrage amendment.

State governments operate about a half dozen of the women's history sites offering interpretive programs. These include the Prudence Crandall House in Canterbury, Connecticut, where Crandall opened the first academy for African American girls, and the home of the author Marjorie Kinnan Rawlings in Florida. The Nebraska State Historical Society administers in Red Cloud the Willa Cather Historical Center, which includes a museum and six properties. One is Cather's childhood home and another is the Pavelka farmstead, which served as the setting for her novel *My Antonia*.

Most of the approximately fifty sites that focus primarily on women are historic house museums, the most predominate form of history museum in the United States.[6] While we can learn much about individuals from the houses in which they lived, there is a concerted effort today also to develop historic sites that were workplaces and meeting places. Among the existing women's history sites that are not houses are the Wesleyan Chapel, where the first women's rights meeting in this country took place; the oldest extant kindergarten, located in Watertown, Wisconsin, and founded by Margarethe Schurz; and the Rika roadhouse, where Erika Wallen, known as Rika, ran a shelter for travelers on the old Richardson Highway in Alaska.

Many historic properties that do not concentrate primarily on women do include women as part of their educational and interpretive programs. For example in "Beyond John Wayne: Using Historic Sites to Interpret Western Women's History," Heather Huyck notes how Fort Laramie illustrates several significant components of women's history. Many families on their westward trek stopped at Fort Laramie to renew supplies. The famous Whitman missionary party, which included Narcissa Whitman and Eliza Spalding, stopped there. But for many women, such as Mrs. Collins who ran a cooperative officers' mess, the laundresses, and the officers' wives, Fort Laramie was home. The history of women's experiences and struggles at historic forts reveals that women lived both traditional and nontraditional lives, adapting to and helping to shape the frontier.[7]

Patricia West, a former member of the staff at the Martin Van Buren National Historic Site in Kinderhook, New York, has written in *The Museum Studies Journal* about the efforts to bring to life not only Van Buren's life but also the lives of the female members of his family and their young Irish house servants. Some may argue, West states, that house servants are only peripheral to the central purpose of commemorating Van Buren. But no one group, even the rich and powerful, can be correctly interpreted in isolation. Van Buren's life-style would have been impossible without inexpensive domestic servants. West urges that in interpreting sites of famous men that "we explore the inevitable interrelationship between, for example, an Irish servant woman and an ex-president." Not only is the interpretation more accurate and less prone to aggrandizement, but West insightfully claims that a deeper sense of historic context and community emerges as a result.[8]

Lowell National Historic Park in Lowell, Massachusetts, although not primarily about women, is an important site for understanding women's past. As the nation's first industrial city, Lowell pioneered in developing a textile manufacturing complex. The 1977 National Historic Landmarks nomination form focused almost exclusively on the mills, machine shops, and canals and locks that provided the necessary power source for converting raw cotton into finished cloth. Yet, as the subsequent study of women's history has emphasized, young unmarried women from rural New England operated the looms and provided the critical skilled labor force for the textile companies. In 1978 a major part of the Lowell Locks and Canals Historic Landmark District became a unit of the National Park Service. Today the research and interpretive program of Lowell includes a strong component on women's history. Lowell National Historic Park brings to life the work, supervision, and housing of the Lowell Mill Girls, as they were called, and plays an important role in recalling women's entry into the industrial work force.

The recent trend to give increased attention to the women associated with historic sites exists at state and local sites as well as national historic parks. At the Hearst San Simeon State Historic Park in California, for example, the emphasis is on the publishing tycoon William Randolph Hearst. However this state park also gives attention to Julia Morgan, the Hearst Castle architect, who spent twenty years designing and planning the roads, docks, and buildings and incorporating sections of dismantled European palaces and cathedrals into the castle. Many of the Shaker historic sites across the country highlight Ann Lee, the sect's founder, and the role of women in the Shaker community. At a local level, the Hempsted House, in New London, Connecticut, which was the residence from 1678 to 1937 of ten generations of one family, examines both the lives of the female as well as the male family members. Unfortunately many historic site curators feel that they have only a brief amount of time to convey much information to the public about the primary figures and events associated with a property and do not have time to undertake new research about women or to incorporate into their interpretive programs, what they consider, women's marginal roles.[9]

One historic house museum that has made the successful transition to incorporate new research and shift its male-focused interpretive program to a female focus is the Ximenez-Fatio House in St. Augustine, Florida. Owned by the National Society of Colonial Dames, this house was built in 1798 by a wealthy Spanish citizen and was first used to interpret the last years of the Spanish occupation and the life of Andres Ximenez. John A. Herbst examined how new research has revealed that in 1825 the building became a guest house, and for the next fifty years, a succession of respectable women who had fallen on hard times financially owned and operated it. In the early nineteenth century, operating a guest house was one of the few socially acceptable occupations for middle- and upper-class women. Besides drawing attention to significant aspects of women's history, the extensive new research documented that Florida received its first wave of tourists in the 1820s. "Armed with current research based on sound documentary evidence," Herbst described how "the local Colonial Dames leadership set in motion a plan for refocusing the interpretation to reflect the building's operation as a hotel and to illuminate the themes of women's history and tourism."[10]

Yet, considering the many historic sites in this country, the number devoted to women's past is exceedingly small. Only a meager beginning has been made in using buildings to enrich Americans' understanding of women's past. However, before more historic sites, well preserved and interpreted, are likely to appear, there must be concerted efforts to identify and research properties associated with women. Background work of surveys and studies of particular structures must precede efforts to develop public educational programs.

This volume builds on a small beginning and attempts to challenge two rapidly expanding fields—historic preservation and women's history—to work together in promoting a more comprehensive understanding of women's past. Collaborative efforts between preservationists and historians, in cases when it does occur, prove mutually beneficial. Attention to historic structures assists historians in grasping some of the spirit, the passions, and the life force that was a part of specific places. A greater exposure to historical research also enables preservationists to understand the historical context and significance of the events that took place in particular buildings. In *The Past Is a Foreign Country* David Lowenthal makes the case that tangible resources from the past are an essential bridge between then and now. "A past lacking tangible relics," he writes "seems too tenuous to be credible."[11] An appreciation of the historical significance of buildings is as important for the preservationist as for the historian.

Material culture, the study of the artifacts of a culture, with buildings being the most prominent artifacts, and its related field, historic preservation, have in the last twenty-five years demonstrated that tangible, three-dimensional, historic objects and structures can be touchstones for enriching our understanding of the past. Brooke Hindle, senior historian at the Smithsonian Institution's National Museum of American History, noted in his presidential address at the 1982 annual meeting of the Society of Historians of Technology that historians are becoming more alert to the potential of using three-dimensional resources. "To the historian," he observed "there can be no more entrancing promise than new sources that can provide truer historical insights, because in our soberer moments, we all know that what we call 'history' is mostly conjecture based on fragmentary evidence."[12] The head of the American Studies department at Notre Dame, Thomas J. Schlereth, stresses that "objects can provide us with numerous and valuable insights into the past." He warns that "to neglect such data in any modern historical inquiry is to overlook a significant body of research evidence."[13]

Indeed, some scholars have begun to use structures as research documents. Buildings may be examined from many viewpoints and reflect social function, technological development, aesthetic taste, and economic factors.[14] Kathleen Neils Conzen has proposed, for example, that an examination of the built environment could shed light on the extent to which leisure-time and consumption activities, as opposed to the workplace alone, defined significant social patterns.[15] But by and large the research potential of structures has been utilized to a lesser extent than objects, such as tools, furniture, pots, and toys.

Despite this unrealized research potential, recent decades have witnessed a significant growth in an appreciation for tangible resources. In 1966 the National Historic Preservation Act was passed, greatly strengthening federal preservation policy. In the following decade several new scholarly journals appeared that specialized in research using tangible resources. Colleges and universities are offering many new courses and programs in the fields of material culture and historic preservation. Edith Mayo, curator at the National Museum of American History of the Smithsonian Institution, has noted that "the use of objects as source materials for scholarship has been increasingly legitimatized by the growth of American Studies programs which are now in the forefront in their work with objects."[16] All of these developments combined have given a strong impetus in recent decades to the study of three-dimensional objects and structures.[17]

At the same time in the 1960s that the historic preservation movement was gaining recognition and support, the rejuvenated women's movement spawned an array of political and social concerns. Just as the earlier civil rights movement sparked an increased interest in African American history, the women's movement focused attention on the previously neglected field of women's history. Marjorie Lightman, who served for many years as the executive director of the Institute for Research in History, noted in Congressional testimony in 1985 that "there is no other single area of research in the humanities that has grown so rapidly, has so widespread a constituency and so significant potential for altering the disciplines," as women's studies.[18] Thousands of courses in women's history are offered each year on college campuses across the country, from community colleges to Ivy League schools. But women's history is no longer just ghettoized into its own sphere, for textbooks and lectures now integrate that scholarship into the larger historical experience.[19] Scholars in the past two decades have also identified a wealth of manuscript and archival sources for the study of women's history. While these sources are often subsumed in collections of fathers or husbands or under record groups or organizations not specifically concerned with women, they have significantly enhanced the study of women's past.[20]

Women's history began with an emphasis on compensatory history, to bring to light women's contributions to American society. Current scholarship on women's history, however, not only shows how women shaped American history but also how American history affected women and affected the definitions of womanhood and manhood. "The compensatory approach to women's history," states Elizabeth H. Pleck, a professor of women's history, "no matter how necessary as a remedy for the invisibility of women and their accomplishments, places too much emphasis on those women whose lives departed most from the typical female experience through activism in public life."[21]

More than 95 percent of the population leave behind no diaries or letters—only their furniture, domestic tools, crafts and houses.[22] Since written records primarily represent the elite of the past, we must rely on methods other than those of traditional history if we wish to understand the ideas, assumptions, and attitudes of most people. Tangible objects and structures allow historians to widen the parameters of historical study to include the day-to-day experiences of working, schooling and child-rearing. As Carroll Smith-Rosenberg, a historian of women's history, has noted, material culture provides social historians, and women's historians especially, a means for shifting the research interest from the public sector to "private places" that is, the household, the bedroom, the nursery, kinship systems, and voluntary associations.[23] Indeed material culture offers a way of achieving the social historian's goal of expanding historical inquiry beyond great men and women to include ordinary people and everyday activities. "In spite of the richness and diversity of the historical record," James Deetz argues, "there are things we want to know that are not to be discovered from it. Simple people doing simple things, the normal, everyday routine of life and how these people thought about it, are not the kinds of things anyone thought worthy of noting."[24] The assumption underlying material culture research is that objects and structures made or modified by humans, consciously or unconsciously, directly or indirectly, reflect the belief patterns of individuals who made, commissioned, purchased, or used them, and by extension, the belief patterns of the larger society of which they were a part.[25]

Yet Thomas J. Schlereth, in his review of current trends in the study of American artifacts, bemoans that material culturalists have only begun to grasp the full applications of the social history perspective and that social historians have remained largely indifferent to material culture scholarship.[26] On the one hand, specialists in material culture have not been known for their analytic rigor or depth, too often content only to describe—a tendency denigrated as "pots and pans" history. On the other hand, historians are usually bound to the written word. They research written documents and write articles and monographs. Seldom do they use artifacts and structures, or even oral histories and photographs, as part of their research design.

If the field of women's history, there are several notable exceptions to the tendency of academic historians to disregard the built environment and structures as viable research documents. Gwendolyn Wright, Dolores Hayden, and Helen Horowitz have studied, respectively, housing designs, domestic space, and the physical fabric of women's colleges to shed light on women's past. In *Building the Dream: A Social History of Housing in America*, Wright has examined thirteen prototype houses, from a Puritan to a 1950s suburban design, to explore the ways in which architecture encourages and protects particular attitudes toward family and social relationships.[27] Hayden, in her seminal book, *The Grand Domestic Revolution*, also emphasizes how house designs and culture affect each other. Her focus is on the feminists of the turn of the century who sought, with few long-term successes, to redesign houses to change the physical and economic context of cooking, cleaning, and the raising of children.[28] Horowitz examines dormitories and academic buildings in *Alma Mater* to gain new insights into both the philosophy of education and the social experiences at women's colleges.[29]

More preservationists and others interested in material culture are also employing social history, and especially women's history, in their work. For example, women's contributions to city building is the subject of Darlene Roth's research on Atlanta. "In every community in America," Roth contends, "there are structures on the landscape which are the result of collective female efforts and testimony to what women's organizations think of their communities and how they perceived their role in them—schools, orphanages, libraries, parks, clinics, gardens, social and recreational centers, monuments, memorials, club houses, headquarters buildings, and similar institutions." These structures, Roth asserts, reveal women as bearers and preservers of culture and founders and administrators of humanitarian organizations. However, in her inventory of sites associated with women in Atlanta, Roth found that none of the philanthropic structures that women built in Atlanta in the period 1880 to 1920 remained intact in their original form and location. What remained was knowledge of the location of the buildings and a general sense of the character of the structures. "The relocation, transformation, and ultimate disappearance of the buildings associated with the early women's charities," Roth explained, "speak eloquently of the fundamental changes which occurred in women's public activities at this time, in Atlanta as elsewhere." The professionalization of social services made the lady philanthropists obsolete. The women who had administered the charity organizations became, as Roth puts it, "mere supports, its gray ladies and fund raisers;" the structures forgotten. But Roth affirms that "if these buildings and structures lack significance as individual architectural statements, they do not lack significance as collective social statements . . . to the fragile viability of separate female institutions."[30]

Aware of the many threats facing the preservation of structures associated with social history, the Wisconsin State Historic Preservation Office in the mid-1980s conceptualized a framework for surveying structures in the state that included a component on women's history. The comprehensive plan highlighted the need to identify properties associated with women's organizations and particularly with women's reform and suffrage activities. Targeting the period from the mid-nineteenth century to the early twentieth century, this cultural resource management plan acknowledged that many sites that should be included in the inventory would remain obscure and "threatened by their virtual lack of identification and appreciation." This situation, the preliminary study explained, resulted from the fact that few women's organizations occupied their own buildings and that "these aspects of social history held little interest for the majority of historians and preservationists."[31] Finally the plan alerted future surveyors that modern changes in approaches to health and human services have meant that historic buildings have been either dramatically altered or abandoned and demolished. Despite the thoughtful development of this inventory strategy, the Wisconsin plan has thus far elicited no specific studies on women's sites.[32]

In 1986 the Public History Program of West Virginia University received a grant from the Humanities Foundation of West Virginia for a project that would identify sites associated with West Virginia women and prepare a brochure that could be used in various convention and visitors' centers in the state.

Completed in 1988, the handsome brochure provides information on twenty-seven sites associated with historically significant West Virginia women and includes a state map to assist those who wish to visit these sites. In preparing a summary report on the project, Barbara J. Howe, the project director and a history professor at West Virginia University, noted that the original goal had been to find a building that could be associated with each woman. This proved an impossibility because so many had been destroyed. Thus in some cases, researchers had to resort to state highway markers and graves. In three instances the brochure notes that "no site has yet been identified." As well as discussing the extreme difficulty in locating information, even on relatively well-known women, Howe expressed disappointment that many identified buildings were in such poor condition they would not generally meet the physical integrity requirements of landmark registering programs.[33]

Darlene Roth's research on Atlanta, the work of the Wisconsin State Historic Preservation Office, and the West Virginia project highlight the dilemmas facing those concerned about the preservation of sites associated with women's history. But the research of Gail Lee Dubrow, who is completing a dissertation titled "Preserving Her Heritage: American Landmarks of Women's History," indicates that diligent surveyors will find resources associated with women's history. In a case study that assessed the possibilities for increasing the public visibility of women's history in Boston, Dubrow surveyed approximately two hundred sites and found dozens of surviving buildings. The most significant of these sites and buildings, she argues, potentially could be organized into a coherent itinerary that would heighten public awareness of women's history through an integrated program of preservation, public art, and public historical interpretation. Dubrow's research suggests the pervasiveness of women's history landmarks in every American city. "Hidden in a Boston alley I discovered the former headquarters of the Boston Women's Trade Union League. Across the street from Copley Square are the one-time offices of the *Woman's Journal* and the Massachusetts Woman Suffrage Association." But she found that local and state preservation offices knew little about these sites.[34] She furthermore surmised that very few would receive landmark status based on architectural significance, since many had been neglected and altered. She concluded that only if special attention is paid to historical significance would many of the sites she located be candidates for an official landmark designation.[35]

The destruction of historic structures, which has so often been the case in women's history, has not prevented Dolores Hayden from commemorating the places associated with Biddy Mason. A former slave and midwife, Mason became one of the first African American women in Los Angeles to purchase land and build a house. She was also the founder of the first predominantly African American church in Los Angeles. The site of Biddy Mason's 1866 homestead is now a parking garage. "But to know that Biddy Mason lived on a specific site in downtown Los Angeles, to visit that place, and to imagine her life and see around us the changes time has wrought would," Hayden asserts, "instill in us a reverence for the human condition."[36] Through a small nonprofit organization, the Power of Place, Hayden has successfully completed the installation of a photomural on the wall of the parking garage where Mason's house once stood. A sequence of images on an eighty-by-eight-foot wall chronicles Mason's life. Maps of an expanding Los Angeles are juxtaposed with Mason's life. The Mason site is one of thirty sites in downtown Los Angeles that the Power of Place has identified for preservation. All thirty are tied to the broad theme of economic activity. One-third of the sites have no structures, one-third are standing but have no official historic designation, and one-third currently have a historic designation but there has been little appreciation of their association with women. Donna Graves, the executive director of the Power of Place, is heading the project to reinterpret the historical significance of the Embassy Auditorium, the first home of the Los Angeles Symphony, which was also the site in women's history of pivotal labor and political rallies and meetings. Through the installation of public art and public historical interpretation, the project hopes to bring to the public the rich association of this building with women's organizations and activities.[37]

Historic structures can be a catalyst for studying and remembering the past. In writing about the National Park Service's role in teaching history, Heather Huyck stresses that "historic sites are both a historical resource in themselves and a means of communicating history." Over one hundred million people visit the historic national parks each year, and untold others visit the over ten thousand historical sites, societies, and museums located throughout the United States. "Here in the incredible diversity of museums and sites," Huyck says "American people learn our history."[38]

Although scholars and nonprofit groups have and will continue to contribute to the preservation of historic sites associated with women's history, federal policy plays a key role. Ary L. Lamme in *American Historic Landscapes* identifies government action as the most effective way of "upholding the rights of Americans to retain their historic landscapes." The complicated task of preserving historic sites involves the skills of a wide range of trained professionals and necessitates, Lamme states, that "preservation leadership should come from both the private and public sectors."[39]

The priorities and interests of scholarly pursuits in women's history and those of federal policymakers have, however, had somewhat different orientations. While much of the recent women's history and material culture research has been on broad social trends and ordinary people, federal programs, to the limited extent to which they do deal with women, have in most cases emphasized the preservation of sites associated with notable women.

The Department of Interior—through the units of the National Park Service, the National Historic Landmark Program, and the National Register of Historic Places—has a mandate to identify and preserve properties of historical significance. The 356 units of the National Park Service are owned and administered by the federal government. National Historic Landmarks (NHL), which in 1990 numbered 1,942, are privately owned and in many cases closed to the public. However, landmark designation does identify a site as nationally significant and helps to focus attention on places of exceptional value. This in turn frequently leads to increased public attention to these sites and in a few cases to their elevation to National Park status. The largest category of historically designated properties in the United States is the National Register of Historic Places, which lists over 55,000 districts, sites, and structures that are significant in American history, architecture, archeology, engineering, and culture. Administered by the National Park Service, the National Register is the official list of the nation's cultural resources worthy of preservation. While NHL designation is restricted to those sites of national significance, the National Register also includes those of local, state, and regional significance.[40]

In analyzing the National Parks and NHLs associated with women, one is immediately struck by the few sites devoted to understanding women's past. Of the 356 units of the National Park System, 60 percent are archeological and historic sites. Yet only four parks focus on women. And of the 1,942 NHLs, less than 2 percent are designated because of their association with women. Over one-fourth of NHLs are designated for architectural significance and approximately one-seventh are associated with America's military past. Despite a rising consciousness resulting from increased familiarity with the expanding field of women's history, the National Park Service and the National Historic Landmarks Program have been very slow in recognizing historic structures associated with women's experiences and contributions.

Gail Lee Dubrow was one of the first scholars to analyze national, state, and local registers to evaluate the status of women's history in the designation of landmarks. In the paper "Preserving Her Heritage: American Landmarks of Women's History," presented at the 1987 annual meeting of the National Council on Public History, Dubrow analyzed the extremely small number of designations that focus on the experiences, struggles, and accomplishments of women. And among the few existing women's history landmarks, she noted that most are located on the eastern seaboard between Maine and Virginia.[41]

Besides the lack of regional balance, Dubrow found few sites that indicated the ethnic diversity of American history. Explicit references to Native American women's presence in California appeared at only one site, and that one presented a distorted view. California Historical Landmark No. 549 in Mendocino County, "Squaw Rock," also known as Lover's Leap, is associated with the legend of a nineteenth-century Native American woman who, holding a great stone, jumped from the precipice onto her faithless lover, who was with another woman. "The problem with the status of women's history landmarks is not limited to an inadequate percentage of designated sites and buildings," states Dubrow, "rather, it extends to the inaccurate and distorted images of women which too frequently appear."[42]

While a long-term goal is to promote additional women's history sites open to the public with sound interpretive programs, one immediate strategy for moving toward this goal is to increase the number of National Historic Landmarks that are associated with women's history. In 1987 the National Park Service History Division staff found that of the 1,942 NHLs, approximately forty were associated with women.[43] Nine of the landmarks commemorate the lives of notable women writers such as Emily Dickinson, Willa Cather, and Harriet Beecher Stowe. Another nine focus on women as educators. Structures associated with leaders of the suffrage movement account for seven of the designations. The homes of Frances Willard and Carry Nation, leaders of the temperance movement, and two of the most famous nineteenth-century settlement houses—Hull House in Chicago and Henry Street Settlement House in New York City—are NHLs. The remaining sites include the homes of Florence Mills, the famous nineteenth-century singer, and Juliette Gordon Low, the founder of Girl Scouts, as well as Constitution Hall of the Daughters of the American Revolution, the Harriet Tubman Home for the Aged, and Rankin Ranch, the home of the first woman to serve in the U.S. Congress. The Sewall-Belmont House, which is now an affiliated area of the National Park Service, and two units of the National Park Service—the Maggie Walker and the Clara Barton sites, are included in the list of NHLs associated with women.

The clustering of sites around subject areas such as writers and leaders of reform movements reflects the emphasis within the NHL program on selecting sites as a part of broad thematic studies. The Rules and Regulations of the Department of Interior specify that potential NHLs are to be identified primarily by means of theme studies or special studies that "provide a contextual framework to evaluate the relative significance of historic properties and determine which properties meet the National Historic Landmarks criteria." The criterion of national significance in the federal guidelines has six categories. Most of those designated because of historical significance fall under the first two categories. The first states that sites must be "associated with events that have made a significant contribution to, and are identified with, or that outstandingly represent, the broad national patterns of United States history and from which an understanding and appreciation of those patterns may be gained." The second criterion pertains to sites associated "importantly with the lives of persons nationally significant in the history of the United States." The regulations also state that only in cases of exceptional importance will properties qualify for designation that have achieved significance within the past fifty years.[44]

The landmark theme studies provide the knowledge base and the bench marks for evaluating historic properties and sites and for weighing the broad parameters provided by the established criteria. In the 1950s the NHL program, which had been established in 1935 by the Historic Sites Act, initiated its first thematic studies. Most of the theme studies concentrated on military and political history and westward expansion—subjects that generally focus on men. Of the approximately fifty theme studies undertaken by the National

Park Service History Division, only three have had more than a minimal representation of women. These were the 1964 study of social and humanitarian movements, which was updated in the 1970s; the 1971 study of American writers; and the African American study conducted in the mid-1970s.

Thirteen of the existing NHLs associated with women represent African American women, most evolving from the African American study. In the early 1970s, as the National Park Service began preparation for the 1976 Bicentennial, the relatively few African American NHLs proved to be an embarrassment.[45] Pressure from a politically powerful coalition of African Americans led the National Park Service to depart from its usual practice of conducting its own Historic Sites Surveys and thematic studies and to award an outside contract to the Afro-American Bicentennial Corporation.[46] Sixty-one new NHL designations resulted from this contract. Almost half of the sites associated with African American women commemorated educators. This accounts for the fact that seven of the nine sites associated with women and education focus on African American women.

Just as outside prodding prompted the National Park Service to address the need to increase the number of NHLs associated with African American history, pressure from the public, the historical community, and Congress led the National Park Service to undertake a special landmark study on women's history. In 1976 Marion Tinling and Linda Ruffner-Russell wrote an article for *Historic Preservation*, the widely circulated magazine of the National Trust for Historic Preservation, in which they called attention to the pitifully few NHLs devoted to women's history. Ironically, they noted, women had been the early instigators of historic preservation, yet the sites that commemorate women's contributions and experiences had been ignored.[47]

A decade later leadership of the Organization of American Historians (OAH) raised the issue of the need for more NHL study on women. In 1985 Joan Hoff, then the executive secretary of the Organization of American Historians, and I, in my capacity as director of the National Coordinating Committee for the Promotion of History (NCC), met with Dennis Galvin, the deputy director of the National Park Service, to discuss the need for a greater representation of women in the NHL designations. While the National Park Service recognized the problem and agreed to work cooperatively with the OAH and NCC on increasing the representation of women, they assigned no resources or staff to the project.[48]

Representative Bruce Vento, the Chair of the House Subcommittee on National Parks and Public Lands which oversees the National Park Service and the federal historic preservation programs, has been in the forefront of noting the scarcity of sites associated with women and urging that increased attention be placed on sites associated with women's experiences and contributions.[49] During a 1988 House of Representatives hearing of the Subcommittee on National Parks and Public Lands, chaired by Representative Vento, committee members discussed the operation of the National Historic Landmark Program and raised questions about the selection and development of landmark theme studies.[50] This led the full committee, the House Committee on Interior and Insular Affairs, to recommend in their comments on the FY '89 budget that "the National Park Service establish an ongoing and substantial cooperative effort with the major professional and scholarly societies to research and publish National Historic Landmark Theme Studies." The Congressional report urged this action because "such theme studies will help direct NPS priorities, provide professional scrutiny and stretch scarce research dollars."[51] After further discussions between representatives of the historical community and the House Interior Appropriations Subcommittee, chaired by Representative Sidney Yates, Interior Appropriations Legislation for FY '89 included modest funding for a study on women's history landmarks.[52]

On February 9, 1989, representatives of the National Park Service, the Organization of American Historians, and the National Coordinating Committee signed a cooperative agreement, this time with fiscal and staff support, to work on a women's history landmark project. The stated objective of the project was "to broaden public support for historic preservation by involving historians and their professional organizations in the study, identification, nomination of, and the dissemination of information about, potential National Historic Landmarks on the role of women in United States history."[53]

It is important to note that this project of identifying sites represents only an initial step toward the final goal of using historic structures to enrich an understanding of women's past. While it is hoped that new federal, state, or private programs may evolve from this effort, which will support additional historic sites associated with women, until such support occurs there will be few public interpretive programs associated with these sites. Yet one should not undervalue the essential role of a survey and the importance of the identification step as a building block for the future.

As a participant in the cooperative women's history landmark project, I can report that considerable progress has been made on preparing nomination forms for the designation of specific sites. The basic goal of the project has been to recognize omissions and to fill in existing gaps in the identification of structures that document and commemorate women's experiences. The project began by developing a data base of over five hundred possible sites for consideration. Lynn Sherr and Jurate Kazickas's *The American Woman's Gazetteer*, published in 1976, and the 1986 encylopedic *Women Remembered: A Guide to Landmarks of Women's History* by Marion Tinling provided a starting point for the project.[54] Both books, organized by states, provide information on many markers, monuments, and sites that would not qualify for NHL designation. However, those two resources are an invaluable resource to anyone interested in sites associated with women. With selected sites from these two books, the project added suggestions from State Historic Preservation Offices, women's history specialists, and other interested historians and preservationists. Notices and requests for suggestions appeared in numerous historical publications. A major effort has been made to identify sites associated not only with famous and exceptional women but also with those more representative of their time and place. Following a careful winnowing process, many historians participated in the preparation of the first group of nomination forms that will soon go to the National Park Service's Advisory Board for consideration of NHL designation.

The twenty-three properties include such structures as Wendover, the building in rural Kentucky that served as the first clinic and the administrative headquarters of the Frontier Nursing Service and the Trades Hall of Nannie Helen Burrough's National Training School for Women and Girls in Washington, D.C., which offered African Americans in the early twentieth century a unique combination of academic, religious, and vocational education.[55] With additional funding provided by Congress in the FY '90 budget, work is currently underway on the nomination of approximately thirty more sites.

In most cases the project has concentrated on the preparation of nomination forms for new NHLs. However for one structure, the Oscar W. Underwood House in Washington, D.C., the project updated information on an existing landmark nomination form which had omitted any reference to its significance in women's history. The 1976 nomination form for this house states as the historical significance of this property that it was the residence from 1914 to 1925 of Oscar W. Underwood, the Democratic leader of the House of Representatives who authored the Underwood-Simmons Tariff, passed in 1913, and who in 1912 was a contender for President. The decision for landmark status never referred to the fact that this building also served from 1924 to 1952 as the home of the Washington College of Law, the first coeducational law school established by women in the United States. Emma Gillett and Ellen Spencer Mussey began the Washington College of Law in 1898 as a response to the discrimination against women at all of the District of Columbia's law schools, with the exception of Howard University. For the next twenty-five years the school used rented and crowded facilities. In 1924 they undertook a major building fund and after much searching purchased 2000 G Street. "Three large classrooms, a kitchen, and a ladies tearoom transformed the old mansion into a school building."[56] Because any history of women's entry into the legal profession would be incomplete without recognition of the role played by the Washington College of Law, it is important that the official NHL designation also include appropriate aspects of women's history.

The general criterion for selection of NHLs is broad, leaving considerable room for varying interpretations. Whether an individual's contributions have national significance, the degree to which a building meets the desired level of integrity, and which site could best represent a national trend or a particular person—all are debatable issues. As the women's history landmarks project has progressed, a number of policy issues concerning the selection of sites have surfaced.

The federal policy embodied in the National Park System and the National

Historic Landmarks Program is aimed primarily at identifying and preserving sites of national significance to assist the American people in remembering and recalling their past. Before a site can be studied to glean the insights that complement the written documents, it must be identified and preserved. With a severe shortage of resources and the professional historians needed to provide the research, the National Park Service in recent years has fallen into somewhat of a holding pattern. For example, whereas there were more than twenty thematic NHL studies completed in the 1960s, fewer than ten were prepared in the 1980s.[57] Inadequate funding is certainly one of the most pressing of the current problems. But because limited funding has reduced the number of sites being studied, one could argue that the current situation requires an even closer examination of the policy issues surrounding the practices and standards for selecting sites for NHL nomination.

Much debate over NHL designations surrounds the historically elitist and architectural orientation of the program. In *Historic Preservation: Curatorial Management of the Built World,* James Marston Fitch notes that until recently almost all preservation programs have been preponderantly upper class and urbane in their emphasis, with a bias toward palaces, castles, cathedrals, and parliaments—the seats of the powerful and famous.[58] The landmark program in the United States is no exception. The large majority of NHLs focus on notable individuals and architecturally substantive buildings designed by architects of recognized status. In *The American Mosaic: Preserving A Nation's Heritage*, Antoinette J. Lee, who is currently a member of the staff of the office of the National Register of Historic Places, explores some of the unresolved issues in the identification of ethnic historic sites. She touches on issues that also affect the selection of women's history sites. One is the criticism from historians of African American and other ethnic historic sites that architectural historians and other preservation professionals are unwilling to designate sites with little pure architectural integrity. "They argue," Lee points out "that sites cannot be evaluated on the same basis as sites associated with the dominant culture."[59] Whereas the great houses of important men identified as NHLs more than twenty years ago frequently had not been significantly altered, properties associated with ethnic and women's history have not fared as well. In reviewing the history of the National Historic Landmarks Program, Barry Mackintosh, a historian with the National Park Service, noted that a number of properties landmarked as part of the 1970s African American project were substandard sites lacking physical integrity and having insufficient association between the sites and the subjects and events they were to commemorate. Although prior to the African American project, he recognizes that "virtually no landmarks honoring black Americans then existed," he concludes that the addition of sixty-one African American landmarks "was not reached without tension among the parties involved and damage to the integrity of the landmarks program."[60]

The NHL proclivity for grand houses over workplaces that in many cases

Villa Lewaro, Irvington, New York. Home built by Vertner Woodson Tandy
for Madame C. J. Walker. (Photograph by Myrna Harris, courtesy of
National Park Service)

have been altered and do not have the same level of physical integrity is illus-
trated by the selection of a site for Madame C. J. Walker. Founder of the
Walker cosmetology products, one of the most successful African American
businesses in the United States in the early twentieth century, Walker was the
first American woman to become a millionaire. With her wealth she built a palatial country home and began plans for an impressive headquarters building.
The headquarters building in Indianapolis was completed after Walker's death,
by her daughter A'Lelia Walker, who followed her mother as president of the
company. In 1975 Walker's country home, Villa Lewaro, in Westchester
County, New York, designed by the noted African American architect Vertner
Woodson Tandy, received NHL designation. But it is the company's headquarters building, which housed the Walker Manufacturing Company, the Walker
Beauty Shop, a pharmacy, and various other shops, as well as the Walker
Theater—supporting African American artists and offering entertainment to
those excluded by segregation from most movies and theaters—that sheds the
most light on Walker's business skills, her insights into marketing, and her philanthropic values.

The emphasis on the notable individuals and events of national significance

Madame C. J. Walker Building, Indianapolis, Indiana. Headquarters of the
Walker Manufacturing Company. (Photograph courtesy of Madame C. J. Walker
Urban Life Center)

and the stress on a high level of physical integrity of structures has made it difficult to move beyond compensatory history, which concentrates on the
achievements of exceptional women. Although there is a provision for sites associated with broad national patterns of United States history (the designation
of a one-room schoolhouse, for example, would involve an in-depth study of
all one-room schoolhouses in the country to identify the one which would be
most representative), with limited resources, the extensive surveys needed to
identify representative sites are an impossibility.

Efforts to include more sites associated with places of work are com-
pounded by the problems of meeting high standards of architectural integrity.
Social and technological changes have altered the places where people worked
more than fifty years ago. Even for an elite structure such as the observatory at
Vassar built for Maria Mitchell, the staff of the National Park Service raised
questions about the integrity of the building because the telescope, now in the
Smithsonian, had been removed.[61]

The desire to keep historic structures frozen in time and set apart from the
contemporary environment is, David Lowenthal suggests, neither possible nor
desirable. "We should not deceive ourselves," he writes, by thinking "that we

can keep the past stable and segregated." Stability and change are both essential factors of life. Lowenthal reminds us that "nothing ever made has been left untouched, nothing ever known remains immutable; yet these facts should not distress but emancipate us." The primary issue for historic preservation policy should be toward developing strategies that will enable people to understand and appreciate their links to the past and should be less directed toward the fight to keep old buildings unchanged. "Every relic," Lowenthal asserts, "is a testament not only to its initiators but to its inheritors, not only to the spirit of the past but to the perspectives of the present." We cannot function without familiar environments and links with the recognizable past. But if we recognize that old structures are continually refashioned, then, Lowenthal concludes, we will "be less inhibited by the past, less frustrated by a fruitless quest for sacrosanct originals."[62] The search for pristine originals of women's past is frustrating and near impossible, yet the need for identifying and landmarking sites that can connect us to women's struggles, experiences, and accomplishments is great.

The small number of sites identified as significant in women's history and the even fewer sites with public programming have stimulated the preparation of this volume. The intent of this collection of essays is to focus attention on historic structures associated with women's history and to provide the contextual framework for making judgments about sites that are of national significance.

A key component in the process of selecting specific sites for nomination as NHLs is the preparation of thematic studies. In weighing decisions about which sites should be nominated for landmark status, the essays included in this volume provided project researchers with the broad historical background needed in making judgments about what is of national significance. For example, of the more than five hundred sites in the project's data base there are numerous women's schools and colleges. Most, however, had primarily local or regional significance. The essay on "Women and Education" provided an overview and major benchmarks in the national development of women's education. This facilitated the evaluation of historic properties and sites for their possible nomination to landmark status.

When funding for the NHL program was more plentiful in the 1960s and 1970s, published volumes accompanied the completion of National Historic Landmark theme studies.[63] Designed to inform the general public about the preservation movement, the volumes in that series reached a wide audience with total sales of more than a quarter of a million copies. *Soldier and Brave*, a study of the military-Indian affairs in the Trans-Mississippi West, was the first volume published in the series. Ray Allen Billington, a prominent Western historian, wrote the introduction, and the staff of the NPS historical office prepared the site descriptions. The eleven volumes published prior to the discontinuance of the publications program in 1978 all followed a similar format, with a beginning narrative of historical background of approximately one hundred pages and then brief one- or two-paragraph descriptions of the specific sites, which included National Park units and National Historic Landmarks as well as sites considered but not recommended for NHL status. The termination of the NHL publications changed the format of the NHL thematic studies. The NPS replaced the extensive historical background essay written by a noted historian with a very short introduction, sometimes only two or three pages long; and instead of having brief descriptions of all sites considered, the new thematic studies include only a compilation of the official nomination forms prepared for the designation of the new NHLs.

This volume attempts to develop a new model for the NHL thematic studies. Reflecting the Congressional mandate that the NHL program establish "an ongoing and substantial cooperative effort with the major professional and scholarly societies,"[64] the women's history landmark project has relied on specialists outside the NPS who could present the study in a broad historical context. The following chapters—on women in architecture, arts, community, education, politics, religion, and work—strive to combine the most recent scholarship in women's history and knowledge of historic sites associated with women's experiences and contributions. They are pioneering essays, for relatively little research exists on structures associated with women's history.

There is an urgency to this task for those who care about women's history because many buildings associated with significant events and people are deteriorating or have already been destroyed. During 1904 and 1905 Henry James, after living for many years in Europe, returned to the United States and described in *The American Scene* his pilgrimage to sites important in his life. On viewing a new large building in New York where his birthplace and childhood home had been he wrote "the effect for me, in Washington Place, was of having been amputated of half my history." When in Boston he sought out the house where he lived for two years as a young man just beginning his literary career. Although most of the houses at Ashburton Place had been razed, he found standing the house where he lived and was able "to recover on the spot some of the ghostly footsteps." He wrote that the place was "a conscious memento, with old secrets to keep and old stories to witness for, a saturation of life as closed together and preserved in it as the scent lingering in a folded pocket handkerchief." A month later James returned to the house "to see if another wif of the fragrance were not to be caught," but he found a "gaping void" for the house had been leveled. "It was," he wrote, "as if the bottom had fallen out of one's own biography, and one plunged backward into space without meeting anything."[65]

Just as tangible buildings connected James with his past, buildings associated with women's history make important connections, offering visitors an opportunity to consider anew their collective and formative pasts. Additional research by the scholarly community and more attention to women's history by private and public preservation leaders will be needed if those on a pilgrimage of women's history sites are to be spared James's experience of finding a "gaping void," of feeling that "one's past has been amputated," and being "plunged backward into space without meeting anything."

The historians who wrote essays for this volume accepted the assignment with some reservations, as I could offer them no models to emulate. The goal of each essay was to provide a synthetic overview of the specific subtheme of women's history including within the essay, where appropriate, consideration of historic structures, to glean insights into women's experiences and contributions.

In the field of historic preservation the progression from preparing a review of the historical context to the actual identification and preservation of structures, and then to the development of an interpretive program is long, difficult, and complex. Yet it is unrealistic to dream of more public historic sites associated with women without being cognizant of the difficult road ahead. The intent in preparing this volume has been to stimulate increased efforts to connect women's past to tangible resources and to appreciate better how "the sense of place" helps Americans to get in touch with important parts of their past. Increased interest in integrating women's history scholarship with material culture studies has the potential of strengthening both disciplines. To Brooke Hindle, a senior historian at the National Museum of American History, the challenge of this kind of endeavor is to produce a better and more useful history. "It will be truer and more useful than the present histories," Hindle concludes, "precisely because the abstractions will be tied by an intricate web to the real world of material culture."[66]

NOTES

1. Sandy Weber, "Angels or Agitators? Avoiding Stereotypes in the Interpretation of Women," *Trends* 25 (1988): 45–48.

2. Robert A. Webb, "Manassas Tragedy: Paving Over the Past," *Washington Post*, 13 March 1988, section C. See also Edward Tabor Linenthal, *Sacred Ground: Americans and Their Battlefields* (Urbana: University of Illinois Press, 1991).

3. National Park Service National Historic Landmark nomination form for the Triangle Shirtwaist Factory, New York City, prepared 26 September, 1989, National Historic Landmark Program, National Park Service.

4. Sarah Orne Jewett, as quoted by Marion Tinling, *Women Remembered: A Guide to Landmarks of Women's History in the United States* (New York: Greenwood Press, 1986), xi.

5. From consulting staff and directories of the major national historical and museum associations, I was unable to locate any survey or list of public historic sites associated primarily with women. The following analysis is based on information and an informal working list that I developed in the course of preparing this volume.

6. The American Association of Museums (AAM) has recently undertaken a national survey of museums. Although the results have not yet been published, they have identified 2,083 historic house museums. The AAM survey did not specifically identify women's history sites.

7. Heather Huyck, "Beyond John Wayne: Using Historic Sites to Interpret Women's History," in *Western Women: Their Land, Their Lives*, ed. Lillian Schlissel, Vicki L. Ruiz, and Janice Monk (Albuquerque: University of New Mexico Press, 1988), 303–30.

8. Patricia West, " 'The New Social History' and Historic House Museums: The Lindenwald Example," *Museum Studies Journal* 2 (Fall 1986): 22, 26.

9. This opinion surfaced frequently at a National Park Service training workshop for Chiefs of Interpretation for the National Capital Region held at Chincoteague, Virginia, 27 September 1990.

10. John A. Herbst, "Historic Houses," in *History Museums in the United States: A Critical Assessment,* ed. Warren Leon and Roy Rosenzweig (Chicago: University of Illinois Press, 1989), 98–113.

11. David Lowenthal, *The Past Is a Foreign Country* (New York: Cambridge University Press, 1986), 247.

12. Brooke Hindle, "Presidential Address: Technology through the 3–D Time Warp," *Technology and Culture* 24 (July 1983): 450–64.

13. Thomas J. Schlereth, ed., *Material Culture Studies in America* (Nashville: American Association of State and Local History, 1981), xiv.

14. Fay D. Metcalf and Matthew T. Downey, eds., *Using Local History in the Classroom* (Nashville: American Association of State and Local History, 1982), 87–88.

15. Kathleen Neils Conzen, "The New Urban History: Defining the Field," in *Ordinary People and Everyday Life: Perspectives on New Social History*, ed. James B. Gardner and George Rollie Adams (Nashville: American Association of State and Local History, 1983), 80.

16. Edith Mayo, "Focus on Material Culture," *Journal of American Culture* 3 (Winter 1980): 597.

17. See Schlereth, *Material Culture Studies*, for an overview.

18. House Comittee on Education and Labor, *Joint Hearing for Senate Subcommittee on Select Education and House Subcommittee on Post Secondary Education, House Committee on Education and Labor*, 99th Cong. 2d sess., 1985, H. Rept. 99–64, 473–78.

19. Elizabeth H. Pleck, "Women's History: Gender as a Category of Historical Analysis," *Ordinary People*, 51–66.

20. Andrea Hindling and Ames Sheldon Bower, eds., *Women's History Sources: A Guide to Archives and Manuscript Collections in the United States* (New York: Bowker, 1979).

21. Pleck, "Women's History," *Ordinary People*, 54.

22. Metcalf and Downey, *Using Local History in the Classroom*, 85.

23. Carroll Smith-Rosenberg, "The New Woman and the New History," *Feminist Studies* 3 (1975): 185–98.

24. James Deetz, *In Small Things Forgotten: The Archeology of Early American Life* (Garden City, N.Y.: Anchor Press, 1977), 8.

25. Schlereth, *Material Culture Studies*, 74.

26. Ibid., 3.

27. Gwendolyn Wright, *Building the Dream: A Social History of Housing in America* (Cambridge: MIT Press, 1983).

28. Dolores Hayden, *The Grand Domestic Revolution: A History of Feminist Designs for American Homes, Neighborhoods, and Cities* (Cambridge: MIT Press, 1981).

29. Helen Lefkowitz Horowitz, *Alma Mater: Design and Experiences in the Women's Colleges from Their Nineteenth Century Beginnings to the 1930s* (New York: Knopf, 1984).

30. Darlene Roth, "Feminine Marks on the Landscape: An Atlanta Inventory," *Journal of American Culture* 3 (Winter 1980): 680, 685.

31. Barbara Wyatt, ed., *Culltural Resource Management in Wisconsin* (Madison: Wisconsin State Historic Preservation Office, June 1986), 1–4.

32. Paul Lusignam, staff of the Wisconsin State Historic Preservation Office, telephone conversation with author, 1 August 1990.

33. Barbara J. Howe, "West Virginia Women's History: Identifying and Publicizing National Historic Landmarks," Final Narrative Report for Humanities Foundation of West Virginia Grant #85–54–85, 24 February 1988; Patricia Lee Hankins, "Women of West Virginia," pamphlet published by the West Virginia University Public History Program, December 1987.

34. Gail Lee Dubrow, "Restoring a Female Presence: New Goals in Historic Preservation," in *Architecture: A Place For Women*, ed. Ellen Perry Berkeley and Matilda McQuaid (Washington, D.C.: Smithsonian Institution Press, 1989), 169–70.

35. Gail Lee Dubrow, telephone conversation with author, 24 July 1990.

36. Jane Browne Gillette, "Power of Place," *Historic Preservation* (July/August 1990): 44.

37. Ibid.

38. Heather Huyck, "National Parks Lead in History Teaching," *Organization of American Historians Newsletter* 10 (January 1982): 4.

39. Ary L. Lamme, *American Historic Landscapes: Community Power and the Preservation of Four National Historic Sites* (Nashville: University of Tennessee Press, 1989), 189.

40. Two excellent resources on federal historic preservation policy are Robert E. Stipe and Antoinette J. Lee, eds., *American Mosaic: Preserving a Nation's Heritage* (Washington, D.C.: U. S. Committee International Council on Monuments and Sites, 1987); and Norman Williams, Jr., Edmund H. Kellogg, and Frank B. Gilbert, eds., *Readings in Historic Preservation: Why? What? and How?* (Burlington, Vermont: Center for Urban Policy Research, 1982).

41. Gail Lee Dubrow, "Preserving Her Heritage: American Landmarks of Women's History" (paper delivered at the annual meeting of the National Council on Public History, Washington, D.C., 25 April 1987).

42. Ibid.

43. "Women and Minority National Historic Landmarks," *Trends* 25 (1988): 49–52.

44. *Code of Federal Regulations*, (CFR, 1989 ed.) Title 36, Part 65, "National Historic Landmarks Program."

45. Barry Mackintosh, *The Historic Sites Survey and National Historic Landmarks Program: A History* (Washington, D.C.: National Park Service, 1985), 72.

46. Gail Lee Dubrow, "Preserving Her Heritage: American Landmarks of Women's History" (Ph.D. dissertation-in-progress, Graduate School of Architecture and Urban Planning, University of California, Los Angeles, 1989 draft).

47. Marion Tinling and Linda Ruffner–Russell, "Famous and Forgotten Women," *Historic Preservation* 28 (July–September 1976): 18.

48. "Memorandum of Agreement between National Park Service and National Coordinating Committee for the Promotion of History and Organization of American Historians," 29 May 1986.

49. "Vento Takes Charge," *National Parks* 60 (March/April 1986): 22.

50. House Subcommittee on National Parks and Public Lands, Committee on Interior and Insular Affairs, held hearings on 23 February 1988 to consider the NPS FY '89 budget. The hearing record was not published.

51. House Committee on Interior and Insular Affairs, *Report to the Committee on the Budget*, 100th Cong. 2d sess., 1988, H. Rept. 100–4, 73.

52. The FY '89 Interior Appropriations Legislation earmarked $60,000 for a Women's History National Historic Landmarks Study.

53. "Cooperative Agreement between National Park Service, National Coordinating

Committee for the Promotion of History, and Organization of American Historians," 2 February 1989.

54. Lynn Sherr and Jurate Kazickas, *The American Woman's Gazetteer* (New York: Bantam, 1976) and Marion Tinling, *Women Remembered*.

55. The twenty-three sites for which forms have been prepared are: *Arts:* Zora Neale Hurston House, FL; Mabel Dodge Luhan House, NM; Laura Ingalls Wilder House, MO; Sarah Orne Jewett House, ME; *Community:* General Federation of Women's Clubs Building, Washington, DC; Margaret Sanger Clinic, NY; United Charities Building, NY; *Education:* Nannie Burroughs School, Washington, DC; Prudence Crandall House, CT; Pine Mountain Settlement School, KY; M. Carey Thomas Library (Bryn Mawr College), PA; Washington College of Law, Washington, DC; *Politics:* Carrie Chapman Catt Residence, NY; Mary Dewson Residence, NY; Emma Goldman Residence, NY; Francis Perkins residence, Washington, DC; *Work:* Wendover (Frontier Nursing Service), KY; "Mother" Jones Prison, WV; Brandywine and Terricina (Rebecca Lukens), PA; Vassar College Observatory, NY; New England Hospital for Women and Children, MA; Brown Building (Triangle Shirtwaist Factory), NY; Madame C. J. Walker Building, IN.

56. "Building the Washington College of Law," *The Advocate: Magazine of American University* (Fall 1984): 15.

57. Mackintosh, *The Historic Sites Survey*, 73–74.

58. James Marston Fitch, *Historic Preservation: Curatorial Management of the Built World* (New York, McGraw-Hill Book Company, 1982), 23–24.

59. Antoinette J. Lee, "Discovering Old Cultures in the New World: The Role of Ethnicity," in *The American Mosaic*, 202.

60. Mackintosh, *The Historic Sites Survey*, 73–74.

61. Memorandum from National Park Service Historical Office staff to Page Putnam Miller, 2 October 1989.

62. Lowenthal, *The Past Is a Foreign Country*, 69, 410–11.

63. See section on "The Publications Program" in Mackintosh, *The Historic Sites Survey*, 89–94.

64. House Committee on Interior and Insular Affairs, *Report to the Committee on the Budget*, 100th Cong. 2d sess., 1988, H.Rept. 100–10, 73.

65. Henry James, *The American Scene* (New York: St. Martin's Press, 1987), 65, 164–65.

66. Brook Hindle, "How Much Is a Piece of the True Cross Worth?" in *Material Culture and the Study of American Life*, ed. Ian M. G. Quinby (New York: Norton for the Winterthur Museum, 1978), 20.

2 • Women and Architecture

BARBARA J. HOWE

Ann Pamela Cunningham, Catharine Beecher, and Julia Morgan were once towering figures in their respective fields, and all left important legacies for the American public. However, except for Beecher, they and their contemporaries are absent from most women's history texts. We have studied Beecher's writings about nineteenth-century homes, but we have not studied equally the work of Cunningham or Morgan in preserving or designing homes, the tangible remnants of our past.

All three women had strong opinions about the American built environment as they worked to preserve, theorize about, or design buildings that reflected their values. Together with many other women who shared their causes, they represent the three themes in this study of women and architecture: women as leaders and participants in the movement to save our nation's built environment through historic preservation, women as promoters of a better domestic architecture through theory and design, and women as architects of both public and private buildings.

In each of these categories, structures exist that illuminate women's contributions. Unfortunately, few of these structures are open to the public or, if open, have interpretive programs that link the women responsible for their preservation or design to scholarship in women's history. For example, the fruits of women's labors in the historic preservation movement stand as national treasures and are visited by large numbers each year. However, the focus of interpretation is more often on the events that took place in the building than on the efforts to preserve it. Likewise, the Harriet Beecher Stowe House in Hartford, Connecticut, may be the only building open to the public which interprets women's role in domestic design, but Stowe is far more famous as the author of *Uncle Tom's Cabin* than as a domestic designer. There is a growing interest in the identification of structures built by pioneer women architects, but only their public buildings are likely to be accessible today. Interpretation of an architect's role often consists of simply a plaque giving the architect's name and the date of construction.

The year 1940 marks a convenient conclusion to this study because most landmarks are designated only after existing for fifty years. The coming of World War II diverted resources from historic preservation and domestic architecture concerns to the wartime economy. After the war, the formation of the National Trust for Historic Preservation (chartered by Congress in 1949) changed the focus of historic preservation efforts by providing a national organization for those interested in private not-for-profit preservation endeavors. At the same time, suburban expansion and federal urban renewal policies drastically changed the face of the landscape as new houses were built in suburbs and old sections of cities destroyed.

No study of this length can hope to include every possible example. Emphasis here is on those organizations and individuals whose work is nationally recognized in some manner, that is, by inclusion in works such as the multivolume *Notable American Women*, Marion Tinling's *Women Remembered: A Guide to Landmarks of Women's History in the United States*, or Charles B. Hosmer, Jr.'s, histories of the historic preservation movement.

Of the three forums for women discussed in this chapter, historic preservation is the best known.[1] It is also one of the easiest to discuss because the results of their work, the buildings saved or lost, are clearly visible, even though women's work in their preservation may not be as well known. Working through organizations or as individuals, women were at the forefront of the voluntary sector of the historic preservation movement from their earliest efforts in the mid-nineteenth century through the 1930s. Although men were more likely to hold paid professional positions in the historic preservation movement, women who worked in communities across the country, generating publicity, raising money, and buying and restoring properties, helped to save many of the nation's most treasured landmarks today, including Mount Vernon and Monticello.

Nineteenth-century women, charged with being the guardians of the society's culture and morals, took their responsibilities seriously. For example, Louisa Tuthill's 1848 volume, *History of Architecture from the Earliest Times; its Present Condition in Europe and the United States; With a Biography of Eminent Architects and a Glossary of Architectural Terms by Mrs. L. C. Tuthill. With Numerous Illustrations*, the first history of architecture published in the United States, is dedicated " 'To the Ladies of the United States of America, the acknowledged arbiters of taste.' " Tuthill hoped that the ladies would promote an *American* architecture that fit the American landscape, used indigenous building materials, and was designed by American architects.[2]

Much of women's leadership in historic preservation, as in other causes, came through voluntary associations in the nineteenth century, a *modus operandi* that has continued to be critical to the preservation movement. Sarah Josepha Hale, for example, led a women's committee to raise funds to complete Boston's Bunker Hill Memorial.[3] Although women were less organized in the South than in the Northeast, sustained organizing efforts for historic preservation began in the South.[4]

Preservation, whether public or private, usually consisted of buying properties, then finding appropriate uses for them, often as museums. For many years, government efforts to save historic properties were secondary to private causes, as voluntary associations and individual involvement usually protected the country's "shrines" until well into the twentieth century.

The movement to save George Washington's home at Mount Vernon is the best known example of women's leadership in historic preservation as well as one of the earliest examples of such voluntary efforts. Mount Vernon also provides an excellent example of an existing National Historic Landmark that deserves to be categorized under the themes of women's history and historic preservation, in addition to its significance as the home of our first president. It is unlikely that Mount Vernon would have survived with the requisite high degree of original integrity to receive this designation without the efforts of the Mount Vernon Ladies' Association (MVLA), organized under the efforts of Ann Pamela Cunningham, which still owns and operates the home.

On December 2, 1853, Ann Pamela Cunningham appealed to the women of the South to save Mount Vernon from possible development as a hotel. She heard about the dilapidated condition of the estate from her mother, who saw it from a boat on the Potomac River and wrote to her daughter, "Why was it that the women of this country did not try to keep it in repair, if the men could not do it? It does seem such a blot on our country!"[5] A South Carolinian, Ann Cunningham at first hoped the women of the South would rise up to save Mount Vernon and that she could stay behind the scenes, but at age thirty-seven she became involved in a battle that would last the rest of her life.

In 1855, Virginia's governor, Joseph Johnson, used his annual message to tell Virginians that a group of ladies from throughout the South had collected money to purchase Mount Vernon, a "noble purpose" that would adorn "the brow of female philanthropy." The legislature chartered the Mount Vernon Ladies' Association of the Union on March 17, 1856, with a charter that allowed the Commonwealth of Virginia to own the property after MVLA purchased it. Two years later, the commonwealth amended the charter to allow the association to hold title to the property. With that act, noted Charles B. Hosmer, Jr., "Virginia left the work of saving Mount Vernon in the laps of the women of the nation."[6]

Working with the Washington family did not prove easy, because John Washington thought the property should be paid for by the Commonwealth of Virginia, but Cunningham, as regent, organized the women through a vice-regent in each state. Vice-regents (in thirty states, both North and South, by

Ann Pamela Cunningham and the Vice-Regents of the Mount Vernon Ladies' Association. Mount Vernon, Virginia, 1873. (Photograph courtesy of the Mount Vernon Ladies' Association)

1860) appointed "lady managers" in each county, town, or village in the state.[7] Cunningham's tactic of appointing prominent women as vice-regents was one that was used by other preservation groups after the Civil War. Today, for example, the National Trust for Historic Preservation counts the First Lady and all living former First Ladies as honorary members. Finally, in June 1856, John Washington agreed to sell the property to the association instead of directly to the state. Almost all the money needed was on hand by December 1859, raised in part from 139 fund-raising speeches by popular orator Edward Everett.

During the Civil War, Mount Vernon was guarded, and thereby preserved, by a superintendent and Sarah C. Tracey, secretary of the MVLA, who lived on the estate. After the war, with Cunningham still in control, the MVLA proved itself a national organization. Cunningham succeeded in getting federal dollars in 1869 to compensate the MVLA for the loss of revenue from its tourist boat, confiscated by Union troops during the war. Before Cunningham retired from the MVLA in 1874, she set about collecting the records of the group so that its history could someday be properly written, making the MVLA one of the few early preservation groups with adequate records.

Vice-regents continued to raise money for the MVLA through projects in their own states. Kansas women raised $1,000 to reconstruct the servants' quarters (presumably really slave quarters). Other women donated from their own funds: Phoebe Hearst, mother of journalist William Randolph Hearst, gave $6,000 to drain and fill the swamp near the mansion. Alice Longfellow, daughter of poet Henry Wadsworth Longfellow, paid for an architect to restore the library and also helped furnish it.[8]

The MVLA did not escape criticism for its work. Attacks came from those who felt they should not have to pay admission to see Mount Vernon. Defenders of the MVLA claimed attackers just wanted control of a political patronage position as guardian of Washington's home. Despite the criticism, the MVLA was the first successful national preservation effort and one of the first successful women's organizations in the United States, with the ladies "amazed to find themselves 'making speeches and passing resolutions like men!' " — a rarity in the mid-nineteenth century.[9]

Ann Pamela Cunningham came to be recognized as a national leader among women, and almost every early preservation group had ties to the MVLA. William Murtagh notes that "most preservation efforts throughout the end of the nineteeth century were characterized by the kind of pietism and private support typical of the Mount Vernon effort."[10] Two groups tried unsuccessfully to emulate its achievements — the Valley Forge Association, organized in 1878, and the Ladies' Hermitage Association, established a decade later. The Ladies' Hermitage Association, however, kept Andrew Jackson's home from being converted into a home for Confederate veterans when, in 1889, the governor of Tennessee turned it over to the association.[11]

The Association for the Preservation of Virginia Antiquities (APVA), the first large state-focused private preservation group to appear in the South, was informally founded in 1888 by Mary Jeffery Galt and formally organized the following year by Cynthia Beverley Tucker Coleman. Although open to men and women, the APVA had a predominantly female membership. The APVA's first purchase was the Powder Magazine in Williamsburg, which it owned until 1985.[12]

In 1890, APVA member Mrs. Joseph Bryan formed the Confederate Memorial Literary Society to save the White House of the Confederacy and persuaded the city of Richmond to give the group the building in 1894. The society opened the house as a Confederate Museum in 1896; an NHL, it is open to the public as part of the Museum of the Confederacy. For almost 100 years, visitors saw the society's efforts to preserve the history of the Confederacy. In 1990, however, the almost-century-old setting disappeared, with the women's efforts interpreted as a museum exhibit itself, when the White House was restored to its appearance at the time Jefferson Davis and his family resided there.

Patriotism and preservation have been inexorably linked on the agendas for several organizations, with the best known being the Daughters of the American Revolution (DAR).[13] Organized in 1890, the DAR became an important national women's force for historic preservation. Working through local chapters and state societies around the country, the group's objectives included "the acquisition and protection of historical spots, and the erection of monuments," making the DAR the first national organization to protect historic sites around the country.[14] In 1892, DAR chapters organized to save Philadelphia's Betsy Ross House, which is open to the public as a museum.[15]

Elsewhere, members marked and preserved sites related to colonial and Revolutionary War events, such as Cowpens National Battlefield in South Carolina and Yorktown battlefield, National Park System units that are already designated as NHLs, although for reasons other than their significance to the historic preservation movement. Over the years, DAR members cooperated with organizations such as the APVA to protect Jamestown Island.[16] The Philadelphia chapter of the DAR received sole custody of Independence Hall from the city of Philadelphia in 1896 and opened the "restored" second floor of the building to the public in 1898.[17] In 1900, New York City DAR chapters organized a "Women's Auxiliary" to cooperate with the all-male American Scenic and Historic Preservation Society (ASHPS), which had been organized in New York in 1895 after the model of the British National Trust. The Women's Auxiliary had three goals: city purchase of Fraunces Tavern, Morris Mansion (Washington's headquarters), and Poe Cottage.[18]

The DAR commemorated more than the era of the American Revolution. During 1928–1929, their National Old Trails Road project placed plaques along the National Road (roughly the alignment of U.S. Route 40 from Cumberland, Maryland, to Illinois) and installed twelve "Madonna of the Trail" statues across the country to honor women who had made the westward trek in the nineteenth century.[19] Bent's Old Fort, now a unit of the National Park System, was originally a DAR project.[20] The DAR also focused on sites honoring "Real Daughters"—the daughters of Revolutionary War soldiers. Properties protected by the DAR around the country are documented in Mollie Somerville's *Historic and Memorial Buildings of the Daughters of the American Revolution*.[21] There are also innumerable bronze markers that visitors will find at historic sites across the country that have been placed there by the Daughters of the American Revolution.

Historic preservation efforts were on the agenda of at least some of the women's clubs that flourished throughout the country in the early twentieth century. Usually affiliates of the General Federation of Women's Clubs (GFWC) or the National Association of Colored Women (NACW), these clubs took seriously their mission to better the communities in which they worked by promoting art, libraries, public health, home economics, and similar causes. While preservation was not a primary focus of their work as it was, for instance, for the DAR, women's clubs provided a readily available pool of educated, organized women who could be mobilized easily. Preservation interests of these groups ranged from safeguarding archeological resources to protecting the home of a major African-American leader.

The Denver Woman's Club was active in one such preservation effort. Virginia Donaghe McClurg (1857–1931) first visited Mesa Verde in 1882 and organized her own expedition to the site four years later; she is credited with the discovery of Balcony House there. After years of lobbying to protect the site, she persuaded the Denver Woman's Club to organize the Colorado Cliff Dwellings Association and served as a leader of the group from 1895 to 1930. The association arranged for the government to purchase the land from the Ute tribe, negotiated the sale, and built a road into the new national monument. Lucy Evelyn Peabody (1865–1934), a rival of McClurg, became known as the Mother of the Mesa Verde because of her advocacy of this site as a national, rather than a state, park.[22]

The National Association of Colored Women (NACW) vowed in 1916 to save the home of Frederick Douglass in Anacostia, a suburb of Washington, D.C. Helen Douglass inherited the house upon her husband's death, but a legal technicality forced her to organize the Frederick Douglass Memorial and Historical Association to guarantee its protection. When the association's trustees could not pay off the mortgage after her death, the NACW stepped in to help as a matter of " 'race loyalty' " and as a tribute to their ancestors.[23]

The Mount Vernon Ladies' Association model also continued to be used into the 1920s, as evidenced by the Robert E. Lee Memorial Foundation, organized in 1929 to save Stratford Hall, the general's birthplace. Two of its leaders, May Lanier (Mrs. Charles Day) and Ethel Armes, tried to get the national United Daughters of the Confederacy (UDC) to buy the home. Failing that, they purchased the stately home with its extensive grounds through the William Alexander Chapter of the UDC, which then turned over ownership to the foundation on July 19, 1929. The foundation was modeled so closely on the MVLA that Lanier asked the older group for a list of its vice-regents when seeking leadership for her own organization.[24] Stratford Hall, an NHL as a site related to the South's most famous son during the Civil War, is also significant for women's history.

These early preservation efforts focused on individual sites of, usually, national significance that were protected often by wide expanses of land traditionally associated with the building, i.e., Stratford Hall and its surrounding plantation lands. However, buildings of less than national significance also deserved protection, particularly in urban areas where "progress" threatened to demolish old buildings that stood in the way of new construction projects. During the early twentieth century, some women began to realize that these historic buildings, individually or in groups, should be saved, even if there was no clear *national* historic significance. In directing their energies to that end, they became pioneers in what is still the most challenging aspect of the historic preservation movement, protecting urban historic districts from development pressures.

One of the most famous urban preservation efforts began in Charleston, South Carolina. Susan Pringle Frost (1873–1960), the first woman on the

Charleston Real Estate Exchange, recognized the need to revitalize that city's historic core. While preservation in any community with resources as rich as Charleston's must include many advocates and partners, Frost was an important predecessor of the numerous development corporations and individuals who use private investment as a means of preserving historic structures. An active member of the Charleston Federation of Women's Clubs, she began buying real estate in Charleston in 1909 because of her interest in the civic agenda of the women's clubs and her family roots in the city's history. Her purchases included properties on Tradd Street, St. Michael's Alley, and East Bay, as well as the Miles Brewton House and the Joseph Manigault House, both of which are NHLs because of their architectural significance.

One of the first to recognize the potential of a restored historic district in Charleston, Frost also realized that public awareness was an important part of historic preservation. Therefore, she formed the Society for the Preservation of Old Dwellings (now the Preservation Society of Charleston) in 1920 and served as its president for seven years. She also served on the city's zoning commission for nine years.[25] Unfortunately, Frost's efforts are not well interpreted to those who frequent the sites she worked to preserve.

In the 1920s, urban preservation issues evolved from a focus on a particular building to an examination of the more complex and interrelated resources of a city. While Frost worked in Charleston, in 1924, a small group of women gathered in San Antonio, Texas, to form the San Antonio Conservation Society to save the city's Greek Market House from demolition. Although unsuccessful at preserving the Market House, the women proceeded to save a natural resource, the last great bend in the San Antonio River, and the ruins of the Spanish Governor's Palace.[26]

Los Angeles's Olvera Street, now a major tourist attraction, was saved through the efforts of Christine Sterling (d. 1963). Sterling first discovered the street in 1926, when the Avila adobe, the oldest and one of the most historic houses in Los Angeles, was a flophouse condemned by the health department. She persuaded the city of Los Angeles to initiate its historic preservation program in this section, although it took years for the work to be completed. It was not until 1952 that the forty-acre district was designated as a state and city park.[27]

Elizabeth Thomas Werlein (1883–1946) led the efforts to preserve New Orleans's French Quarter. She published *The Wrought Iron Railings of Le Vieux Carre, New Orleans*, a pictorial booklet, in 1910. After her husband's death in 1917, she became very active in a range of women's activities, including the Woman's Commitee of the New Orleans Liberty Loan drives, the Woman's Division of the Council of National Defense for New Orleans, the League of Women Voters of Louisiana (first state president, 1920), and the Professional Women's Committee of the Roosevelt National Campaign Committee (1932). She also worked as public relations director from 1924 to 1930 for a southern chain of motion picture theatres.

In New Orleans's French Quarter, where she eventually lived at 630 St. Ann Street, she supported community organizations such as Le Petit Theatre du Vieux Carre. While she interested some of her friends in restoring houses in the French Quarter, the area became a center for speakeasies and prostitutes during Prohibition, thwarting preservation efforts. Werlein then organized the Vieux Carre Property Owners Association in 1930 to combat these problems and pushed for the enactment and enforcement of zoning regulations and building codes. If work was done without her personal approval, she turned to the courts if needed. Werlein is credited with promoting interest in the Vieux Carre and spearheading restoration efforts there. The Vieux Carre NHL Historic District is a tribute to the work that she and others did to preserve historic sites related to the War of 1812.[28]

Throughout the 1930s, women remained active in preservation efforts around the country, continuing their tradition of philanthropic work but also beginning to gain valuable paid professional experience. Those with personal or family financial resources, such as Louise du Pont Crowninshield (1877–1958), provided financial assistance to save individual buildings.[29] Crowninshield persuaded her father, Col. Henry A. du Pont, to purchase Eleutherian Mills, the original home of E. I. du Pont that is now part of the Winterthur Museum complex near Newark, Delaware.[30] Antoinette Downing wrote the architectural history of Rhode Island before World War II and organized the College Hill project in Providence, Rhode Island, one of the earliest and most successful attempts to use preservation as a tool for urban revitalization. Women also began to find professional employment in the field as Colonial Williamsburg, Inc., developed its professional staff. The federal government opened many positions to women during the New Deal, and a few were hired by the new Historic American Buildings Survey program, organized in 1933.[31]

Women's participation in the historic preservation movement, then, was not an isolated phenomenon. Women across the country and across the decades have assumed the responsibility of protecting the country's built environment. Women's organizations played an important part in this endeavor and gave women important experience in leadership and fund-raising that was vital to their success in the preservation movement. The women who led the preservation movement recognized their traditional role in a concern for protecting the country's heritage and yet knew that carrying out that role meant, perhaps, stretching the traditional "proper" definitions of women's activities to accomplish their goals.

They deliberately left us tangible reminders of our country's past. However, in preserving the structures they thought important to teach us about their view of the past, a past dominated by white male politicians and military leaders, they left us buildings that can also be used to interpret a much broader view of history. As historic sites reflect the scholarship of the "new social history," we can tell many more stories about these buildings and their inhabitants, about the mothers and wives and sisters of the "great men," about the slaves and servants who kept the buildings and lands operating, and, perhaps most often neglected, about the women whose efforts preserved the buildings for us.

While some women were active in preserving our nation's historic structures, others directed their attention to designing a better environment for contemporary living. Doris Cole, in *From Tipi to Skyscraper*, argues that although women have been sparse in the ranks of formally trained architects, they have been "active, influential participants in developing and formulating America's architecture" through their concern for "improving the social, physical, and moral character of their families and nation." Women writers and housing reformers often chose to focus on "the daily, ordinary problems of living" or theoretical designs instead of the formal plan of structures that were actually constructed. Cole labels this area of concern "social architecture."[32] The word "home" is important here because it is the concept of home that is important, not the standard definition of a house. Again, the range of examples used here is illustrative of women's activities in these arenas but is in no way comprehensive.[33]

Many of the writers and theorists addressing the issue of domestic space wrote in the late nineteenth and early twentieth centuries, a time of intense discussion about housing alternatives and other political and economic theories, including socialism, nationalism, and capitalism. While the focus of this chapter is on housing designs, it is important to note that these were often linked to broader theories about the economy or family structure and gender roles. Those ideas may be explored further in the references cited in the notes.

Urban growth produced early apartment buildings in major cities, and Andrew Jackson Downing published his *Cottage Residences* in 1842, but the discussion of alternatives to architect-designed houses for individual families exploded only after the Civil War. Builders' and architects' journals, as well as popular magazines such as *Ladies' Home Journal*, provided a ready outlet for essays and designs. Part of the discussion centered around the design of the home itself, as nineteenth-century styles like the Queen Anne Revival gave way to Colonial Revival homes and then to the bungalow before World War I. Designs for houses were simplified, with fewer and smaller rooms that could be maintained without servants, while providing modern improvements such as central heating, electricity, sanitary bathrooms, and efficient kitchens.

"High style" architecture has long been associated with specific values and uses; for example, Gothic Revival for educational or religious structures but not for commercial use, or Classical Revival for governmental buildings. The multiroom houses of the late nineteenth century separated family from visitors and servants, but they also separated family members from each other. This segregation ended in early twentieth-century designs, when smaller spaces forced family members together; writers advocated togetherness in the living room instead of separation in study and playroom.[34] At the same time, suburbanization increased as streetcars, and eventually automobiles, linked previously inaccessible areas to downtown workplaces for middle-class commuters.

During the mid-nineteenth century, women examined their role in the home and the organization of their domestic space. Dolores Hayden notes that, from the end of the Civil War to the beginning of the Great Depression, women whom she terms "material feminists" "challenged two characteristics of industrial capitalism: the physical separation of household space from public space, and the economic separation of the domestic economy from the political economy." They worked for day-care centers and kitchenless houses served by public kitchens and community dining clubs, arguing that women could not achieve true equality without "feminist homes" that provided socialized housework and child care.[35] It is important to remember, however, that those who were to be spared the drudgeries of housework were those who had the financial resources to hire other women too poor to enjoy the same option.

Catharine Beecher and Charlotte Perkins Gilman, her grandniece, were the two most important theorists on domestic architecture in the nineteenth and early twentieth centuries, but they were by no means alone. Melusina Fay Peirce belonged to a middle generation between Beecher and Gilman. While Beecher thought the home could be designed to be a better workplace for middle-class housewives, Peirce and, later, Gilman argued for cooperative housekeeping that would free those same women from the rigors of housekeeping so that they could pursue more exciting and lucrative careers. At a minimum, Peirce argued that women should be paid for housekeeping chores. The evolution of their ideas, then, provides a way to assess the importance of the home in the lives of middle-class women who, by the end of the nineteenth century, in the era of the "New Woman" and nascent Progressivism, found more challenging, and lucrative, alternatives than housekeeping to occupy their time.

Catharine Beecher (1800–1878) was one of the first women to publish widely her views on the American home. In 1841, she published the first edition of her *Treatise on Domestic Economy, For the Use of Young Ladies at Home and at School*, the first comprehensive manual for homemakers, in which she described the first servantless house and counseled her readers on "every aspect of domestic life from the building of a house to the setting of a table." At the same time, she provided the first text that standardized the practices of American homemakers, including child care and home health concerns, and initiated household automation. She also, for the first time, "exaggerated and heightened gender differences and thereby altered and romanticized the emphasis given to women's domestic role."[36]

Several of the chapters in *Treatise* deal with the design and construction of a home and its rooms. In chapter 25, "On the Construction of Houses," Beecher writes,

> There is no matter of domestic economy, which more seriously involves the health and daily comfort of American women, than the proper construction of houses.

There are five particulars, to which attention should be given, in building a house; namely, economy of labor, economy of money, economy of health, economy of comfort, and good taste.[37]

Her ideal house plan included, for instance, one stairway instead of the traditional front public stairway and back servants' stairway, a nursery and kitchen located close to each other to save steps, a perfectly square house as the least expensive to build and heat, a central chimney, simple moldings instead of ornate decoration, and a constant supply of fresh air in bedrooms. She also provided scaled drawings of her sample houses for readers. In a series of subsequent chapters, Beecher instructed her readers on the decoration and care of parlors, breakfast and dining rooms, chambers and bedrooms, and the kitchen, cellar, and storeroom.[38]

In 1869, Catharine Beecher collaborated with her sister Harriet to publish *The American Woman's Home: Or the Principles of Domestic Science*. This was, in many ways, a continuation of the earlier *Treatise*, updated to include references to modern stoves and "earth closets" and Harriet's ideas on entryways, decorating, and gardening. Reflecting recent technological developments, the model home featured a warm air furnace in the basement supplemented by small Franklin stoves in each room; a central service core housed the plumbing, ductwork, chimney, and stairway. Catharine's contribution seems to have been her drawings and comments on a combined home-church-school to promote her ideal of the Christian family. One gable-roofed model even had a steeple topped with a cross.[39]

The Harriet Beecher Stowe House at 73 Forest Street, in Hartford, Connecticut, was based on the design ideas of Catharine Beecher and Andrew Jackson Downing, as presented in *The American Woman's Home*. Although the Stowes did not build the house, the 1871 Gothic Revival cottage was an appropriate design, given Catharine Beecher's interest in the ideal Christian family. Stowe moved into the house in 1873, two years after its construction, and decorated it by the principles outlined in her book, using plants instead of drapes on the windows, for example.[40]

Melusina Fay Peirce (1836–1923) was, notes Dolores Hayden, "one of the first women to make a detailed economic critique of domestic life in the United States." While living in Cambridge, Massachusetts, she argued that women were oppressed because their work in the home was unspecialized and unremunerated, a theory that late twentieth-century feminists would also espouse. In the *Atlantic Monthly*, during 1868 and 1869, she developed her arguments for "cooperative housekeeping," in which groups of twelve to fifty women would organize to share all domestic work and charge their husbands for the services rendered. Membership fees would provide the funds needed to build a headquarters so that laundry, cooking, sewing, and baking could be done on a large scale in a central location. Workers, either the cooperative members or former servants, would be paid appropriate wages, with retail prices charged

Illustration of window treatment from *American Woman's Home*.
(Photograph courtesy of James Gardner)

for services. With these basic services centralized, women architects could design kitchenless houses for families. She also hoped that apartments would be built with communal facilities to promote cooperative housekeeping, but this did not materialize.[41]

To implement her ideas, she helped organize the Cambridge Cooperative Housekeeping Society in 1869. The group established its headquarters in the "old Meacham House on Bow Street," Cambridge, in 1870. The laundry and store operated until the society closed in 1871, but the kitchen never opened.[42]

Charlotte Perkins Gilman (1860–1935), grandniece of Catharine and Harriet Beecher, continued her great-aunts' tradition of writing on domestic matters. However, the Beecher sisters doubtless would not have understood Gilman's perspective, for she went far beyond Catharine's romantic emphasis on women's domesticity and "synthesized the thinking of suffragists, home economists, and utopian novelists on the question of the home." Instead of celebrating the home as the healthy domain of an individual family, she argued for "collective domesticity," an idea which appealed to feminists in both the United States and Europe.[43]

Gilman argued that women would work outside the home for wages while being freed from mundane domestic chores, because they lived in kitchenless houses or apartments linked to central kitchens, dining rooms, and day care centers. She preferred these feminist apartment hotels to cooperative communities. She even provided a detailed description for a Feminist Apartment Hotel. The New York Feminist Alliance hired Max G. Heidelberg to design this hotel, but it unfortunately was never built. There are no known sites built to Gilman's designs, but several floor plans in Dolores Hayden's *The Grand Domestic Revolution: A History of Feminist Designs for American Homes, Neighborhoods, and Cities* illustrate possible ways to design communal kitchens and living quarters. Gilman espoused her ideas in several major publications, including *Women and Economics: A Study of the Economic Relation between Men and Women as a Factor in Social Evolution* (1898), *What Diantha Did* (1909–1910), *Moving the Mountain* (1911), and *Herland* (1915).[44]

Women such as the Beecher sisters and Charlotte Perkins Gilman were interested in improving domestic architecture and women's economic role in the home. They accepted the idea that the family's health and happiness depended on the woman's role as homemaker and guardian. This was a very conservative definition of women's responsibilities, but these women infused the traditional roles with often radical redefinitions of the ways in which those roles could be carried out. Cooking and laundry did not have to be done in isolated kitchens. There were better ways to design a home to promote better health and economize on labor. Other than identifying buildings that house cooperative societies or communal kitchens, or the homes of the women noted, it is difficult to isolate sites for designation as NHLs for domestic architecture. Rather, the success of these women's efforts lay in the untold number of homes that were designed to incorporate some of their ideas, or, impossible to know, the number of homes where wives and servants adopted their techniques for homemaking to better care for their families.

In addition to writing about the design of homes, women have had long careers as housing reformers, an interest growing out of their role as guardians of America's homes.[45] If society determined that they were responsible for providing a proper home for their own families, they found it logical to expand their domestic interest to the homes of the nation's poor as they became active in the Progressive Era's municipal housekeeping campaigns. While some of these housing reformers studied architecture, they are perhaps better known for their writing and action on behalf of housing reform policies than for the design of specific buildings. Thus, while the NHL program includes housing reform under the general theme of Social and Humanitarian Movements, an examination of women housing reformers is an important way to examine women's participation in the traditionally male domain of architecture.

The control of housing had been a primarily private matter in the United States before the mid-nineteenth century, although in the eighteenth century cities such as Boston had regulated control of construction materials to prevent fires. Various tenement laws in the second half of the nineteenth century had attempted to regulate the worst excesses of housing for the poor, although New York's ill-fated Tenement House Law of 1879 created more problems than it solved with its advocacy of the model dumbbell tenement. This design maximized land usage by providing only narrow shafts between buildings for light and air to circulate—and garbage to accumulate. Jacob Riis's *How the Other Half Lives* provided graphic descriptions of the problems of the housing among the urban poor. This led Governor Theodore Roosevelt to appoint New York State's Tenement House Commission, led by settlement house worker Lawrence Veiller, to study New York City's housing problems. The 1901 Tenement House Law, which implemented the commission's recommendations, became the model for all of the country's subsequent housing codes, spreading the idea that poor housing was the result of unscrupulous landlords and careless tenants and that housing must be controlled so that it did not provide threats to the community's health, welfare, and safety.[46]

By World War I, women were gaining prominence as housing reformers, primarily through the work of women such as Edith Elmer Wood (1871–1945). Eugenie Birch argues that female influence led directly to two important features of early housing policy: "the insistence that government was to build homes for the low-income slum dweller because the private sector would not do so" and "the demand that the publicly constructed homes be positively supportive of family life, not merely provision of minimal shelter." As long as women helped to implement public housing programs, Birch notes, "public housing architecture would reflect domestic needs."[47]

Edith Elmer Wood was one of the most important early women housing reformers. Educated at Smith College, she followed the path of many of the first generation of college women by working at the College Settlement in New

York in the 1890s, before her marriage to Albert Norton Wood in 1894. Her first career was as a novelist. While her husband was stationed in Puerto Rico with the U.S. Navy, Wood led an antituberculosis campaign for the island in 1906. She soon determined that the disease could not be eradicated without providing better housing and, therefore, wrote a new housing code for San Juan, thus beginning her career as a housing reformer.

Returning to the United States, she eventually settled in Washington, D.C., and became active in the city's housing reform movement. There, she began to differ from the accepted wisdom of the New York commission as she discovered that the city's alley residents had no alternatives to slum conditions. Forcing them out of the alleys, she concluded, was not the solution.

She decided to become a professional housing reformer in 1914 and attended New York School of Philanthropy and Columbia University to acquire the necessary expertise for this work. Her Ph.D. dissertation in political economy, *The Housing of the Unskilled Wage Earner*, was published in 1919; in it, she advocated the need for a national housing policy to provide low-cost housing because the traditional regulatory methods were not adequate. Housing problems, she concluded, were the result of a breakdown in the country's industrial system, not a moral problem of bad landlords or lazy tenants. Housing must be as much a matter of public policy as public utilities, and housing decisions had to consider density, rent restrictions, and accessibility to jobs in addition to traditional concerns of health and safety.

Wood then proceeded to survey the nation's housing problem, using whatever statistics were available, because the census did not yet include adequate questions on housing or income. She concluded in 1919 that approximately one-third of the nation's residents lived in below normal housing conditions, while one-tenth lived in conditions that were actually harmful to " 'health, morals, and family life.' "[48]

During the 1920s and 1930s, Wood continued to monitor the country's housing problems. Wood was among the first members of the Regional Planning Association of America, organized in 1923 and became a vice-president of the National Public Housing Conference (NPHC) formed in 1931 as a lobbying group for housing issues. In the NPHC, she worked with Mary Kingsbury Simkhovitch (president), Edith Abbot, Mary Harriman Rumsey, Cornelia Bryce Pinchot (all vice-presidents, with Wood), Helen Alfred (executive director), and Catherine K. Bauer, another important housing reformer. Two years later, she helped organize the National Association of Housing Officials. In 1935, the Public Works Administration published her *Slums and Blighted Areas in the United States*, in which she again concluded that one-third of the nation was ill-housed, providing President Franklin D. Roosevelt with the famous section of his 1937 inaugural address: "I see one third of a nation ill-housed, ill-clad, ill-nourished." While most professionals accepted her conclusions and statistics, the real estate industry and housing reformers such as

Lawrence Veiller challenged her work because it led to a conclusion they abhorred: government construction of housing units.

Wood's goal was realized with the passage of the National Housing Act (Wagner-Steagall Housing Act) of 1937, which provided for her plan of slum clearance and construction of the country's first public housing units designed to her ideas. She also supported financial assistance for those who were not poor but needed assistance in acquiring adequate housing; this goal was achieved with the passage of the Housing Act of 1949, in which Congress affirmed the country's responsibility to provide adequate housing for all, and the Housing and Urban Development Act of 1965, which established the cabinet-level Department of Housing and Urban Development.[49] In a sense then, the nation's public housing projects are a monument to Wood's work, albeit a monument that she would surely now find tarnished as the nation's commitment to improved housing for the poor has strayed from the idealism of those New Deal days.

While women were active theorists and planners for a better domestic architecture, they have been much less prominent as the designers of those living spaces. Their legacy is more often in the form of written commentary or sketches than in actual buildings. Architecture traditionally has been defined as a male field in American society, and those women who were able to succeed often did so against great odds. Certainly few, until recently, have received the attention they deserved. This chapter concentrates on the opportunities for architectural education open to those before World War II as an avenue for exploring the options open to women interested in the profession. Further, it discusses those women who comprised what I have chosen to call the first generation of women architects, those women who practiced their profession in the late nineteenth and early twentieth centuries and paved the way for their sisters to follow. Not all were equally important, of course, but too few have received recognition for their work.

Cole's brief 1973 overview, *From Tipi to Skyscraper*, noted that only approximately 2 percent of the architects then practicing were women and that less than one-half of the women who earned architectural degrees were registered architects. Even the work of those few architects was not well known, as Cole labels her book "the first history of women in American architecture."[50] Judith Paine suggests that these women have been so inconspicuous because "prejudice nourished anonymity" and because the women usually practiced alone or in small offices, designing private buildings that were rarely publicized in the architectural press. She suggests that they chose to be inconspicuous "so that their work would be judged on merit, not sex."[51]

Standard sources such as Tinling's *Women Remembered*, the four-volume *Notable American Women*, and the *Macmillan Encyclopedia of Architects* include a paltry list of women architects: Nora Stanton Blatch Barney (1883–1971), Louise Blanchard Bethune (1856–1913), Elisabeth Coit (c.

1892–1987), Mary Jane Elizabeth Colter (1869–1958), Marion Lucy Mahony Griffin (1871–1962), Sophia Gregoria Hayden (c. 1868–1953), Julia Morgan (1872–1957), Minerva Parker Nichols (1861–1949), Lillian Rice (1888–1938), Theodate Pope Riddle (1868–1946), and Hazel Wood Waterman (1865–1948). Almost all have some claim as a "first." Lois Lilly Howe (1864–1964) is not even included in these lists. Standard histories of American architecture, including Alan Gowans's *Images of American Living: Four Centuries of Architecture and Furniture as Cultural Expression*, David P. Handlin's *American Architecture* (only Griffin, Morgan), Leland M. Roth's *A Concise History of American Architecture*, and Marcus Whiffen and Frederick Koeper's *American Architecture* (only Morgan) ignore these women except for the references shown.

Although the list of possible NHLs is not extensive, only three complexes designed by women had been designated by 1990: Colter's Hopi House, Hermit's Rest, Lookout Studio, and Desert View at Grand Canyon National Park; and Julia Morgan's La Cuesta Encantada (William Randolph Hearst's San Simeon estate) in San Luis Obispo County, California; and her Asilomar Conference Grounds in Pacific Grove, California. Clearly, buildings designed by women architects are the best buildings to designate in their honor because they can show us the women's level of skill and ideas about use of space and materials.

Colter's Grand Canyon structures are both the best and least altered, but also among the only remaining examples of her work. Her designs are important because of her interest in archeology and history, here of Native Americans (Hopi) and the Southwest, and because of her desire to design structures appropriate for the country's new national parks, structures that would appear to be part of the landscape instead of in conflict with their surroundings. Hopi House, for example, is a large rectangular multistory sandstone building with small windows and stepped roofs at various levels to resemble a pueblo. Most of the rooms have ceilings of peeled log beams covered with saplings, grasses, and twigs with a mud coating on top, as would a pueblo. Hermit's Rest is a stone structure "tucked into a small man-made earthen mound" so that the building blends with its environment; those portions of the building that are visible are of rubble masonry, structural logs, and some glass. Bright Angel Lodge, or the Lookout Studio, a small building of rubble masonry, is built into the canyon rim. The Indian Watchtower at Desert View, from a distance, appears to be an Anasazi watchtower, although it is much larger than known original towers. The tower is built of uncoursed rubble topped by coursed sandstone, with irregular fenestration. The NHL nomination for the Colter structures includes the historic furnishings and ceremonial objects that Colter collected "to contribute to the nostalgic mood she wanted to create."[52]

In addition to their design characteristics, the structures are important historically because of their significance to the burgeoning tourist trade serviced by the Fred Harvey Company and the Atchison, Topeka & Santa Fe Railroad at Grand Canyon. The National Park Service now recognizes such structures built to serve visitors to the nation's treasures as cultural resources worthy of documentation and preservation in themselves.

In La Cuesta Encantada, Morgan abandoned her usual practical use of space, form, and structure, her belief that buildings should be unobtrusive parts of the landscape, and her focus on simplicity. While designed as a reinforced concrete structure, the building is "thoroughly ostentatious, bristling with ornament, filled with impracticalities. . . ." The nomination form for La Cuesta Encantada focuses primarily on its significance as the home of politician and journalist William Randolph Hearst. Clearly, this recognition of Hearst's importance does not explain the full significance of this site. The Asilomar Conference Grounds is significant to the history of the Young Women's Christian Association because it was designed as the organization's national camp and conference center in the West. It is also recognized as an example of Morgan's work in the Craftsman style, for she designed buildings using local stone and exposed heavy wood truss construction to blend with the trees and beach setting of the center.[53]

Colter received no formal academic training as an architect, while Morgan received the best available in the world by studying in Paris. Women's opportunities for careers in architecture, throughout the United States, were closely linked to their abilities to receive the appropriate training. Formal architectural education for either men or women in the United States did not begin until after the Civil War. Prior to that time, apprenticeships in architectural firms were the normal way for both men and women to gain the requisite experience, and even after the Civil War, Louise Blanchard Bethune and Minerva Parker Nichols received their training through apprenticeships.

In the late 1860s, the country's educational system expanded. The Massachusetts Institute of Technology began in 1868 and included the first recognized school of architecture in the United States. Cornell University and the University of Illinois, both land-grant schools, opened by 1871 under the provisions of the Morrill Land-Grant Act of 1862.[54] Cornell awarded the first recognized university architectural degree to a woman in 1880.[55] Between 1878 and 1894, only eight women completed four academic architectural programs in the United States, and only a few schools, including Syracuse, Cornell, Cooper Union, the University of Illinois, and MIT even admitted women to degree programs in architecture.[56] Harvard University, the University of Pennsylvania, the George Washington University, and Columbia University were among the schools that closed their doors to women interested in studying architecture.[57] Bethune estimated in 1891 that the number of women with architecture degrees could " 'hardly exceed a dozen.' "[58] Even after opportunities were available in the United States, however, the most prestigious education available was at the Ecole des Beaux Arts in Paris.

The American Institute of Architects (AIA), in 1901, began to require that members pass an examination or have a degree from an accredited school of architecture, thereby making it more difficult for men and women to enter the profession through the apprenticeship route. Five years later, the AIA's Committee on Education, dominated by educators and graduates of architecture schools, defined professional education for architects as " 'the breeding of gentlemen of cultivation, learning, and broad sympathies. . . ,' " thereby erecting even higher barriers to women in the profession.[59]

One option for women interested in pursuing careers as architects was the Cambridge School, officially the Smith College Graduate School of Architecture and Landscape Architecture in Cambridge by the 1930s. The school began in 1915 when a Radcliffe graduate, Katherine Brooks, asked Professor Pray, head of Harvard's Graduate School of Landscape Architecture, if she could study there. When Harvard's rules barred her entrance, Pray arranged for Henry Atherton Frost, an instructor in Harvard's Graduate School of Architecture, to be her tutor. Frost and his partner, Bremer Pond, soon found that they were running an informal school as more women showed up to be tutored, so they began to organize, setting up a curriculum and charging tuition. By integrating architecture and landscape architecture, the school became an early proponent of environmental design.

Although Harvard's administration was not enthusiastic, almost five hundred women, and no men, attended the "school" before Smith College officials closed it in 1941–1942. Smith College had assumed control of the school in 1938 when all architectural schools required a university association to be accredited. The school operated at five locations on or near Harvard Square, with its longest tenure (1928–1942) at 53 Church Street, a large frame house which is extant and merits NHL designation for its association with women's architectural education, for it was purchased by a former student, Faith Bemis, to be leased to the school. Here we can see how women helped each other achieve an education, as alumnae and outside supporters contributed funds to build a north-lighted wing with two large drafting rooms to accommodate sixty students. The number of women architects practicing in the Boston area, some of whom are noted below, is a tribute to the opportunities available at the Cambridge School and MIT.[60]

Even if they could obtain an education, women architects faced difficulties. The business aspect of architecture that involved getting commissions, and thereby perhaps mixing with politicians, was considered unladylike and unbecoming to women. Architects need clients with money, and women had little influence in the business world. Nor could women legally sign contracts in some cases, thereby denying the women architects the right to act on their own behalf in this important area.[61]

As the "New Woman" emerged in the 1890s, she joined with other women in the years ahead to use her influence and money to hire women architects for projects that included the construction of women's clubhouses, YWCAs, and private residences. Perhaps the first such use of a commission directed specifically to women architects was that issued for the design of the Woman's Building at the World's Columbian Exposition in Chicago.[62]

The first generation of women architects is here defined as those completing their architectural educations before the AIA cut off the option of apprenticeships in 1901 in a move that is generally considered to have restricted opportunities for women. To understand the evolution of women as architects, the most prominent individual women will be discussed here in approximate chronological order. In each case, the focus is on women who were responsible for the design of complete buildings, not, for example, only the design of individual rooms within those buildings through the design and placement of furnishings or the design of wall coverings.

Harriet Abigail Morrison Irwin (1828–1897) of Charlotte, North Carolina, is one of the earliest women designers to leave a record of her work. In 1869, she received a patent for an "Improvement in the Construction of Houses," her design for a hexagonal building that had no entrance hall, only one central chimney, and rooms that were either diamond- or hexagonal-shaped to maximize light and ventilation, thereby improving the physical health of the residents. One version of these mansard-roofed houses was built about 1869 at 912 West Fifth Street in Charlotte; she also designed at least two other homes nearby. Unfortunately, none of Irwin's buildings are extant. She publicized her work in her novel *The Hermit of Petraea* (1871). Irwin's houses are "evidence of the first dwelling plan patented by an American woman and indicate an initial, crucial step toward women creating a conscious identity as architects."[63]

Louise Blanchard Bethune (1856–1913), the first professional woman architect in the United States, practiced in Buffalo, New York. She learned her trade by studying architecture at Cornell University for two years and then by apprenticing in the office of Buffalo architect Richard A. Waite before opening her own firm. She announced the opening of her firm at the Ninth Congress of the Association for the Advancement of Women held in Buffalo in October 1881. In December, she married Robert Armour Bethune, her partner; they then shared the firm of Bethune & Bethune.

The firm built eighteen public schools in Buffalo and its suburbs, the Woman's Prison at the Erie County Penitentiary, the 74th Regiment Armory (later Elmwood Music Hall), Buffalo Baseball Association grandstand and additions, the police station for Buffalo's Precinct No. 2, industrial and commercial buildings such as the Cataract Power & Conduit Company transformer building and the Jacob Dold wholesale meat packing building, in addition to houses. The Denton, Cottier & Daniels music store, built by the firm and later demolished, was one of the country's first steel and concrete buildings, using steel framing and poured concrete floors to provide a fire-resistant structure. Bethune herself can be definitively credited with only ten buildings of her own design, including the Lockport Union High School (1890, now demolished) and the Hotel Lafayette (1902–1904, still standing).

The French Renaissance-style Hotel Lafayette is considered to be Bethune's masterpiece. The 265-room fireproof hotel was designed originally to house visitors to the Pan-American Exposition, but the hotel did not open until June

1, 1904, due to financial problems. Situated at the corner of Washington and Clinton streets, across from Lafayette Park and "amid quiet surroundings," the seven-story steel-frame hotel has a facade of dark-red brick and white terra cotta trim. The hotel also has concrete floors, a concrete roof, and wrought iron balconies. The only wood used in the construction, assured the owners, was in the doors and window frames so that the building would be "absolutely fireproof." The lobby, 72 feet by 84 feet, was "finished in Numidian marble and mahogany, and the furniture of soft red leather harmonizes with the prevailing color of the room," noted a hotel advertising brochure (ca. 1904). The hotel accommodated the needs of women guests, with a women's reception room near the carriage entrance; a women's parlor on the second floor; a tea room that was "a marvel of daintiness and good taste, and of graceful proportions"; and a second women's reception room, "a symphony in silver and mauve," near the banquet hall and "conveniently" apart from the rest of the hotel. The rooms were all advertised to be "bright; cheerful; spacious; well lighted and well ventilated . . .—specially adapted for families and others desiring the privacy and comforts of a home."[64]

Bethune did not enter the competition for the Woman's Building at the World's Columbian Exposition, agreeing with the American Institute of Architects, which opposed competitions on principle, and arguing that a separate Woman's Building somehow implied inferiority. She also objected to the fact that the honorarium was not equal to that given to men for comparable projects.[65] Bethune was admitted to the Western Association of Architects in 1885, was a major organizer of the Architects Association in Buffalo in 1886, became the first woman to be admitted to the American Institute of Architects in 1888 and, the following year, became its first female Fellow. She also served as vice-president and treasurer of the AIA. Bethune retired in 1908.[66]

Minerva Parker Nichols (1861–1949) was one of America's first professional women architects. She studied at the Philadelphia Normal Art School, graduating in 1882, and at the Franklin Institute in Philadelphia before beginning her career by drafting with Philadelphia architect Frederick G. Thorn, Jr., in January 1882. Parker took over Thorn's practice when he retired in 1888, married Unitarian minister William Nichols in 1891, and continued the office until 1895. During that time, she specialized in designing private homes, some of which can be found in the Philadelphia suburbs of Radnor, Cynwood, Berwyn, Germantown, and Overbrook. These combined medieval features with detailing based on the work of Eastlake and Furness. In *Housekeeper's Weekly*, for June 10, 1893, she argued that each room of a house needed its own style to express its unique purpose and the temperaments of its occupants. In addition, her commissions included two factories for Geano and Raggio, a Philadelphia spaghetti manufacturer, and the Browne and Nichols School in Cambridge, Massachusetts.

Nichols entered the competition for the Woman's Building at the Chicago

Hotel Lafayette, Buffalo, New York. Most acclaimed building by architect Louise Blanchard Bethune. (Photograph by Joseph Stallone, courtesy of Adriana Barbasch)

Columbian Exposition in 1893 but was apparently unsuccessful in winning the competition for several reasons. First, she had already produced a Moorish design for the Isabella Pavilion, modeled on the Alhambra where Queen Isabella was buried, for the Queen Isabella Association, which claimed to be promoting the interests of women at the fair; while the building was built, it was not to Nichols' design. Second, Frances Dickinson submitted Nichols's design for the Isabella Pavilion to Bertha Honore Palmer, president of the Board of Lady Managers, even though the design did not blend with the neoclasical motif for the rest of the fair complex.[67] Nichols also designed clubhouses for New Century Clubs in Philadelphia (1893, now demolished) and Wilmington, Delaware (extant); the first was "vaguely Renaissance" in style, and the second colonial. After leaving Philadelphia in 1896 with her husband, she continued her practice on an occasional basis with projects for friends and relatives.[68]

Sophia Gregoria Hayden (ca. 1868–1953), born in Chile and raised in Jamaica Plain, Massachusetts, entered MIT in 1886 and became the first woman to complete the four-year course in architecture there, receiving the Bachelor of Architecture degree in 1890. That same year, she taught mechanical drawing in Jamaica Plain. In 1891, at twenty-one, she won first prize in the competition to design the Woman's Building for the World's Columbian Exposition with a design based on the Renaissance Museum of Fine Arts she had designed for her MIT thesis. The building is no longer standing, but Hayden's design, claimed the judges, had the requisite " 'balconies, loggias and vases for flowers' " that produced a design that was " 'the lightest and gayest in its general aspect, and consequently best adapted for a joyous and festive occasion.' "[69] While she won the competition, Hayden's work as architect on the Woman's Building was far from easy, and she apparently suffered some type of nervous breakdown by the time the building was dedicated in 1892, leading the *American Architect* to question whether women had the stamina to pursue careers as architects. Hayden designed a Memorial Building for the Women's Clubs of America in 1894, but this was never constructed. She married artist William Bennett soon thereafter. Her obituary did not take notice of her career as an architect.[70]

Perhaps the best known and most prolific woman architect was Julia Morgan (1872–1957), who helped to further open the field of architecture to women.[71] Growing up in a comfortable style in Oakland, California, her mother motivated her to excel. Perhaps encouraged by her mother's cousin, architect Pierre LeBrun, she entered the University of California, Berkeley, where she became the first woman student in the College of Engineering; architecture courses were taught in that college. There, she met Bernard Maybeck, a graduate of the École des Beaux Arts who taught an informal architecture course at his home and became a major influence in Morgan's life. Morgan received her degree in engineering in 1894. Leaving for Paris in 1896, Morgan gained admission to the École des Beaux Arts in 1898 as the first woman in the world admitted to the Architectural Section. In 1902, she became the first woman to graduate from that section.

Morgan returned to California, where, in 1902, she became the first woman to earn an architect's license in the state, just one year after the state started to license architects. While working with John Galen Howard on the campus master plan, Hearst Memorial Mining Building, and Greek Theatre at the University of California, Berkeley, she met Phoebe Apperson Hearst. The two Berkeley buildings were part of the campus comprehensive plan designed in a competition financed by Phoebe Hearst.[72] Morgan then remodeled the Hearst Hacienda at Pleasanton and worked with Maybeck to design a castle and "village" at Wyntoon, both for Hearst. It is possible that Hearst persuaded Morgan to open her own practice in 1904; certainly, she helped her get commissions.

Morgan's fame spread as she designed a reinforced concrete Mission-style bell tower (1903–1904) for Mills College, a women's college, and redwood shingle homes. The disaster of the 1906 San Francisco earthquake proved to be an important opportunity for Morgan, who won the commission to rebuild the

Asilomar Conference Grounds, Pacific Grove, California. Administration Building designed by architect Julia Morgan. (Photograph by Aaron Gallup, California Office of Historic Preservation, courtesy of National Park Service)

Fairmont Hotel, now one of the city's most luxurious hotels. Working in a partnership with Ira Hoover between 1907 and 1910, she again established her own office in 1910. She then built residences, churches, clubs, banks, hospitals, offices, stores, and educational buildings, including the Berkeley Baptist Seminary; the home of her sister Emma North in Berkeley (1909); the Ben Reed House in Piedmont (1926); and for Oakland, California's, Mills College, a library (1905–1906), El Campanile (1903–1904), gymnasium (1907–1908), and Alumnae Hall (1916). She designed the "rambling, shingled" St. John's Presbyterian Church (1908–1910) in Berkeley, which has been, says Tinling, an "architectural landmark ever since" its construction.[73] Increasingly, she favored the Spanish Revival style for her work and became adept at the use of steel reinforced concrete for institutional buildings.

Women and women's organizations provided an increasingly important source of commissions for Morgan. She designed a series of residence halls throughout California for the Young Women's Christian Association (YWCA), as well as their Asilomar Conference Center (1913–1928) at Pacific Grove, near Monterey, California. Grace Merriam Fisher, a sorority sister of Morgan's, worked with her on her first YWCA commission, in Oakland, California, in 1915, while Fisher was a member of the YWCA's national board. During World War I, Morgan also built hospitality houses for the YWCA. Her designs for women's clubhouses included the Saratoga Foothill Club (1915) and the Berkeley City Club (1929). During the 1930s, she also designed YWCAs in Salt Lake City and Honolulu. She also received commissions from women's hospitals and retirement homes; for example, she designed the King's Daughters of California Home for Incurables in Oakland, California, in 1912.[74]

While working with Phoebe Hearst on the Berkeley campus buildings, Morgan met Phoebe's son, William Randolph Hearst, for whom she designed La Cuesta Encantada (1919–1940), better known as Hearst Castle. La Cuesta Encantada, Morgan's most famous project, was also her most difficult. Building on an inaccessible site, she began working on the estate in 1919 and spent twenty years on the project, building a dock, warehouses, and roads so that supplies could be brought to the site, providing a method to bring water to the site from its source five miles away, and designing ways to incorporate the sections of European palaces and cathedrals that Hearst had accumulated on his travels to Europe.[75]

In addition to La Cuesta Encantada, she worked for Hearst for over two decades after World War I, gaining almost one-third of her career commissions from him and building her staff to thirty-five to handle the work. These commissions included newspaper facilities in Los Angeles and San Francisco and "pleasure palaces" in California and Mexico, buildings in the Grand Canyon (1925), Wyntoon (1930–1945), and the Phoebe Apperson Hearst Memorial Gymnasium (1924–1926) at the University of California, Berkeley. Hearst endowed the gymnasium with the stipulation that it be designed by Morgan and Maybeck; it was named Hearst Hall in memory of Phoebe Hearst and replaced an earlier structure that burned in 1922.[76] Morgan's work for Hearst ended in the mid-1930s when the publishing company faced financial problems.

Throughout her career, Morgan produced over 800 structures. Her other commissions included the new campus of Principia College in Elmhurst, Illinois, where she collaborated again with Maybeck. Although Morgan's office survived the depression of the 1930s without retrenchment, she was forced to cut back her practice when World War II produced a shortage of building materials. Her last project was a design for a medieval museum in Golden Gate Park in San Francisco; this has not been constructed.

While she avoided publicity, Morgan was a pivotal figure in American architecture in the first half of the twentieth century. She did not consider herself a feminist, but she provided important support to future women architects, as she employed them in her architectural office and offered financial aid, anonymously, to women students. As an architect, her designs for redwood shingle houses "contributed to the emergence of the Bay area shingle style" in the San Francisco region, and she was "a decade ahead of most of her contemporaries in using structure as a means of architectural expression." She did not, however, work in the International style, which was gaining favor around the world in the first decades of the twentieth century.[77] Throughout her work, she became known for her "client-centered approach to design, her use of locally available materials, and her integration of the varied architectural traditions of the West with the sophisticated vocabulary of her Beaux-Arts training."[78] She retired and had many of her records destroyed in 1952, insisting that her buildings were the only record necessary of her career because " 'architecture is a visual, not a verbal art.' "[79]

Mary Jane Elizabeth Colter (1869–1958) was one of the first architects to "recreate the cultural heritage of the region instead of imitating European styles."[80] She became interested in artifacts of Native Americans while growing up in St. Paul, Minnesota. At age seventeen, she went to San Francisco to study art at the California School of Design, and graduated in 1890. She became apprenticed in a architectural office at a time when California architects were developing the Spanish Revival style to suit the California landscape, but she then returned to St. Paul to teach mechanical drawing at Mechanic Arts High School. While visiting in California one year, she met the manager of a Fred Harvey Shop and indicated an interest in working for the company. In 1902, she was hired by the Fred Harvey Company and the Santa Fe Railway as an architect and decorator, working that summer as decorator for the Indian Building next to the Alvarado Hotel in Albuquerque, where Native American crafts were to be displayed to visitors.

After that summer job, Colter returned to teaching in St. Paul until 1904, when she was commissioned to design a Native American building across from the new El Tovar Hotel at the Grand Canyon; known as Hopi House, the building opened January 1, 1905, and Colter again returned to St. Paul to teach. It was not until 1910 that Colter was offered a permanent position as architect and designer with the Fred Harvey Company, designing hotels, restaurants, and union station facilities. While it is not likely that Colter was ever a licensed architect, she worked with licensed architects at the Santa Fe Railway who could do the necessary final drawings for her work.

Her major early works include Hermit's Rest (1914), Lookout (1914), Phantom Ranch (1922), Watchtower (1932), Bright Angel Lodge (1935), Men's Dormitory (1936), and Women's Dormitory (1937), all at the Grand Canyon; her design for the Indian Gardens at the Grand Canyon, her only signed drawings still extant, was never built. Other important projects include the El Navajo Hotel (Gallup, New Mexico, 1923, demolished 1957), decoration of the Fred Harvey shops and restaurants at the Chicago Union Terminal (1924), decoration of the La Fonda Hotel (Santa Fe, New Mexico, 1929), the decoration of the Fred Harvey diners on the Santa Fe's Super Chief train (1936), original decoration and renovation of the Fred Harvey facilities at Kansas City's Union Station (redecoration, 1937), decoration of the Fred Harvey facilities at Los Angeles's Union Station (1939), and decoration of the Painted Desert Inn at Petrified Forest National Park, Arizona. Her La Posada Hotel,

built for the Fred Harvey Company in 1930 in Winslow, Arizona, was her fa-
vorite building; it included eighty rooms, a coffee shop seating 116, a dining
room accommodating seventy-two, and a bar and cocktail lounge. When
threatened with demolition in 1957, the building was saved by the Santa Fe
Railway and converted into its division headquarters.[81] Throughout her career,
Colter specialized in buildings that reflected the Native American and Spanish
tradition of the Southwest, where she practiced until her retirement in 1947.
She also played an important role in encouraging national interest in Native
American arts and crafts.[82]

The women architects discussed above were among the most important
of their generation, but they were not alone. Lois Lilly Howe (1864–
1964) opened her own office in Boston in 1895. She became known for
her work with plaster as an exterior finishing material and documented New
England's vernacular architecture through measured drawings, publishing
these in 1913 in collaboration with Constance Fuller as *Details from Old
New England Houses*. In 1913, Howe opened an architectural practice with
Eleanor Manning O'Connor (1884–1973), also an MIT graduate. They always
hired women graduates of MIT. In 1924, Howe and Manning designed a series
of homes for the Cincinnati, Ohio, suburb of Mariemont, hailed as a " 'National Exemplar in Town Planning.' " Mariemont is a historic district on
the National Register of Historic Places. The all-female firm of Howe, Manning, & Almy organized under that name in 1926 and dissolved in 1936 or
1937.[83]

While women have received little attention as architects, they are even less
well known as landscape architects. Landscape architecture is a separate theme
in the NHL typology, but a few comments are appropriate here because the
subject is not addressed elsewhere in this anthology. The number of women
landscape architects is even fewer than the number of women architects, and
only one, Beatrix Jones Farrand (1872–1959), will be discussed because she
was the premier woman landscape architect of her generation.

Farrand began her formal study of landscape architecture near Brookline,
Massachusetts, by studying with Charles Sprague Sargent, founder and first director of the Arnold Arboretum of Harvard University. Undoubtedly, her family's social position helped her get her first private commissions, which included
work for J. P. Morgan. For almost fifty years, Farrand was the consulting landscape architect for Abby Aldrich Rockefeller's garden at her home in Seal Harbor, Maine. In 1899, two years after beginning her private practice, Farrand
was one of the founding members, with Frederick Law Olmsted and Charles
Eliot, among others, of the American Society of Landscape Architects. Farrand
was influenced in her work by two English landscape specialists, landscape architect William Robinson and landscape gardener Gertrude Jekyll, and by her
aunt, novelist Edith Wharton, who wrote *Italian Villas and Their Gardens*. Farrand's commissions included Dartington Hall in England, Princeton Univers-

ity's Graduate College gardens (beginning in 1916), Yale University's Memorial Quadrangle gardens (beginning in 1923), gardens for Mrs. Theodore Roosevelt and Mrs. Woodrow Wilson, and consulting work at Vassar and Oberlin colleges and the University of Chicago. She retired in 1948.

Farrand's most important work was at Dumbarton Oaks, 3101 R Street, N.W., Washington, D.C., the home of her friend Mildred Bliss. Farrand worked on these gardens from 1923 through the 1930s. In 1940, the Blisses gave Dumbarton Oaks to Harvard University, and in 1944, the estate served as the site of the Dumbarton Oaks Conferences, which led to the formation of the United Nations charter. Although only sixteen acres survive of the fifty-four-acre garden Farrand designed, it is her only design where any large section has survived virtually unchanged. Only a few sites have been designated as NHLs under the theme of landscape architecture; Dumbarton Oaks was considered as a possible NHL in 1976, but a final decision awaits a full theme study.[84]

The pioneering women in architecture and landscape architecture have left more permanent monuments of their own creativity than have those women active in historic preservation and domestic architecture. The buildings and gardens women designed still stand, in some cases, to illustrate their work.

Dumbarton Oaks, Washington, D.C. Gardens designed by landscape architect Beatrix Farrand. (Photograph by Jill S. Topolski)

These architects and landscape architects relied heavily on their network of women friends and colleagues for commissions, and scholars influenced by the women's movement of the late twentieth century have recovered their legacy. It is no accident that, with the major exception of Charles B. Hosmer, Jr.'s, work, many of the references cited here are to women scholars writing over the past two decades.

The buildings cited in this chapter, then, help to tell us how women perceived the built environment and how they understood the concept of domestic and public space. Women understood that buildings associated with the nation's heroes were important tangible reminders of our history that should be preserved as places to teach us about the character of those individuals, that we can better appreciate George Washington's longing to return to Mount Vernon by seeing the beautiful house on a wide expanse of green grass, that we can better understand Thomas Jefferson's inventions by seeing them installed in Monticello. Even conceptualizing the idea of kitchenless houses meant a radical change in thinking about the purpose of the home on the part of writers such as Charlotte Perkins Gilman. Few architects, female or male, were as creative as Harriet Irwin in her design for hexagonal rooms. Few were as versatile as Julia Morgan; and it is Morgan's buildings, as she herself noted, that are the best monuments to that versatility. Dumbarton Oaks tells us more about Farrand's design capabilities than photographs in a book.

There is no doubt that we need better interpretation of the significance of these women preservationists, designers, and architects at the sites themselves. Too often we hear only about the people who lived in the building, not about those who worked to preserve it. In the case of Mount Vernon or the White House of the Confederacy, women's preservation efforts have long outlasted the tenancy of the persons honored. At historic houses, kitchens, servant quarters, and basements where housewives, servants, and slaves cooked are too often not shown to the public because they are used for storage or office space or because there is no safe public access to the spaces. If shown, the pots are brightly polished, the floors swept clean, the beds made. We need to see the conditions that drove women like the Beecher sisters to consider alternatives, and then we need to see how those really worked. Our women architects also deserve full recognition for their accomplishments by appropriate achnowledgment at the sites themselves.

All of the women discussed here, and their sisters in their causes, have left us their tangible legacy that provides a challenge to the future. How many women will form or join a historic preservation organization after visiting Mount Vernon? What new designs for twenty-first-century kitchens may percolate through the mind of a visitor to the Harriet Beecher Stowe house? What young woman will decide to be an architect after visiting a Julia Morgan building? We cannot afford *not* to protect and interpret these buildings, for they are gifts from the past to the future.

NOTES

1. I am indebted to Dr. Patricia Mooney-Melvin, Dr. Jannelle Warren-Findley, and Dr. Heather Huyck, who read earlier versions of the section of this manuscript that relates to the history of women in historic preservation; Dr. Huyck, particularly, provided valuable editorial expertise. Some of the material on women and historic preservation in this chapter is reprinted, with revisions, from Barbara J. Howe, "Women in Historic Preservation: The Legacy of Ann Pamela Cunningham," *The Public Historian* 12 (Winter 1990): 31–41, by permission of the Regents of the University of California, which holds the 1990 copyright.

2. Lamia Doumato, "Louisa Tuthill's Unique Achievement: First History of Architecture in the U.S.," in *Architecture: A Place for Women*, ed. Ellen Perry Berkeley and Matilda McQuaid (Washington, D.C.: Smithsonian Institution Press, 1989), 5–13.

3. Gail Lee Dubrow, "Restoring a Female Presence: New Goals in Historic Preservation," in *Architecture: A Place for Women*, 159–60.

4. Almost every history of women in America discusses the efforts of women in the nineteenth century to organize to solve the country's problems. One such summary is available in Nancy Woloch, *Women and the American Experience* (New York: Alfred A. Knopf, 1984), 167–99. For a women's studies perspective on some of the events to be discussed below, emphasizing the cult of true womanhood as applied to historic preservation, see Margaret Supplee Smith, "Beyond the Domestic Sphere . . . Barely: Early Women Preservationists and Historic Preservation" (paper presented at National Trust for Historic Preservation annual meeting, October 1987, Washington, D.C.).

5. Charles B. Hosmer, Jr., *Presence of the Past: A History of the Preservation Movement in the United States before Williamsburg* (New York: G. P. Putnam's Sons, 1965), 45.

6. Ibid., 43, 44.

7. Ibid., 49–50.

8. Ibid., 55.

9. Ibid., 56–57, 62.

10. William J. Murtagh, *Keeping Time: The History and Theory of Preservation in America* (Pittstown, N.J.: The Main Street Press, 1988), 30.

11. Hosmer, *Presence of the Past*, 57–60, 70, 105.

12. Ibid., 66. For additional information on the formation of the APVA, see James M. Lindgren, " 'For the Sake of our Future': The Association for the Preservation of Virginia Antiquities and the Regeneration of Traditionalism," *Virginia Magazine of History and Biography* 97 (January 1989): 49–74. In 1985, ownership of the Powder Magazine was transferred to Colonial Williamsburg. The Powder Magazine is included within the Williamsburg NHL Historic District.

13. The Society of the Colonial Dames of America, United Daughters of the Confederacy (UDC), and the Daughters of the Republic of Texas, other hereditary groups organized in the late nineteenth century, also preserved historic sites such as the Alamo (Daughters of the Republic of Texas) and Georgia's Fort Frederica (Georgia Society of Colonial Dames of America). Their efforts can be documented through Hosmer's histories of the historic preservation movement and through histories of the organizations. While the UDC focused on preserving history by collecting documents and oral testimonies, the other groups worked to preserve the built environment, as well as the written and photographic record. For a description of the UDC work, as well as the activities of other patriotic groups in the South, see Jacqueline Goggin, "Politics, Patriotism, and Professionalism: American Women Historians and the Preservation of Southern Culture, 1890–1940" (paper presented at American Historical Association annual meeting, December 1989, San Francisco, Calif.).

14. Juliette Boyer Baker, comp. and ed., *West Virginia State History of the Daughters of the American Revolution* (n.p., n.d. [1928]), 5.

15. Floride Cunningham, of South Carolina, was one of the eighteen original members of the DAR; she was a relative of Ann Pamela Cunningham. For information on the Betsy Ross House, see Hosmer, *Presence of the Past*, 88–91. I am indebted to Mollie Somerville, who shared her impressions of the DAR's work in historic preservation during a telephone conversation on 30 August 1989. Ms. Somerville began writing the history of the DAR about 1964, when she was hired by the organization to write its seventy-fifth anniversary history; she has published two subsequent histories, in addition to other publications for the organization. She noted that, despite her efforts and various state DAR histories, the DAR's work in historic preservation is "inadequately written," citing ten issues per year of the DAR's magazine published since 1892 as sources.

16. Mollie Somerville, telephone conversation with Barbara J. Howe, 30 August 1989. Cowpens National Battlefield was established as a national battlefield site on March 4, 1929 and transferred from the War Department to the National Park Service on August 10, 1933 (U.S. Department of the Interior, National Park Service, *The National Parks: Index 1987* [Washington, D.C.: National Park Service Office of Public Affairs, 1987], 35). All references to dates for the authorization or establishment of the National Park Service are from this source.

17. Hosmer, *Presence of the Past*, 88. The Pennsylvania Society of the Colonial Dames of America started to join the effort but decided to restore the Senate Chamber in Congress Hall, next to Independence Hall, instead of tackling that building. Their restoration efforts can still be seen today.

18. Ibid., 96. The ASHPS name was officially adopted in 1901.

19. The Madonna of the Trails statues, still maintained by the DAR chapters, are located in Bethesda, Maryland; Washington County, Pennsylvania; Wheeling, West Virginia; Springfield, Ohio; Richmond, Indiana; Vandalia, Illinois; Lexington, Missouri; Council Grove, Kansas; Lamark, Colorado; Albuquerque, New Mexico; Springerville, Arizona; and Upland, California. The Bethesda statue had to be moved to a new location because of road construction (Mollie Somerville, telephone conversation with Barbara J. Howe, 30 August 1989).

20. Polly Kaufman, telephone conversation with Barbara J. Howe, 24 August 1989. Kaufman is preparing the definitive history of women in the National Park Service; the information supplied in the conversation came from her two chapters on women as "savers," and I am grateful to her for these leads. Bent's Old Fort was established as a National Historic Site on June 3, 1960 (U.S. Department of the Interior, National Park Service, *The National Parks: Index 1987*, 28.

21. Mollie Somerville, comp., *Historic and Memorial Buildings of the Daughters of the American Revolution* (Washington, D.C.: National Society, Daughters of the American Revolution, 1979).

22. Marion Tinling, *Women Remembered: A Guide to Landmarks of Women's History in the United States* (Westport, Conn.: Greenwood Press, 1986), 642–43. The national monument designation was made under the terms of the Antiquities Act of 1906, which "authorized the president to designate resources on public lands as national monuments and provided some protection for prehistoric and historic properties by assigning criminal penalties for unauthorized actions that would disturb them" (Beth Grosvenor, "Federal Programs in Historic Preservation," in *Public History: An Introduction*, ed. Barbara J. Howe and Emory L. Kemp [Malabar, Fla.: Robert E. Krieger Publishing Co., 1986], 132–33).

23. Paula Giddings, *When and Where I Enter: The Impact of Black Women on Race*

and Sex in America (New York: Bantam Books, 1984), 138. The Frederick Douglass Home National Memorial became part of the National Park System on September 5, 1962.

24. For more information on the foundation, see Charles B. Hosmer, Jr., *Preservation Comes of Age: From Williamsburg to the National Trust, 1926–1949*, vol. 1 (Charlottesville: University Press of Virginia, 1981), 190–201.

25. All information on Frost is from Sidney R. Bland, " 'Miss Sue' of Charleston: Saving a Neighborhood, Influencing a Nation," in *Architecture: A Place for Women*, 63–73; and Charles H. Lesser, senior historian, to Page Putnam Miller, 6 November 1989, letter in possession of the author.

26. Hosmer, *Preservation Comes of Age*, vol. 1, 275–79.

27. Tinling, *Women Remembered*, 603.

28. For summaries of Werlein's career, see Hosmer, *Preservation Comes of Age*, vol. 1, 297–305; Gail Lee Dubrow, "Supplementary Sheet: Elizabeth Werlein Residence," undated typescript prepared for Women's History NHL study (citing Mary Gehman and Nancy Ries, *Women and New Orleans* [New Orleans: Margaret Media, 1988], 111–13), in possession of the author; and William G. Wiegand, "Werlein, Elizabeth Thomas," in *Notable American Women*, vol. 3, ed. Edward T. James, Janet Wilson James, and Paul S. Boyer (Cambridge: Belknap Press of Harvard University Press, 1971), 568–69. Hosmer says that the Vieux Carre Property Owners' Association was organized in June 1938 (p. 297), while Wiegand gives 1930 as the date (p. 569). Dubrow states that *The Wrought Iron Railings* booklet was published in 1917, while Wiegand gives the date of 1910.

29. Hosmer, *Preservation Comes of Age*, vol. 2, 142–43, 176.

30. Tinling, *Women Remembered*, 306. This site is already a National Historic Landmark. The National Trust for Historic Preservation has since named its most prestigious preservation award, recognizing superlative lifetime achievement in the field, for Crowninshield.

31. Helen Duprey Bullock first worked in Williamsburg, Virginia, in 1929 and became an archivist there. Two women who worked with HABS were Henrietta Dozier (1872–1947), who worked on the documentation of historic structures in Saint Augustine, Florida, and Georgia Bertha Drennan, who worked on the Louisiana survey and eventually served as the office supervisor for the project. For Dozier, see American Architectural Foundation, *"That Exceptional One,"* 18; and Matilda McQuaid, "Educating for the Future: A Growing Archive on Women in Architecture," in *Architecture: A Place for Women*, 254–55, 257. For Drennan, see Samuel Wilson, Jr., "The Survey in Louisiana in the 1930s," in *Historic America: Buildings, Structures, and Sites* (Washington, D.C.: Library of Congress, 1983), 31, 32.

32. Doris Cole, *From Tipi to Skyscraper* (Boston: i press inc., 1973), ix, x.

33. There are numerous works that discuss the changes in American domestic architecture, emphasizing the ideology and technology that accompanied those changes. These include Dolores Hayden, *The Grand Domestic Revolution: A History of Feminist Designs for American Homes, Neighborhoods, and Cities* (Cambridge: The MIT Press, 1981); Margaret Marsh, "From Separation to Togetherness: The Social Construction of Domestic Space in American Suburbs, 1840–1915," *Journal of American History* 76 (1989): 506–27; Colleen McDannell, *The Christian Home in Victorian America, 1840–1900* (Bloomington: Indiana University Press, 1986); Gwendolyn Wright, *Building the Dream: A Social History of Housing in America* (New York: Pantheon Books, 1981); and Gwendolyn Wright, *Moralism and the Model Home: Domestic Architecture and Cultural Conflict in Chicago, 1873–1913* (Chicago: University of Chicago Press, 1980). All have extensive bibliographies for additional references. In addition, of course, the writings of the various theorists and reformers are available. Standard ar-

chitectural histories cover the basic changes in the "high styles" popular for domestic architecture throughout American history, while the extensive literature on vernacular and folk architecture examines the housing occupied by those who lived in areas less influenced by "high styles" and the sometimes academic debates of theorists.

34. Marsh, "From Separation to Togetherness," 517.

35. Hayden, *Grand Domestic Revolution*, 3.

36. Kathryn Kish Sklar, *Catharine Beecher: A Study in American Domesticity* (New York: W. W. Norton & Co., 1973), 151, 152, 153, 154–55.

37. Catharine Beecher, *A Treatise on Domestic Economy* (New York: Shocken Books, 1977, reprint of 1841 ed.), 268.

38. For Beecher's ideas on the construction of the house, see ibid., 268–97; parlors are discussed on pp. 337–49, breakfast and dining rooms on pp. 350–58, chambers and bedrooms on pp. 358–65, and kitchens, cellars, and storerooms on pp. 366–76.

39. Sklar, *Catharine Beecher*, 263–64, xi; Leland M. Roth, *A Concise History of American Architecture* (New York: Harper & Row, 1979), 152. For an illustration of her house-church-school, see Sklar, *Catharine Beecher*, illustrations following p. 174 or McDannell, *The Christian Home*, 38.

40. National Register of Historic Places nomination form for Harriet Beecher Stowe House, prepared for Women's History National Historic Landmarks theme study, 1990.

41. For additional information on Peirce, see Hayden, *Grand Domestic Revolution*, 67–72, 77–79ff; quotation is on p. 67.

42. Ibid., 80–81.

43. Hayden, *Grand Domestic Revolution*, 183.

44. For an overview of Gilman's influence on domestic architecture, see ibid., 183–205. The proposed designs are on pp. 187, 190–191, and 193.

45. This chapter concentrates only on housing reform, as opposed to related efforts to create playgrounds, for instance. That topic is covered in Gail Lee Dubrow's chapter.

46. Eugenie Ladner Birch, "Woman-Made America: The Case of Early Housing Policy," *American Institute of Planners Journal* (April 1978): 132–33.

47. Ibid., 131.

48. Ibid., 133, quoting from *The Housing of the Unskilled Wage Earner*.

49. Eugenie L. Birch, "Wood, Edith Elmer," in *MacMillan Encyclopedia of Architects*, ed. Adolph K. Placek (New York: MacMillan, 1982), 412; and Birch, "Woman-Made America," 130–44, provide an overview of Wood's career.

50. Cole, *From Tipi to Skyscraper*, ix, xi.

51. Judith Paine, "Pioneer Women Architects," in *Women in American Architecture: A Historic and Contemporary Perspective*, ed. Susanna Torre (New York: Watson-Guptill Publications, 1977), 54.

52. Information on Colter's structures is excerpted from section 8 of the National Register of Historic Places Inventory—Nomination Form, prepared by Laura Soulliere Harrison in 1986.

53. Information on La Cuesta Encantada is from Richard W. Longstreth, *Julia Morgan: Architect* (Berkeley, Calif.: Berkeley Architectural Heritage Association, 1977), 9, 29 (quote). Information on Asilomar Conference Grounds is from Walter T. Steilberg, "Some Examples of the Work of Julia Morgan," *The Architect and Engineer of California* 55 (November 1918): 102; and History Division, National Park Service, *Catalog of National Historic Landmarks: 1987* (Washington, D.C.: U.S. Department of the Interior, 1987), 21.

54. Cole, *From Tipi to Skyscraper*, 75.

55. American Architectural Foundation, *"That Exceptional One": Women in American Architecture, 1888–1988* (American Architectural Foundation, 1988), 13.

56. Jeanne Madeline Weimann, *The Fair Women: The Story of the Woman's Building, World's Columbian Exposition, Chicago 1893* (Chicago: Academy Chicago, 1981), 145. Cooper Union admitted women from its founding in 1859, Cornell and Syracuse admitted women to study architecture in 1871, and the University of Illinois admitted women to study architecture in 1873 (Paine, "Pioneer Women Architects," 55).

57. Paine, "Pioneer Women Architects," 56.

58. Weimann, *The Fair Women*, 145.

59. Elizabeth G. Grossman and Lisa B. Reitzes, "Caught in the Crossfire: Women and Architectural Education, 1880–1910," in *Architecture: A Place for Women*, 30. This article provides a brief overview of the problems of architectural education for women in these decades.

60. For a description of the Cambridge School, see Dorothy May Anderson, "The Cambridge School: An Extraordinary Professional Education," in *Architecture: A Place for Women*, 87–98; "The Cambridge School," in *Women in American Architecture*, 91; and NHL nomination prepared for the Cambridge School of Architecture, 53 Church Street, as part of the Women's History National Historic Landmarks theme study. Anderson entered the Cambridge School in 1929. The footnotes for Anderson's article include the names of some Cambridge alumnae, but it appears that the records of this important institution are very slim. Torre's description gives 1941 as the closing date, but classes apparently ended then, while the school officially closed in February 1942. The Cambridge School Corporation was dissolved in 1945.

61. Cole, *From Tipi to Skyscraper*, 74–75.

62. The prospectus soliciting designs can be found in Weimann, *The Fair Women*, 147.

63. Paine, "Pioneer Women Architects," 55; and Beverly Heisner, "Irwin, Harriet Morrison," in *Macmillan Encyclopedia of Architects*, 46–67; quote is from Paine.

64. All quotes are from an untitled and undated pamphlet published by the Lafayette Hotel Company to promote the hotel; photo copy from files of Women's History National Historic Landmarks theme study, National Coordinating Committee for the Promotion of History, Washington, D.C. Additional architectural information is from the National Historic Landmark nomination form for the Hotel Lafayette prepared for the Women's History National Historic Landmarks theme study.

65. Weimann, *The Fair Women*, 147; and Paine, "Pioneer Women Architects," 62.

66. Weimann, *The Fair Women*, 144–45. Information on Bethune's career is from Adriana Barbasch, "Louise Blanchard Bethune: The AIA Accepts Its First Woman Member," in *Architecture: A Place for Women*, 15–25; American Architectural Foundation, *"That Exceptional One,"* 13, 16, 17; Austin M. Fox, "Louise Blanchard Bethune (1856–1913): Buffalo Feminist and America's First Woman Architect," *Buffalo Spree* (Summer 1986), 50–51; and Paine, "Pioneer Women Architects," 61–62. The most complete list of her buildings is Adriana Barbasch, "Louise Bethune, FAIA (1856–1913)," a brochure compiled in 1986 for the Buffalo/Western New York Chapter of the American Institute of Architects to celebrate 100 years of architecture (1886–1986).

67. Weimann, *The Fair Women*, 61, 67, 146.

68. Information on Minerva Parker Nichols is compiled from Cole, *From Tipi to Skyscraper*, 73; and Agnes Addison Gilchrist, "Nichols, Minerva Parker," in *Notable American Women*, vol. 2, 629–30. The most complete list of Nichols's work is in Paine, "Pioneer Women Architects," 63–64.

69. Weimann, *The Fair Women*, 148. For a description of the construction of the building, and alterations from Hayden's design, see 150–56.

70. Ibid., 145. Weimann discusses Hayden's relationships with the Board of Lady

Managers in *The Fair Women*. The Woman's Building controversy is also discussed in Paine, "Pioneer Women Architects," 57–60. Hayden's career in summarized in Judith Paine, "Sophia Hayden and the Woman's Building Competition," in *Women in American Architecture*, 70–71.

71. Information on Morgan's career is compiled from Sara Holmes Boutelle, "Morgan, Julia," *Macmillan Encyclopedia of Architects*, 258; Sara Holmes Boutelle, "Women's Networks: Julia Morgan and Her Clients," *Heresies* 11 (1981): 91–94; Elinor Richey, "Morgan, Julia," *Notable American Women: the Modern Period*, ed. Barbara Sicherman and Carol Hurd Green (Cambridge: Belknap Press of Harvard University Press, 1980), 499–501; Tinling, *Women Remembered*, 591–92, 593, 624; and Richard W. Longstreth, *Julia Morgan: Architect* (Berkeley, Calif.: Berkeley Architectural Heritage Association, 1977).

72. Tinling, *Women Remembered*, 591, 593. Tinling, on pp. 591–592, lists a large number of buildings named for prominent women faculty and staff, as well as Phoebe Hearst, on the University of California, Berkeley campus.

73. Ibid., 593. Elinor Richey, in *Notable American Women: The Modern Period*, also describes this as a "rambling, shingled" building.

74. Sara Boutelle, "Julia Morgan," in Torre, ed., *Women in American Architecture*, 82. Boutelle's sketch of Morgan's career, one of the sources used for this sketch, is found on pp. 79–87.

75. Tinling, *Women Remembered*, 624.

76. Richey, "Morgan, Julia," *Notable American Women: The Modern Period*, 500, 501.

77. Ibid., 501.

78. Boutelle, "Morgan, Julia," *Macmillan Encyclopedia of Architects*, 258.

79. Ibid., 258. Boutelle discusses the problems of documenting Morgan's career in "An Elusive Pioneer: Tracing the Work of Julia Morgan," in *Architecture: A Place for Women*, 107–16. Boutelle gives several dates in her various articles for the destruction of Morgan's records, with 1952 as the latest (Boutelle, "Julia Morgan," in *Women in American Architecture*, 87).

80. Tinling, *Women Remembered*, 587.

81. Ibid., 587.

82. Sara Holmes Boutelle, "Colter, Mary," *Macmillan Encyclopedia of Architects*, 441–42; Virginia L. Grattan, *Mary Colter: Builder Upon the Red Earth* (Flagstaff, AZ: Northland Press, 1980); and William C. Tweed et al., "National Park Service Rustic Architecture: 1916–1942" (National Park Service, Western Regional Office, Division of Cultural Resource Management, February 1977).

83. For more on Howe, Manning, and Mary Almy (1883–1967), who joined the firm in 1917, see Weimann, *The Fair Women*, 145, 149; American Architectural Foundation, *"That Exceptional One,"* 17; Paine, "Pioneer Women Architects," 66, 68; Paine, "Sophia Hayden and the Woman's Building Competition," 73; and Eugenie L. Birch, "Manning, Eleanor," *MacMillan Encyclopedia of Architects*, 91–92. On page 66 of "Pioneer Women Architects," Paine says the firm dissolved in 1936; on page 73, she says the year was 1937.

84. For more on Farrand's work, see "Farrand, Beatrix Jones," *Notable American Women: The Modern Period*, 221–23; and Diana Blamori, "Beatrix Farrand at Dumbarton Oaks," *Heresies* 11 (1981): 83–86. The NHL status of Dumbarton Oaks is noted in an undated memorandum (spring 1990) from Carolyn Pitts to Ben Levy; the memo, in the possession of the author, is her review of a draft of this chapter.

3 ◆ Women and the Arts

BARBARA MELOSH

"Women have always made art," declared Patricia Mainardi in an influential 1973 essay on women as quilt-makers.[1] As she reclaimed these works of women's hands, Mainardi exemplified the revaluation of women's contributions that accompanied the resurgence of the women's movement. Both inside and outside the academy, feminism inspired new attention to women as subjects and creators of art and literature. The feminist critique of sexual inequality provided a new perspective on the canon—those works of art and literature revered as the highest achievements of Western culture. As feminists sought to expose sexism and to develop new ways of seeing women, they also turned critical eyes on the representation of women in popular culture. Television, popular literature, film, and advertising were the subjects of both scholarly analysis and political protest.

Feminist scholarship has reshaped interpretations of American women's history, not only in the specialized domains of scholarly journals and monographs but in museums, films, and popular fiction—media accessible to large audiences.[2] This essay surveys some of the major issues in the reinterpretation of women in the arts and then considers how those revisions might guide the National Park Service's selections of National Historical Landmarks (NHLs). My review emphasizes literary criticism and art history, reflecting the concentration of feminist scholarship in these fields. Feminist literary criticism has focused most intensely on British literature; for the purposes of this essay, I emphasize work on American literature with some discussion of important debates and models generated from interpretations of British literature. The performing arts—theater, dance, and music—are slighted here. With a few notable exceptions, feminist scholars have not extended their analysis to these forms, though the performing arts offer promising material for such work. That broad revision is beyond the scope of this essay, but I do suggest briefly how feminists' interpretations of literature and art history might be extended to embrace the performing arts.

Reinterpretations of women in the arts followed the trajectory of women's history, beginning with efforts to recover female achievement and to write women back into the historical record. Focusing on women's contributions, scholars brought new questions and assumptions to their readings of the works of exceptional women, reexamining the work of those few female writers and artists already acknowledged in the canon: Emily Dickinson, Willa Cather, Carson McCullers, Gertrude Stein, Edith Wharton, Mary Cassatt, Georgia O'Keeffe. Confronting the fact of women's sparse representation in the pantheons of great writers and artists, feminists sought to recover "lost" women— those unjustly excluded from the canon—and to explain women's marginality in the arts. In what might be called canon expansion, feminists rediscovered the work of neglected women and challenged their exclusion. For example, new scholarship retrieved Sarah Orne Jewett and Kate Chopin from the minor leagues of regionalism; writer Alice Walker drew new attention to Zora Neale Hurston, reclaiming Hurston as literary foremother of black women writers and establishing her place among the writers of the Harlem Renaissance. Charlotte Streifer Rubinstein's *American Women Artists* documented the careers of dozens of women overlooked in conventional histories of art.[3] In a recent example, *Women Composers: The Lost Tradition Found* recovers women's contributions in music.[4]

Rejecting assumptions of women's essential inferiority, feminists sought alternative explanations for women's limited representation among the great artists and writers. Influenced by *A Room of One's Own*, Virginia Woolf's powerful 1928 essay on women and writing, other scholars examined the conditions that enabled creative work and noted men's privileged access to the time, privacy, and money that facilitated artistic production.[5] In *Silences*, Tillie Olsen explored obstacles to creative work as confronted by a range of writers, both male and female, and she reflected poignantly on the disjuncture and interruptions that vitiated women's writing.[6] Posing the question, "Why Have There Been No Great Women Artists?" Linda Nochlin's essay explicated the social conditions facilitating artistic production, documenting women's restricted access to training, especially their exclusion from the anatomical drawing of nude models.[7] In *The Obstacle Race*, Germaine Greer assessed the work of women artists and documented the barriers that she argued kept most from real achievement.[8]

The scholarship of recovery, with its emphasis on women's contributions, did not directly challenge the fundamental assumption supporting the artistic and literary canon: the idea of universal and transcendent standards of quality. Still, these scholars chipped away at the authority of the existing canon in two ways. By arguing that male critics had overlooked women's work that met the standards of canonical criticism, feminists raised doubts about the objectivity of criticism and rendered suspect its claims of political neutrality. And, by articulating the exceptional conditions that supported creative work, feminists rejected the Romantic notion of individual genius as the wellspring of artistic achievement, along with its corollary of female inferiority.

In a development that grew out of the political culture of the twentieth-century women's movement, feminist literary critics turned new attention to women's writing as an alternative tradition. For many feminists, participation in the women's movement led to a reaffirmation of distinctive female experiences and traditions. Even as feminists documented and protested sexual inequality, many also gained a new appreciation for "women's culture." For women's historians, women's culture meant the shared activities, experiences, and relationships that flourished among women, often as a consequence of their segregation from public life.[9] Within the women's movement, it referred broadly to a range of activities and ideologies: acknowledging traditional domestic arts such as cooking, quilting, and nurturing; developing and patronizing women-owned institutions (book stores, bars, restaurants); organizing women-only events and separatist institutions. The connecting theme was a self-conscious appreciation of women, a defiant rejection of cultural ideologies that devalued women's lives and disparaged female friendships. Just as the slogan "Black is beautiful" embodied blacks' triumphant repudiation of white standards, so the idea of women's culture proclaimed—and sought to construct—a new valuation of women.

Among feminist scholars, this political bent was manifested in two related critical directions. Firstly, literary critics revised within the canon by reexamining well-known women writers *as* women. In such work, feminist critics discerned the workings of alternative traditions and voices. Patricia Meyer Spacks's *The Female Imagination*, Ellen Moers's *Literary Women*, and Elaine Showalter's *A Literature of Their Own*, for example, placed gender in the foreground by considering women writers as a group and showing how the distinctive experience of gender inflected their work and working lives.[10] The authors in Emily Toth's anthology *Regionalism and the Female Imagination* provided gendered readings of the work of women writers categorized as regionalists, emphasizing women's contributions to this genre and the significance of the female experience for their work.[11]

Secondly, women's culture articulated a reevaluation of femaleness and a critique of patriarchal culture that motivated renewed interest and more respectful attention to women writers and artists who occupied a marginal or outcast status by the standards of the canon. In one expression of this kind of criticism, scholars explored differences among women and alternative traditions among women writers themselves. In an early example, Jane Rule's *Lesbian Images* explored writing of and about women doubly outcast, as women and as lesbians.[12] Scholars such as Barbara Christian, Gloria T. Hull, Hazel Carby, and Mary Helen Washington recovered the distinctive subjects and voices of black women writers, explicating the intricate connections of race and sex in their lives and work.[13] Ranging beyond the writers recognized by the canon, some feminist literary critics also set aside canonical notions of "literature," turning their attention to female writers working in forms such as the nineteenth-century sentimental novel, Gothic fiction, or romance novels. In *The Land Before Her*, Annette Kolodny argued that women's writing about the frontier revealed ways of imagining the landscape that departed from conventional metaphors of conquest and domination in men's writing.[14] Elizabeth Hampsten's *Read This Only to Yourself* looked at midwestern women's private writings—letters and diaries—to discern distinctly female concerns and stylistic conventions.[15] Ann Douglas's *The Sentimentalization of American Culture* presented a dissenting interpretation of women's culture in its negative assessment of nineteenth-century conventions of female domesticity and sentimentality.[16]

Feminist art historians also moved beyond the canon to examine painting traditions associated with genteel femininity, such as watercolor and embroidery, and to extend art criticism beyond elite forms, such as oil painting and sculpture, to craft traditions like quilting and ceramics.[17] Artist Judy Chicago took up these themes in her controversial work *The Dinner Party*, honoring a pantheon of female historical figures through the imagery of female genitalia and the media of needlework and ceramics.

In another direction, feminist scholars took up the question of women's literary and artistic production through a criticism centered on formal or linguistic issues. This work examines the relationship of women writers to a literary tradition defined by male writers and standards, and more pervasively, by language itself, theorized as embodying and reproducing patriarchy. Examining nineteenth-century British women writers in *The Madwoman in the Attic*, Sandra M. Gilbert and Susan Gubar portrayed their subjects as hobbled by a literary tradition and a language not their own.[18] They found the struggle for a female voice inscribed in women's writing, often in significant absences or densely coded forms. Similarly, Margaret Homans's essay "In Her Very Own Howl" portrayed women writers in an ambiguous relationship to language, one that reproduced their ambiguous status as both insiders and outsiders in their own culture.[19]

Other critics worked from the same premise about language as dominance, but rejected the deterministic view of women entrapped by the structures of language. Instead, they emphasized women writers' agency and resourcefulness in revising tradition and remaking language. In *Writing Beyond the Ending*, for example, Rachel Blau DuPlessis argued that women writers revised and subverted the conventions of romance, resisting the containment of female characters and the dichotomy of female love and male quest.[20] For Alicia Ostriker, women's rebellion against patriarchy found voice in poetry that centered on an authentic female vision and self.[21] Art historians Rozsika Parker and Griselda Pollock went farther to suggest that marginality was sometimes enabling for women, freeing their creative work from the constraints of established traditions.[22]

Both in the women's movement and among feminist scholars, the concept of women's culture affirmed sexual difference; at the same time, feminists held widely divergent views on the sources and implications of differences between men and women. For some, such as Elaine Showalter, women's differences are rooted in the historical and social conditions of inequality. But in another influential mode of criticism, some feminist scholars view difference as more fundamental, transcending the historical or social conditions of female subordination. The post-structuralist emphasis on language, though it does not necessarily posit sexual difference as essential, nonetheless portrays differences as deeply embedded, as the fundamental principle in language and culture. Many post-structuralists have taken on Jacques Lacan's revisions of Freud to emphasize the psychology of difference in theory that reinterprets the positions of the mother and daughter in the Oedipal relationship. In one tendency within this criticism, French feminists have produced theory that places strong emphasis on the female body as the repressed term in language and culture, and on an imagined female language that would embody what is now repressed. In contrast to sociological or historical interpretation of inequality, this variety of post-structuralist criticism portrays sexual difference as radical and essential, rooted not in historical particularity but in the psychology of female sexuality and reproduction.[23]

A heated debate has surrounded this body of theory. Some women's historians have denounced its essentialism and called for a more materialist account of gender rooted in changing historical experience. Others are concerned that the emphasis on sexual difference might lead feminist scholars to underestimate important differences of class and race. Another criticism holds that linguistic theory has made itself inaccessible and unaccountable, couched in esoteric terminology and arcane argument.[24]

Even as feminist critics explored women as writers and artists, they also developed new critical strategies that emphasized feminist ways of reading or viewing.[25] Scholars began by debunking the universal claims of canons and evaluative criticism. Mary Ellman's *Thinking about Women* dissected literary criticism with wry humor, demonstrating the sexist prejudgments embedded in critical language.[26] Literary histories of the canon traced the rise and fall of critical orthodoxies, revealing the subjectivity and historicity of evaluative criticism. Paul Lauter, for example, found canon formation closely linked to a process of professionalization that legitimized the authority of white male critics. Shifting literary standards excluded the work of women, even those who had been formerly recognized in literary histories, and rendered black literary traditions invisible.[27] In art history, Roszika Parker and Griselda Pollock probed the origins of the Western canon and argued that women's marginality was crucial to the formation and definition of the Romantic artist and the ideal of great art.[28] Parker and Pollock documented the growing exclusion of women artists and the critical deprecation of their work in the nineteenth century.

Feminist scholars returned to familiar literature and art with new questions and interpretations. In *The Lay of the Land*, Annette Kolodny investigated the recurring metaphors of conquest and domination, and the trope of the land as female, in American literature.[29] Judith Fetterley's *The Resisting Reader* offered new readings of canonical works in American literature, grounded in a feminist perspective and historical consciousness.[30] Gendered readings yielded new ways of seeing women artists as well.[31] In an innovative work of art criticism, Pollock interpreted the inscription of gender in the subject matter and formal strategies of Impressionist painters Berthe Morisot and Mary Cassatt.[32] In her essay "Modernity and the Spaces of Femininity," Pollock begins with an analysis of content, interpreted through women's social experience. Comparing the subjects of Morisot's and Cassatt's paintings with those of their male counterparts, she documents the women's tendency to depict the private spaces of house and garden. Pollock notes women's more restricted movement in public spaces; women artists had limited access to the streets and cafés so often featured in the work of male Impressionists. In a persuasive visual rhetoric, Pollock then shows how Morisot and Cassatt reproduced the constriction of women's position through their manipulation of the spectator's gaze. While male artists painted from an expansive perspective that surveys and spans the scene, Morisot and Cassatt often confine the spectator's view, disclosing the scene through a restricted vantage point.

As some feminist critics took on the assumptions and methods of deconstruction, they eschewed evaluative criticism altogether. Annette Kolodny urged "a playful pluralism" that celebrated the multiple meanings disclosed by new readings of literary texts and affirmed the feminist reader's critical insight as outsider to the predominantly male enterprise of literature.[33]

Others moved beyond the text itself in ways that suggest fruitful interpretive strategies for public historians. Feminist applications of reader-response criticism sought to document the meanings generated by readers other than literary critics. Janice A. Radway's innovative *Reading the Romance* provided an ethnography of a group of romance readers that took account of their readings and analyzed what the act of reading meant to these women.[34] Parker and Pollock called for a revised social and historical criticism to situate the work within the conditions of its creation and reception. This work calls our attention to the enterprises of publishing and patronage that support literary and artistic production; to informal social organizations like salons, women's clubs, reading groups; to galleries, bookstores, libraries, and community theaters.

Finally, feminists have taken up questions of representation and grappled with a fundamental concern of social and historical criticism: the relationship of representation and social life. In one approach, images of women stood as evidence of ideology. Kate Millett's *Sexual Politics* dissected the marginal and often degraded positions of women characters in canonical works of male writers, indicting a literature pervaded by sexism.[35] John Berger's *Ways of Seeing* posited one influential model in its interpretation of the charged relationship of artist, model, and patron in the painting of the nude. Berger argued that the male artist's privileged access to the nude model was vicariously shared and reenacted in the male patron's viewing of the painted model.[36] Post-structuralist critics extended this analysis with Lacanian interpretations of the gaze as the reenactment of the male child's view of the primal scene, elaborating the different positions of male and female in the Oedipal triangle. In her classic essay "Visual Pleasure and the Narrative Cinema," Laura Mulvey examined the camera's replication of the male gaze and the filmic repression of the female spectator and subject. The visual strategies of film, she argues, assume a male spectator, and therefore place female spectators outside the defining concerns of the cinematic work. While men are implicitly portrayed and positioned as acting, desiring subjects, women are rendered marginal, and can see the narrative film only as voyeurs—women watching, as outsiders, scenes cast in terms of male desire—or as fetishists—female spectators who identify with the male gaze and accept its terms of woman as other.[37] The display and spectacle of theater, and the presence of actors and audience, make dramatic production a promising subject for this kind of analysis; Sue-Ellen Case's *Feminism and Theatre* and Jill Dolan's *The Feminist Spectator as Critic* stake out some important questions.[38] Feminist art historians have also taken up this genre of psychoanalytic criticism.[39]

For some, such exercises were diagnostic: Literary images of women reflected social ideologies that legitimated male domination, a view that assumed an essentially passive role for art. Other work emphasized the significance of gender ideology for cultural history, demonstrating the pervasive use of gender representation in allegory or symbols of national identity. In *Imaging American Women*, for example, Martha Banta analyzed the uses of representations of women in American art and literature from 1876 to 1919, examining sexual ideology as a vehicle for nationalist ideology.[40] Others saw literature and art as complicit: representation was itself a form of social action. Catherine Besley's essay "Constructing the Subject," for example, posited literature as one powerful source for the creation of cultural meanings about gender. Parker and Pollock took a similar position on the role of visual art, portraying art as one site for the ongoing redefinition of gender.

Such formulations built on earlier social-historical criticisms, especially Marxist theories of culture, that emphasized the role of ideology. But feminist critics' concern with the "construction of gender" signaled an important difference. Recent work generally accords greater weight to literary and artistic representation. Post-structuralist criticism gives language a powerful, even determining role, shifting the ground in historical and social criticism of art and literature. In interpretations that emphasize the "construction" of gender, representation is neither mirror nor vehicle of existing ideology, but a primary site for the production of meaning, including cultural categories of sexual difference.

Feminist critics and public historians alike share an interest in "text," audience, and interpretation. If the written text and crafted work are the focus of most literary and art criticism, architecture and site offer another kind of text with rich possibilities for interpretation in National Park Service landmarks. Such visible and tangible survivals have long provided evocative material for historical interpretation. From George Washington's teeth to Hearst's Castle, objects associated with well-known Americans stir the curiosity and the historical imaginations of visitors.

Feminist work on women as writers and artists suggests important new ways of interpreting the historical evidence of site, building, and objects. In Virginia Woolf's *A Room of One's Own,* domestic space is both a metaphor and a material condition for the privacy and leisure that enables writing. Writers' and artists' houses can offer important clues about their working lives and domestic environments. Studies and studios, writing desks and easels evoke the labor and working conditions of literary and artistic production. The size and character of domestic architecture convey other crucial historical evidence. Large, grand houses with servants' quarters signal the affluence that facilitates work that is often poorly or irregularly compensated. Gardens, kitchens, and nurseries open up opportunities to explore the traditional domains of women's responsibilities.

Interpreting the household through buildings and site provides an opportunity to convey important biographical evidence. Women such as Sarah Orne Jewett benefited from the encouragement of supportive fathers, or, like Georgia O'Keeffe, from the patronage of husbands. The resources of affluent families facilitated the work of writers such as Edith Wharton. Others, like Jewett, Gertrude Stein, and Willa Cather, chose other women as their partners. Emily Dickinson's reclusive life is dramatized for visitors who visit Amherst, Massachusetts, to see the house and room where she lived out her self-imposed confinement. Orchard House in Concord, Massachusetts, where Louisa May Alcott struggled to support her impecunious father Bronson, provides the occasion to interpret the economic constraints of this writer's life, and to consider the possibilities for financial independence created by an expanding literary marketplace and a growing female readership. The same site includes the building that housed the Concord Summer School of Philosophy and Literature, organized by Bronson Alcott, Ralph Waldo Emerson, and Frank Sanborn. The NPS interpretation can use this building to suggest the intellectual milieu of social reform within which Louisa May Alcott came of age, as well as to underscore the ventures that preoccupied Bronson to the detriment of his family's financial welfare.

The site itself may enhance the interpretation of life and work. Many writers took their settings and subjects from the communities and the land around them,

Willa Cather House, Red Cloud, Nebraska. (Photograph courtesy of National Park Service)

just as artists often worked from the contours, colors, subjects, and light of their local visual environments. Willa Cather's childhood home in Red Cloud, Nebraska, can help visitors imagine the midwestern landscape and frontier history that inspired some of her work.[41] The NHL site encompasses the Cather house, which the family rented from 1884 to 1904; a historic district of Red Cloud, including public spaces mentioned in her fiction; and a stretch of the prairie, the wide landscape that figured prominently in her fiction. Red Cloud was also the site of Cather's important early rebellion against conventions of womanhood: in 1888, at the age of fourteen, she renamed herself William, cropped her hair, and began to dress as a man, a style she maintained through her first two years at the University of Nebraska. Her transgressive self-presentation remains vivid in local Cather lore, according to her biographer Sharon O'Brien.[42] The Maine setting enhances visitors' appreciation for the atmospheric fiction of Sarah Orne Jewett, who wrote of the changing landscape of nineteenth-century rural New England. Georgia O'Keeffe's quarters and studio in Abiquiu, New Mexico, offer another compelling example. O'Keeffe carefully crafted her domestic and studio space according to her own aesthetic and drew inspiration for her painting from the land around Abiquiu.

Sarah Orne Jewett House, South Berwick, Maine. (Photograph courtesy of Society for the Preservation of New England Antiquities)

In dramatically different ways, four historic sites offer eloquent visual testimony to the significance of domestic space for women's creative work. Buildings provide texts that enhance our understanding of the lives of Emily Dickinson, Sarah Orne Jewett, Georgia O'Keeffe, and Zora Neale Hurston.

Emily Dickinson's home on Main Street in Amherst, Massachusetts, constituted the geographic boundaries of her experience by the late 1860s, after which she seldom left the grounds. Generations of readers have been fascinated by the enigmatic "recluse of Amherst," whose unbounded imagination flourished within the narrow confines of this house.[43] The substantial brick building gives evidence of the material conditions that enabled her work; the family's house was a visible sign of her father's wealth and his commanding position in Amherst. Facing south and west, her bedroom looked out on the main street and the grounds of her brother Austin's house; her writing table and the bureau where she kept her carefully bound manuscript poems remain in the room. Dickinson's house thus suggests both her unusual biography and the larger social conditions that Woolf stipulated as necessary for the development of creative work.

Sarah Orne Jewett, a New England writer, died in the house where she was born, but she traveled widely beyond its bounds and established an independent life as a single woman. Built in 1774, the house in South Berwick, Maine, exemplifies the high style of elite eighteenth-century New England families. The Georgian building has an elaborate front hall and carved staircase, an ornately crafted entrance that attests to the wealth and aesthetic of a maritime elite. The house belonged to Jewett's grandfather, and both she and her sister Mary were born there. Her father, Theodore Jewett, later built a house next door where his family lived. In 1887, the original house was deeded to Mary, who set up housekeeping with Sarah; the two extensively redecorated the house and lived there for the rest of their lives. The house was bequeathed to the Society for the Preservation of New England Antiquities in 1931. Mary preserved Sarah's bedroom as it was at her death in 1909, and it remains unchanged, a valuable document of the writer's personal tastes and domestic setting.

Inherited wealth enabled Sarah Orne Jewett to live and work in financial ease; nineteenth-century women's culture offered her an alternative to marriage. Jewett's writing was enabled by her sister Mary, who shouldered most of the work of their joint household, freeing Sarah to work and travel. Jewett shared a loving relationship with Annie Fields, and lived part of each year in Fields's Boston house. Their letters, intimate and affectionate, attest to the emotional comradeship the women shared.[44]

Georgia O'Keeffe built a room of her own on the New Mexico land that inspired many of her remarkable paintings. O'Keeffe first traveled to New Mexico in 1929, staying with Mabel Dodge Luhan in the Taos residence described below. She returned in the summer of 1931, renting a cottage near Abiquiu, an isolated spot in the arid hills. By 1934 she was returning every year. In December 1945, she persuaded the Catholic Church to sell her a derelict building and three acres at Abiquiu. The door in one wall intrigued her, later providing the subject for a series of paintings. Over the next four years she rebuilt the adobe house and patio. In 1949, three years after the death of her husband and patron, photographer Alfred Stieglitz, she moved there permanently.

New Mexico was O'Keeffe's chosen venue, her alternative to the hectic life in New York, where she and Stieglitz spent each winter, and the bustling family life at Lake George, where they lived during the summer. O'Keeffe chafed under the distractions of sociable Lake George summers and felt suffocated by the green, enclosing landscape. When Stieglitz became romantically involved with the young matron Dorothy Norman, O'Keeffe had new reason to escape Lake George. Thereafter, her periodic separations from Stieglitz provided distance from his infatuation, respite from his increasing dependence, and the solitude she needed for her work. In Abiquiu, O'Keeffe crafted the place that most closely expressed her aesthetic and that sustained her art.[45]

The small green house in Fort Pierce, Florida, occupied by Zora Neale Hurston, provides an instructive contrast to the substantial dwellings of Dickinson and Jewett, and to the Abiquiu house that O'Keeffe designed to conform to her

Zora Neale Hurston House, Fort Pierce, Florida. (Photograph by Jill S. Topolski)

deliberate aesthetic of simplicity. The School Court house serves to commemorate a now-celebrated African-American writer, and to remind us of the financial hardship that disabled and sometimes silenced American writers.

Zora Neale Hurston is perhaps the most widely read figure in the expanded canon; her 1937 novel, *Their Eyes Were Watching God*, has found a broad and enthusiastic new audience. Dismissed by most critics in her own time, Hurston's work was recovered from obscurity by the contemporary writer Alice Walker and eagerly embraced by contemporary audiences as well as by critics committed to the recovery of literary traditions that flourished outside the boundaries of a white, male canon. Set in rural Florida, Hurston's fiction celebrates an alternative language and culture, even as it renders the divisions of sex and class within the black community.

In addition to her accomplishments as a writer of fiction, Hurston did pioneering work in folklore. The first black graduate of Barnard, she held a B.A. in anthropology, and she collected folklore of black traditions in Florida, Alabama, Louisiana, and the Bahamas; later she traveled to Haiti and Jamaica to document folk traditions.[46]

Hurston's biography reminds us forceably of the bias of class and survival in history rendered through material culture. Her family's home in Eatonville, Florida, the first incorporated town established by black people, no longer stands. As an adult she moved often, and never owned a house. Though she enjoyed some literary success, her earnings were limited and she often turned to friends and patrons for financial help. Hurston's troubled relationship with a white patron illustrates a recurring problematic for black intellectuals seeking access to the resources and recognition of mainstream culture. Charlotte

Osgood Mason sponsored Hurston's research for five years, but then sought to control Hurston's use of the material she had collected.

The School Court house proposed for NHL status captures the precarious conditions of Hurston's life. A fifty-foot square concrete block structure in a block of similar houses, the building was erected in 1957 by C. C. Benton, Hurston's physician. Benton offered the house rent-free to Hurston, who moved there in 1958. Though her biographer Robert Hemenway cautions against "the impulse to romanticize" by exaggerating the poverty of her final years, he records that "after 1957 she survived on unemployment benefits, substitute teaching, and welfare assistance. In her very last days Zora lived a difficult life—alone, proud, ill, obsessed with a final book she could not complete."[47] Unable to care for herself after a stroke, Hurston moved into the county welfare house in October 1959, and died there three months later.

In commemorating figures such as Dickinson, Jewett, O'Keeffe, and Hurston, these current and proposed NHLs honor women's achievements as writers and artists. Other landmarks indicate an expanded definition of art and literary history. One proposed site, Mabel Dodge Luhan's compound in Taos, New Mexico, illustrates the role of women as patrons. The proposal to grant NHL status to the Pewabic Pottery in Detroit, Michigan, acknowledges founder Mary Chase Perry (Stratton) as entrepreneur and artist, refusing conventional divisions between fine arts and the implicitly lesser pursuit of crafts. Another proposed NHL would honor Laura Ingalls Wilder, author of popular children's books, a nomination that recognizes the accomplishment of a woman writer in a field traditionally considered marginal to the canon of great books.

As elite women became guardians of culture in the nineteenth century, patronage emerges as a significant subject for a women's history of the arts. Wealthy women's leisure was a form of conspicuous consumption, and involvement in the arts an approved feminine pursuit. As patrons and collectors, wealthy and socially prominent women helped to shape the arts. The elaborate homes and grounds of patrons embody the elite economic status that enables support of the arts, and such houses also may contain valuable collections of art, visual evidence of a collector's aesthetic, interests, and relationships with artists. Large public spaces—drawing rooms, ballrooms, salons, dining rooms—evoke the social rituals of wealthy patrons of culture. Decor, furnishings, and architecture all convey contemporary aesthetics of domestic space. The MacDowell Colony, for example, a current NHL, embodies these characteristics of patronage, and its rural setting illustrates the enduring valorization of nature in the American literary tradition.

A proposed NHL, Mabel Dodge Luhan's home in Taos, New Mexico, offers an exceptionally rich site for interpretation. Luhan both exemplified and helped to create a distinctive style of American literary radicalism. A writer herself, Mabel Dodge is best remembered for her more traditional female role

Mabel Dodge Luhan House, Taos, New Mexico. (Photograph courtesy of Las Palomas de Taos)

as patron of the arts. She moved from the bohemian circles of New York City's Greenwich Village to Taos in 1917, where her home soon became the center of a growing artistic colony. A few years later she married Antonio Luhan, a Pueblo Indian of the Tiwa tribe. Luhan is significant as a patron of numerous writers and painters, and visits to Taos influenced the work and careers of others, including D. H. Lawrence, Willa Cather, and Georgia O'Keeffe. Luhan also exemplifies the romantic primitivism of the 1920s—the celebration of the American Indian as exotic other, as uncorrupted nature and spiritual corrective to the ills of civilization deplored by many modernist writers and artists. The site provides a striking opportunity for integrating cultural and political history, for Luhan's enthusiasm for Pueblo life directly influenced federal policy toward American Indian populations during the 1920s and 1930s. In 1920, John Collier visited Luhan and left deeply impressed by her vision of Pueblo culture as ideal community. Collier became the architect of New Deal policy for American Indians, setting out an ideal of cultural pluralism against the dominant policy of promoting assimilation.[48]

The main building itself expresses Luhan's eclectic aesthetic, her spirited independence, and her self-definition as patron of the arts. The Big House, a three-story, twenty-two-room building, was designed by Mabel Dodge and built by Antonio Luhan. The original building was begun in 1918 and completed in 1922, then expanded over the next ten years with a series of additions. In no single conventional style, the adobe structure echoes elements of Pueblo and Spanish Colonial building traditions,[49] an apt testament to Luhan's taste and eclecticism. Traditional building materials and methods—adobe and wood—embody her fascination with the land and its history. The sprawling Big House, surrounded by smaller guesthouses when Luhan occupied it, attests to her role as patron of visiting artists and writers. The large common rooms of the Big House, including the Rainbow Room and a living room, served as Luhan's salons, spaces for guests to meet and share the exhilarating talk that she inspired and thrived on. The Luhan's living quarters, with separate bedrooms and a sleeping porch, recall Mabel Dodge's upper-class origins and suggest that she valued privacy and independence within marriage.

Mary Chase Perry (Stratton) built on genteel female accomplishment to establish herself as an artist and entrepreneur, achievements embodied in the Pewabic Pottery in Detroit, Michigan. China painting, a popular amateur pursuit of well-bred young women, drew Perry's interest, and she soon was teaching from her own studio. Harry Caulkins, a neighbor, had developed a new high-heat furnace for firing dental products, and he provided technical assistance when Perry set up her first pottery in 1904. William Stratton, her friend and later her husband, designed and built the present site of Pewabic Pottery in 1907. There Perry continued the experimentation that yielded her innovative firing techniques and original glazes. Her work with architectural tiles won her a number of prestigious commissions in Detroit (some of this work is still extant) and across the country. In 1918, at the age of 51, she married Stratton, a long-time friend.[50]

Used for years as a teaching facility of the University of Michigan, Pewabic Pottery resumed production in 1985 under the direction of Mary Roehm. The site also houses some of Stratton's records and a collection of her work. In the midst of industrial Detroit, it exemplifies the traditional values of craft production, part of the early twentieth-century Arts and Crafts movement that set itself against the machine-paced work and standardization of industrial production.[51]

Laura Ingalls Wilder's house in Mansfield, Missouri, nominated for NHL status, is now a museum commemorating this popular children's writer. In this ten-room clapboard farm house, Wilder wrote *Little House in the Big Woods*, published in 1932 when Wilder was sixty-five. Six others followed, all based on Wilder's own experiences growing up on the midwestern frontier. During the 1930s, Wilder's only child, Rose Wilder Lane, returned to her parents' Mansfield home. A close collaborator on the Little House books, Rose left diaries that reveal her ambivalent relationship with her mother and that illuminate the poignant history of a daughter, established as a writer, who midwifed her mother's work, ultimately much more widely read than her own.[52] The plain

Pewabic Pottery, Detroit, Michigan. Mary Chase Stratton at work in production ca. 1906. (Photograph courtesy of Pewabic Pottery Collection)

house and still rural character of the site help to recapture the conditions in which Wilder lived and worked. A museum on the site contains family memorabilia and many of Laura Ingalls Wilder's papers and manuscripts.

Even as the NPS sustains a commitment to adding new landmarks, it can integrate the interpretation of women's history into existing sites. Many historic sites offer evidence of women's participation in literature and the arts. Books in the family library, theater programs, paintings purchased to display in the home, club memberships, costumes for pageants or community theater all demonstrate women's activities as readers, patrons, spectators, and amateurs. Historic homes evince an aesthetic usually shaped by the woman in charge of the household and contain objects crafted by women. China painting, watercolors, quilts, embroidery—all provide evidence of women's artistic activities and their place in cultural definitions of femininity. In historic sites commemorating male artists and writers, interpretive material and tours should ask visitors to ponder the household arrangements that facilitated men's creative work.

Feminist scholarship provides a new base and a constantly enlarging body of research for broadening the interpretation of history in NPS sites. In turn, public historians have a special opportunity—and a responsibility—to convey these findings to visitors. In the process, the constituency for NPS sites is likely to change and grow as previously marginalized groups find their history recognized and commemorated. The NPS will perform an invaluable service in remembering and recovering the history of women. At the same time, these new sites and fresh interpretive approaches can advance the NPS's educational mandate, promoting an enlarged and broadened sense of history among NPS visitors.

NOTES

1. Patricia Mainardi, "Quilts: The Great American Art," *Feminist Art Journal* 2, no. 1 (Winter 1973): 1, 18–23.

2. For an excellent overview of the scholarship of women's studies, see Ellen DuBois et al., *Feminist Scholarship: Kindling in the Groves of Academe* (Urbana: University of Illinois Press, 1987); for a survey of representations of women's history in museum exhibitions, see Barbara Melosh, "Speaking of Women: Museums' Representations of Women's History," in *History Museums in the United States*, ed. Warren Leon and Roy Rosenzweig (Urbana: University of Illinois Press, 1989), 183–214.

3. Charlotte Streifer Rubinstein, *American Women Artists* (New York: Avon, 1982).

4. Diane Peacock Jezic, *Women Composers: The Lost Tradition Found* (New York: The Feminist Press, 1989); and see also her very useful bibliography of other scholarship on women and music, 243–47.

5. Virginia Woolf, *A Room of One's Own* (New York: Harcourt Brace Jovanovich, 1981; 1st publ. 1928).

6. Tillie Olsen, *Silences* (New York: Delacorte Press, 1979).

7. Linda Nochlin, "Why Have There Been No Great Women Artists?" (1971), in *Women, Art, and Power* (New York: Harper and Row, 1988), 145–78.

8. Germaine Greer, *The Obstacle Race* (New York: Farrar, Straus, Giroux, 1979).

9. The idea of women's culture was articulated in Carroll Smith-Rosenberg's widely cited examination of nineteenth-century women's relationships, "The Female World of Love and Ritual," *Signs* 1, no. 1 (1975): 1–29.

10. Patricia Meyer Spacks, *The Female Imagination* (New York: Alfred A. Knopf, 1975); Ellen Moers, *Literary Women* (Garden City, New York: Doubleday, 1976); Elaine Showalter, *A Literature of Their Own* (Princeton, New Jersey: Princeton University Press, 1977).

11. *Regionalism and the Female Imagination*, ed. Emily Toth (New York: Human Sciences Press, 1985).

12. Jane Rule, *Lesbian Images* (Freedom, California: Crossing Press, 1982).

13. This subject has developed a rich and sophisticated critical literature. See, for ex-

ample, Barbara Christian, *Black Women Novelists: The Development of a Tradition, 1892–1976* (Westport, Connecticut: Greenwood, 1985); Gloria T. Hull, *Color, Sex, and Poetry* (Bloomington: Indiana University Press, 1987); Hazel Carby, *Reconstructing Womanhood* (New York: Oxford, 1987); and Mary Helen Washington, *Invented Lives* (Garden City, New York: Doubleday/Anchor, 1988).

14. Annette Kolodny, *The Land Before Her* (Chapel Hill: University of North Carolina Press, 1984).

15. Elizabeth Hampsten, *Read This Only to Yourself* (Bloomington: Indiana University Press, 1982).

16. Ann Douglas, *The Sentimentalization of American Culture* (New York: Knopf, 1978).

17. See Lise Vogel, "Fine Arts and Feminism," *Feminist Studies* 2 (1974): 3–37. On the historical emergence of privileged forms and the denigration of craft as feminine, see Rozsika Parker and Griselda Pollock, "Crafty Women and the Hierarchy of the Arts," in *Old Mistresses: Women, Art and Ideology* (New York: Pantheon, 1981), 50–81.

18. Sandra M. Gilbert and Susan Gubar, *The Madwoman in the Attic* (New Haven, Connecticut: Yale University Press, 1979).

19. Margaret Homans, "In Her Very Own Howl," *Signs* 9, no. 2 (Winter 1983): 186–205.

20. Rachel Blau DuPlessis, *Writing Beyond the Ending* (Bloomington: Indiana University Press, 1985).

21. Alicia Ostriker, reply to Margaret Homans, *Signs* 10, no. 3 (Spring 1985): 597–600; and see also Ostriker, "The Thieves of Language: Women Poets and Revisionist Myth-Making," *Signs* 8, no. 1 (August 1982): 68–90.

22. Parker and Pollock, *Old Mistresses,* 19–20.

23. For a good introduction to these theorists, see Ann Rosalind Jones, "Writing the Body: Toward an Understanding of l'ecriture feminine," *Feminist Studies* 7, no. 2 (Summer 1981): 247–63; the same issue contains other articles on major figures Monique Wittig and Luce Irigaray. For translations and explication of some key critical work, see *New French Feminisms*, ed. Elaine Marks and Isabelle de Courtivron (Amherst: University of Massachusetts Press, 1980).

24. For good discussions of recent theory, see *Signs* 14, no. 1 (Spring 1988), a special issue titled "Feminism and Deconstruction"; for a critical view, see especially Barbara Christian, "The Race for Theory," 67–79. For other excellent commentaries, see Judith Newton, "Family Fortunes: 'New History' and 'New Historicism,' " and Judith Walkowitz, Myra Jehlen, and Bell Chivigny, "Patrolling the Borders: Feminist Historiography and the New Historicism," both in *Radical History Review* 43 (Jan. 1989): 5–22, 23–43. Some key differences between post-structuralists and social historians are represented in an exchange in *Signs* 15, no. 4 (Summer 1990); see Joan W. Scott, *"Heroes of Their Own Lives: The Politics and History of Family Violence*, by Linda Gordon," 848–52; Gordon, "Response to Scott," 852–53; Gordon, *"Gender and the Politics of History*, by Joan Wallach Scott," 853–58; Scott, "Response to Gordon," 859–60.

25. For an excellent anthology with a range of viewpoints and approaches, see Elaine Showalter, *The New Feminist Criticism* (New York: Pantheon, 1985).

26. Mary Ellman, *Thinking about Women* (New York: Harcourt, Brace and World, 1968).

27. See Paul Lauter, "Race and Gender in the Shaping of the American Literary Canon: A Case Study from the Twenties," in *Feminist Criticism and Social Change: Sex, Class and Race in Literature and Culture,* ed. Judith Newton and Deborah Rosenfelt (New York: Methuen, 1985), 19–44; Ana Lauter, *Canons and Contexts* (New York: Oxford University Press, 1991).

28. Parker and Pollock, "Critical Stereotypes: The Essential Feminine or How Essential Is Femininity," in *Old Mistresses*, 1–49.

29. Annette Kolodny, *The Lay of the Land* (Chapel Hill: University of North Carolina, 1975).

30. Judith Fetterley, *The Resisting Reader* (Bloomington: Indiana University Press, 1978).

31. For a good overview, see "Introduction: Feminism, Femininity and Representation," *Looking On: Images of Femininity in the Visual Arts and Media*, ed. Rosemary Betterton (London and New York: Pandora, 1987), 1–16.

32. Griselda Pollock, "Modernity and the Spaces of Femininity," in *Vision and Difference: Femininity, Feminism and Histories of Art* (London and New York: Routledge, 1988), 50–90.

33. Annette Kolodny, "Dancing Through the Minefield: Some Observations on the Theory, Practice, and Politics of a Feminist Literary Criticism," *Feminist Studies* 6, no. 1 (Spring 1980): 1–25.

34. Janice A. Radway, *Reading the Romance* (Chapel Hill: University of North Carolina Press, 1984).

35. Kate Millett, *Sexual Politics* (Garden City, New York: Doubleday, 1970).

36. John Berger, *Ways of Seeing* (New York: Penguin, 1977).

37. Laura Mulvey, "Visual Pleasure and Narrative Cinema," *Screen*, vol. 16, no. 3 (Autumn 1975): 6–18; see also Mulvey, "Afterthoughts on 'Visual Pleasure and Narrative Cinema' Inspired by *Duel in the Sun*," *Framework*, nos. 15, 16, 17 (1981): 12–15. For an extended application of Mulvey's theory, see Mary Ann Doane, *The Desire to Desire: The Woman's Film of the 1940s* (Bloomington: Indiana University Press, 1987).

38. Sue-Ellen Case, *Feminism and Theatre* (New York: Methuen, 1988) and Jill Dolan, *The Feminist Spectator as Critic* (Ann Arbor: UMI Research Press, 1988).

39. See, for example, Pollock's "Woman as Sign: Psychoanalytic Readings" and "Screening the Seventies: Sexuality and Representation in Feminist Practice—a Brechtian Perspective," both in *Vision and Difference*.

40. Martha Banta, *Imaging American Women* (New York: Columbia University Press, 1987); see also Marina Warner, *Monuments and Maidens: Allegory of the Female Form* (New York: Macmillan, 1985).

41. See Judith Fryer's *Felicitous Space* (Chapel Hill: University of North Carolina Press, 1986) for a reading of the uses of space in the fiction of Willa Cather and Edith Wharton.

42. Sharon O'Brien, *Willa Cather: The Emerging Voice* (New York: Oxford University Press, 1987), 97. For an excellent discussion of Cather's persona of William, see 96–114; for O'Brien's thoughtful analysis of Cather's sexuality and her conclusion that Cather was a lesbian, see 117–46.

43. Biographers have speculated endlessly on the reasons for her self-imposed seclusion. The biographical and critical literature on Dickinson is voluminous. Two works illustrate the wide range of interpretation of Dickinson's reclusiveness. John Cody's *After Great Pain: The Inner Life of Emily Dickinson* (Belknap/Harvard University Press, 1971), written by a practicing psychiatrist, emphasizes abnormal psychosexual development. Cynthia Griffin Wolff takes a different tack by arguing that Dickinson consciously chose her seclusion to enable her art; unfettered by the demands of conventional womanhood, Dickinson could pursue the development of her formidable talent; see Wolff, *Emily Dickinson* (New York: Borzoi/Knopf, 1986).

44. See Warner Berthoff, "Sarah Orne Jewett," in *Notable American Women*, 1670–1950, eds. Edward T. James and Janet Wilson James (Cambridge: Belknap Press of Harvard University Press, 1971), 274–76. For a recent critical and biographical in-

terpretation of Jewett, see Sarah Way Sherman, *Sarah Orne Jewett: An American Persephone* (Hanover, N.H.: University Press of New England, 1989).

45. Biographical information is from Roxana Robinson, *Georgia O'Keeffe: A Life* (New York: Harper and Row, 1989); on O'Keeffe's dissatisfaction with Lake George, see 260–62, 286, 317, 361; on Stieglitz's relationship with Dorothy Norman, see 299–302, 318–19, 357–58; on Abiquiu house, see 448–50, 473–77.

46. This material is drawn from Cheryl A. Wall's excellent biographical sketch, "Zora Neale Hurston," in *Notable American Women: The Modern Period*.

47. Robert E. Hemenway, *Zora Neale Hurston: A Literary Biography* (Urbana: University of Illinois Press, 1977), 322.

48. See Lois Palken Rudnick, *Mabel Dodge Luhan: New Woman, New Worlds* (Albuquerque: University of New Mexico Press, 1981), 143–89; for a summary of Collier's philosophy, see 262. For a discussion of Indian policy under the New Deal, see Robert Berkhofer, *The White Man's Indian: Images of the American Indian from Columbus to the Present* (New York: Alfred A. Knopf, 1978), 176–86.

49. NPS nomination form for Mabel Dodge Luhan site, Taos, New Mexico, 1.

50. Biographical information is from NPS nomination form for Pewabic Pottery, Detroit. A brief entry for Mary Chase Stratton may be found in Peter Hastings Falk, *Who Was Who in American Art* (Madison Conn.: Sound View Press, 1985), 602.

51. On the recent revival of Pewabic Pottery, see Daniel Cohen, "Modern Mosaic," *Historic Preservation*, (March–April 1990): 30–36; on the Arts and Crafts movement in the United States, see Eileen Boris, *Art and Labor: Ruskin, Morris, and the Craftsman Ideal in America* (Philadelphia: Temple University Press, 1986).

52. Anita Clair Fellman, "Laura Ingalls Wilder and Rose Wilder Lane: The Politics of a Mother-Daughter Relationship," *Signs* 15, no. 3 (Spring 1990): 535–61.

4 ◆ Women and Community

GAIL LEE DUBROW

Perhaps the greatest legacy of women's organized building efforts can be gathered under the theme of community.[1] Both the women's organizations that carried out programs of local reform and the community institutions that they founded merit greater recognition than they have been accorded in the past through landmark designation and historic preservation programs. While the tangible remains of women's work as community-builders have survived to the present day in the form of clubhouses, association buildings, group homes, community kitchens, and social settlements, many significant examples of these building types are not adequately represented on landmark registers, nor is their historical significance otherwise publicly commemorated. As a result, visitors to historic sites and buildings too often have been presented with a distorted view of women's history, leaving with an incomplete picture of the varied roles played by women in the nation's development.

Recent historical scholarship has placed new emphasis on women's formative role in the social, economic, political, and cultural lives of their respective communities. Increased awareness of the scholarship in women's history is likely to lead preservationists to a variety of sites, structures, buildings, districts, and objects previously unimagined. A review of new scholarship on the history of women in the community underscores the need for preservation planners to familiarize themselves with recent developments in women's history and highlights the tangible benefits that will accrue in the process.

The concept of community is complex and has been loaded with diverse associations.[2] The term usually refers to a group sharing common social traits. It connotes a sense of belonging achieved through social bonds and interactions that shape the group into a distinctive social entity. These ties may or may not be defined by a shared physical space or common geographical area. It is only in recent years, with the rise of new scholarship in women's history, that gender has received serious consideration as an analytic category in histories of various communities. There has been a virtual explosion of scholarly interest in the impact of women on communities and on the effects of community involvement on women's lives. Scholars focusing on women's participation in community settings have expanded our knowledge of the female experience beyond the customary arenas of work and family. This has resulted in a more sophisticated understanding of women's struggle to reshape the boundaries of the public domain.

A growing body of scholarly literature has focused on women's organized efforts to carry out the basic functions of communities, including the provision of basic economic needs, socialization, social control, social participation, and mutual support,[3] and beyond that, to assert political influence over American civic life. Before women won formal political rights, they reached beyond the constricted domain of the household to define their own social responsibilities to larger communities. However, because of sex-segregation, these activities largely were conducted in a separate female sphere.

The benevolent activities of women's religious auxiliaries and secular associations presupposed that women felt an ethical, social responsibility for the welfare of "less fortunate" individuals in the community. The clubs and associations formed by middle- and upper-class women contributed to the development of myriad community institutions such as maternity homes, orphan asylums, day nurseries, kindergartens, schools, residences for working women, clinics, social settlements, and old age homes. Many of these institutions met the needs of women and children living in poverty, particularly those who lacked or had lost access to the social and economic privileges that traditional marriage conferred. Because many of the philanthropic institutions established by women's groups gradually came to be seen as legitimate and essential public services, it is apparent that organized women contributed greatly to the development of the modern welfare state.

Recent scholarship traces the origins and explains the significance of women's voluntary activities in the community. In *Born for Liberty: A History of Women in America*, historian Sara M. Evans writes, "grounded in daily lives which brought circles of female kin and neighbors together for rituals of birth and death," these female-dominated institutions "nourished a female culture where women could act, both privately and publicly, on a value system increasingly at odds with those of dominant males."[4] In fact, in 1906, one advocate of the women's club movement, seeking to distinguish traditionally male "patriotic" concerns with law, war, government, and finance from organized women's activities coined the companion term "matriotism" in an effort to suggest women's more peaceable, but no less transformative, political involvement in social reform and civic affairs.[5] Community activity served as a critical context for the development of a female political culture because of women's exclusion from male-dominated political institutions and women's lack of formal political power during the greater part of American history.[6]

In this chapter, several key elements of the built environment significant in the history of women and community are surveyed, including sites and buildings from the women's temperance movement, women's clubhouses and meeting places, association buildings, organized homes for working women, and the social settlements. This selection is intended to be suggestive, rather than representative or comprehensive. It draws from the wealth of historical sources and scholarship now available to document middle-class white, and to a lesser extent, black women's community-building activities. At the same time, it recognizes the need for what is now an emerging wave of historical scholarship that will lay a foundation for future surveys of sites associated with the community participation of white ethnic women as well as women of color—Native American, Latina/Chicana, and Asian American women—which promises to widen and transform existing conceptions of gender and community derived from partial readings. This chapter is offered as a glimpse into the variety of tangible resources that could be commemorated, interpreted, and preserved by those who are interested in increasing the public visibility of women's history at historic sites and buildings.

Before the most recent wave of scholarship in women's history, chronicles of the temperance movement generally fell into one of two categories. Either they were written by critics who tended to underestimate the significance of the movement, while sensationalizing and ridiculing its leaders,[7] or they were eyewitness accounts and official histories written by Woman's Christian Temperance Union (WCTU) members, which tended to sanctify the movement's leadership.[8]

The problems that have characterized past efforts to interpret and preserve sites associated with temperance as a theme ultimately can be traced to conceptual limitations in the scholarly literature. Unfortunately, past scholarship on the temperance movement that focused on the leadership, according to historian Jill Conway, overlooked "the grass-roots nature of the movement and the breadth of participation [which] were obviously key factors in its success."[9]

These problems with the scholarly literature hindered past efforts to interpret and preserve sites associated with temperance and limited the variety of building types that have been preserved. The places chosen to commemorate the women's temperance movement, especially the private residences of movement leaders, have echoed the narrow emphasis on notable individuals that in times past defined much of women's history. Through the process of selective preservation, the residences of temperance leaders such as Eliza Thompson, Carry A. Nation, and Woman's Christian Temperance Union president Frances Willard literally have come to "stand" for the larger movement. The residence of "Mother" Thompson, who led the 1873 uprising of women in Hillsboro, Ohio, is listed on the National Register.[10] Temperance crusader Carry Nation's turn-of-the-century residence in Medicine Bow, Kansas, was designated as a

Frances Willard Rest Cottage/ Woman's Christian Temperance Union headquarters, Evanston, Illinois. (Photograph from *Historic Rest Cottage*, Evanston, Illinois: Woman's Christian Temperance Union, 1911, courtesy of Schlesinger Library, Radcliffe College)

National Historic Landmark in 1976.[11] Frances Willard's Rest Cottage in Evanston, Illinois, which also served as national headquarters for the Woman's Christian Temperance Union, was designated a National Historic Landmark in 1965 and subsequently included in the Historic American Buildings Survey;[12] the two-story Gothic cottage serves as a museum for the national and world WCTU, and the interior furnishings date to the period of Willard's occupancy.

However, new scholarship suggests intriguing future possibilities for the identification, designation, interpretation, and preservation of the movement's landmarks. Scholars recently have begun to place the women's temperance movement in the broader context of women's history. In the first full-length scholarly study, *Woman and Temperance: The Quest for Power and Liberty* (1981), historian Ruth Bordin documented the WCTU's significance as "the national voice through which women expressed their views on social and political issues" during the last quarter of the nineteenth century.[13] Bordin also shifted interpretive emphasis away from the WCTU's leadership to focus on the feature of the movement that has the greatest untapped preservation potential: its vast grass-roots force.

In response to concerns over the destructive consequences of male intemperance on the lives of women and children, temperance crusaders converted female moral authority in the home into a vehicle for increasing women's power in the public sphere. Employing a variety of direct action tactics, including "hatchetation," which involved the seizure and destruction of liquor barrels, organized women leveled an unprecedented attack on the bastions of male solidarity. In an effort to reconstruct public life and reformulate social institutions in the absence of alcohol, reformers established an expansive temperate counterculture during the last quarter of the nineteenth and the beginning of the twentieth century. Were preservationists to look beyond the leadership to explore the national significance of this grass-roots social movement, they would find a rich array of tangible resources previously ignored.

Carry Nation's home in Medicine Bow, Kansas, is the only site that marks the spirit of direct action that infused the early years of the temperance crusade. Yet this placid residence fails to convey the drama that swept across hundreds of towns during the winter of 1873–1874 when, in the words of Frances Willard, "like a Western prairie fire," thousands of women engaged in protests against saloons and liquor dealers.[14] In a militant action that secured the hatchet as the symbol of the growing women's temperance movement, crusaders in Washington Court House, Ohio, forced a dealer to discard his supply of liquor, after which

> axes were placed in the hands of the women who had suffered the most, and swinging through the air, they came down with ringing blows, bursting the head of the casks, and flooding the gutters of the street. One good woman, putting her soul into every blow, struck but once for a barrel, splashing Holland gin and old Bourbon high into the air amid the shouts of the people.[15]

Such was the success of the crusade, in Ruth Bordin's analysis, that

> within three months of the Hillsboro march, women had driven the liquor business out of 250 villages and cities. In Ohio 130 towns had experienced crusades; Michigan had 36, Indiana 34, Pennsylvania 26, New Jersey 17. By the time the marches ended, at least 912 communities in 31 states and territories had experienced crusades.[16]

The designation of Carry Nation's home fails to capture the dynamic quality of female protest that occurred in main street confrontations with liquor dealers and in front of male-dominated saloons. One effort was made by the Woman's Christian Temperance Union in Wichita, Kansas, to erect a fountain on the site of Carry Nation's first arrest. Ironically, it was overturned by a beer truck in a 1945 traffic accident, and only recently has the fountain been moved and restored.[17] Whether in Wichita, Kansas, or Hillsboro, Ohio, there is a need for more accurate public interpretations of the militant aspects of women's history on the downtown streets where they occurred.

Similarly, the lone designation of Frances Willard's bucolic Rest Cottage as a landmark of the WCTU fails to capture what unquestionably was one of the most significant features of the WCTU's success: the relationship between Willard's effective national leadership and the grass-roots efforts of hundreds of thousands of women organized into regional branches and local chapters. New interpretive focus on the organization promises to reveal tangible evidence of the temperate counterculture constructed by American women.

The WCTU's transition from evangelical origins to its emergence as a nationally significant social and political movement was expressed in the built environment, as the WCTU moved out of the Protestant churches and invented a new institution: the secular temperance temple. Plans for building the first temperance temple began in July 1887, when Matilda Carse, president of both the Chicago WCTU and the Woman's Temperance Publishing Agency, founded the Woman's Temperance Building Association. Three years later, in 1890, the Association began construction on a twelve-story office building in Chicago's Loop. Designed by Burnham and Root, the building was intended to be "self-liquidating: office and meeting space for the Union and its related activities would be provided, but would occupy a small part of the building, and the substantial rental income from the other floors would eventually retire the bonds," which were purchased by Chicago financiers and WCTU members.[18] The red granite and terra-cotta office structure served as national WCTU headquarters from 1892 to 1898.[19]

Regional WCTU branches and local chapters adapted a variety of institutions to serve as substitutes for the saloon. Scattered throughout California, for example, were temperance temples, coffee houses, reading rooms, restaurants, and even a temperance ice cream parlor, located in San Francisco.[20] Sometimes existing buildings were adapted for new uses; but in many cases new buildings were constructed specifically for the purpose.

On April 28, 1889, the Southern California Chapter of the WCTU dedicated a four-story temperance temple at Broadway and Temple Street in downtown Los Angeles. Built on a more modest scale than the Chicago headquarters, the local temple outlasted the national one on which it was modeled. The building served as regional and local headquarters for the organization. A variety of groups leased the auditorium, which had a capacity of six hundred; the rental of furnished rooms brought in added income; and a popular temperance restaurant operated out of the basement.[21] The fourth floor was converted into the Frances E. Willard Home for Girls in 1919. It provided temporary shelter for approximately six hundred delinquent girls per year who otherwise would have had to serve jail sentences, presumably for minor offenses.

What remains of the WCTU's building programs? Eventually the temperance temples in Chicago and Los Angeles were demolished. The fate of the Los Angeles temperance temple suggests that these buildings, in many ways, were bellwethers of their times. During the 1920s the city of Los Angeles forced the WCTU to remove ten and twelve feet from the Broadway and Temple Street sides of the building, respectively, in order to accommodate street widening. In 1933, the building's brick structure and elaborate parapet were easy targets for Southern California's devastating earthquake, which so severely damaged the upper two stories of the temple that city inspectors insisted that they be removed. The physically diminished temple received yet another blow, this time politically, when Prohibition finally was repealed. The WCTU's substantial loss of power to control the sale of alcoholic beverages had some embarrassing consequences in Los Angeles, according to the official historical record published by the Southern California WCTU's State Executive Committee.

> The cafe on the Temple Street side of the building gave some trouble after repeal because the leases read that the tenants could not sell alcoholic beverages "according to law." The tenant obtained a permit to sell beer and wine with meals, and put a sign in the window. This was printed in *Time* magazine and caused quite a stir.[22]

The eventual death of the cafe owner allowed the WCTU to save face by leasing the premises to a more compatible tenant. Finally, in 1947, Los Angeles County Supervisors purchased the temple that the WCTU had occupied for sixty-seven years and razed it for civic center expansion. No longer a vital organization nationally, at the time of this study the vestigial Los Angeles branch still maintained headquarters in a three-story residence that it had occupied since 1950.[23]

Because of the wealth of tangible resources once associated with the WCTU, there is a need for further documentation of the built environment associated with a movement that, by 1920, absorbed the energies of more than eight hundred thousand women,[24] yielded a constitutional amendment, exercised profound local influence in many parts of the country, and clearly altered the course of American history.

The omission of grass-roots aspects of the women's temperance movement from the list of themes covered in past state and local preservation surveys leaves open the question of whether temples, restaurants, reading rooms, and homes survive in other cities. However, the ready availability of primary and secondary sources clearly indicates that such a survey is possible. If and when representative examples are found, they should be nominated for National Register designation, and considered for inclusion in the National Historic Landmark program.

Histories of women's efforts to establish clubs, associations, and homes for working women suggest yet another rich array of potentially significant properties where women's history can be publicly interpreted. These women's organizations arose in both black and white communities, and while many parallels may be found that transcend race, an examination of the historic built environment associated with each group suggests some revealing differences in resources and priorities. While the following surveys highlight the abundant resources that are likely to be revealed in surveys of sites significant in the history of the white Protestant and African American women's clubs and associations, emerging scholarship on women's contributions to other communities—Native American, Chinese American, Italian American, and more—promises to challenge past understandings of organized women's activities that were based largely on the experiences of white, middle-class women. It will provide a foundation for more expansive, multiethnic surveys in the future.

Beginning in 1868 with the founding of Sorosis in New York City and the

New England Woman's Club in Boston, middle-class white women founded clubs that would serve as centers for literary and cultural exchange in their own communities. Complex and contradictory institutions, women's clubs both reinforced Victorian ideals of womanhood and deliberately undermined the conventional separation of male and female spheres by providing women with a point of entry into the public domain. In *The Clubwoman as Feminist: True Womanhood Redefined*, Karen J. Blair chronicled the emergence of the American women's club movement during the second half of the nineteenth century.[25] According to Blair, women's clubs achieved their influence

> not [by] rejecting the traditional imagery of the lady, but consciously building upon it. Their modifications made the role more palatable, for clubwomen transformed ladyhood by providing an intellectual and social self-improvement program outside the realm of the household, designed to nurture the skills that would enable women to demand reforms for women and for all people in a society that had relegated them to the sidelines.[26]

Thus over time, the relatively innocuous social and cultural bonds that originally united clubwomen matured into effective political alliances, as women's clubs moved from self-improvement into more ambitious campaigns for civic improvement and social reform. Because the women's club movement is important for understanding both women's history and their contribution to American civic life, historic places associated with the movement's origins, spread, diversity, and consolidation merit serious attention from historic preservation agencies.

Although much has been written about Sorosis in New York City and the New England Woman's Club in Boston,[27] little effort has been made to document or preserve the sites and buildings that were associated with these first American women's clubs. Setting the pattern for nineteenth-century women's clubs, the first organizational meetings of Sorosis and the New England Woman's Club were held in the parlor of an organizer's home, at Jane Croly's and Harriot Hunt's residences respectively.[28] Thereafter, larger regular meeting places were secured. Twice-monthly meetings of Sorosis were held at Delmonico's Restaurant in New York City.[29] In contrast, the New England Woman's Club, with its interlocking membership in a host of other Boston-based women's organizations, typically secured rooms in buildings shared with allies in the women's rights movement.[30]

Fortunately there are two places in Boston where the New England Woman's Club can be commemorated. The New England Woman's Club and other women's reform organizations that began in the postbellum period, such as the Massachusetts and the New England Woman Suffrage Associations, their organ *The Woman's Journal*, and the Women's Educational and Industrial Union, first chose Tremont Place, and then the more spacious Quincy Parlors nearby on Park Street, for their early headquarters in the period from 1868 to

1905. Although ineligible for landmark designation because these historic buildings have been replaced by more recent construction,[31] the site still merits public interpretation for a number of reasons.

First, by 1868 when the New England Woman's Club was founded, suburban expansion and the radial orientation of the city's fledgling public transportation system frustrated middle- and upper-class women's traditional remedy for domestic isolation, the practice of paying social calls. Thus, Caroline Severance and other founding members secured a central location for the New England Woman's Club to overcome spatial barriers to female solidarity. Reflecting on the early choice of location, the first president of the New England Woman's Club, Caroline Severance, wrote

> There were no days "at home" as now, when one could be certain of finding the friend, who might at that very hour be wending her way by steam car to the City, across it by horse car, and again by steam to one's suburban home, only to find her friend away. The loss of time, and strength, and the delights of meeting one another, intensified my unquenched desire to create the opportunity for easy and frequent intercourse.[32]

The choice of Park Street as a site for public commemoration of the New England Woman's Club would recognize the historical significance of the club's proximity to the Park Street Station. Other compelling reasons for introducing public interpretation of women's history at Park Street include this site's close proximity to and association with the Massachusetts State House, the Boston Commons, and Brimstone Corner, all of which were important settings in women's campaigns for social reform.

The Chauncy Hall Building, opposite Copley Square on Boylston Street, is the only extant building that served as headquarters for the New England Woman's Club.[33] Built in 1909, it was occupied by the club through 1929 and housed related women's organizations during the final decade of the woman's suffrage campaign.[34] Despite the fact that modifications to the facade of this four-story brick building have diminished the historical integrity of its architecture, the building merits consideration for listing on local, state, and national registers of historic buildings in light of the significance of the New England Woman's Club in the history of the women's club movement.

The myriad local clubhouses that have survived to the present day are tangible reminders that the women's club movement spread to nearly every village, town, and city in the nation.[35] Approximately twelve hundred women's clubhouses reportedly existed in 1933, the individual value of which ranged from three hundred dollars to three million dollars.[36] Compared with other building types significant in women's history, women's clubhouses are relatively well represented on local, state, and national landmark registers. Michigan alone added three women's club buildings to the National Register during the early 1970s.[37] The Kalamazoo Ladies' Library Association Building, dedicated in 1879, is reputed to be the first building in the nation "erected exclusively by and for a woman's club,"[38] a claim that has yet to be verified in a comparative study. This library building is representative of an important contribution made by women's clubs to the cultural lives of their respective communities. According to Karen J. Blair, "the American Library Association reportedly credited women's clubs with . . . initiating seventy-five percent of the public libraries in existence in the United States in 1933."[39]

The fact that many women's clubs hired noted architects to design their buildings has strengthened arguments for listing them on landmark registers. Landmark nominations for women's club buildings such as these illustrate a problem in the assessment of their significance. Aesthetic merit and the historical significance of the architect have tended to overshadow the women's history that led to the clubhouses' construction in the first place. A case in point is the Outdoor Art Club building in Mill Valley, California, designed in 1904 by internationally known American architect Bernard Maybeck and noted more for the architectural significance of its unusual roof truss system than for its historical significance.[40]

An active involvement in historic preservation led a number of women's clubs to adopt historic structures for their club buildings. The Woman's Club of Santa Clara, California, acquired and restored for their own use the only remaining adobe in the valley.[41] Other women's clubs contributed to the development of regional architecture through the intentional use of revival styles or characteristic local building materials in newly constructed club buildings. Hazel Wood Waterman, who designed the San Diego Wednesday Club House, relied on the Mission revival style to create a fit between the existing architecture of Southern California and her additions to the region's built environment.[42]

Male-dominated architectural firms with solid local reputations were responsible for the bulk of newly designed women's club buildings. California architect Julia Morgan was one of the few exceptions. Sara Holmes Boutelle's book *Julia Morgan, Architect* is the first major work on Morgan, who was without a doubt the most successful of the early twentieth-century women architects. Boutelle's effort to situate Morgan in the context of a network of women's organizations that supported her practice,[43] particularly California women's clubs and the National Board of the Young Women's Christian Association, opens new interpretive possibilities at Morgan-designed buildings such as the Berkeley Women's City Club, constructed in 1929 and entered onto the National Register in 1977.[44]

In larger metropolitan areas, where dozens of women's clubs often coexisted, a number of clubhouses may remain. Seven extant women's club buildings and group residences are listed as Historic-Cultural Monuments in the Los Angeles area alone: the Harbor Area YWCA and the Hollywood Studio Club, designed by Julia Morgan; the Mary Andrews Clark Residence of the YWCA; two branches of the Ebell Club; the Van Nuys Woman's Club Building; and the Friday Morning Club building. The cedar trees planted on Los Feliz Boulevard by the local women's city club also have been designated Historic-Cultural Monuments.[45] Given the abundance of tangible remains from the women's club movement, especially in major cities, and their importance for understanding middle- and upper-class women's lives in the late nineteenth and early twentieth century, thematic group nominations of these cultural resources would be worthy additions to national, state, and local historic preservation inventories. Only one such group currently appears on the National Register, which consists of nine Illinois chapter houses historically associated with the American Woman's League.[46]

In 1890, white women's clubs pooled their separate influences in a General Federation. According to Sara Evans, the two hundred clubs at the General Federation of Women's Clubs' founding convention represented twenty thousand women. By 1900 it had 150,000 members and two decades later it served as a voice for the concerns of a million women.[47] An excellent place for marking this nationally significant historical development is the Washington, D.C., building that was purchased by the General Federation of Women's Clubs and served from 1922 on as its headquarters.[48] It is a four-story Renaissance style building that originally was constructed in 1875 as a residence for Rear Admiral William Radford's retirement years.

By the time of this purchase, the women's club movement had evolved into a hybrid form that combined the longstanding social and cultural interests of late nineteenth-century women's clubs with an emphasis on civic engagement more characteristic of women's clubs in the twentieth century. This complex program shaped both the allocation and use of space in the headquarters building, which combined social, cultural, and political functions. The first floor was devoted to legislative, research, and distribution offices for the organization, along with pantries and a model electric kitchen that was a tangible expression of the General Federation of Women's Clubs' link to the Better Homes movement. The second floor included ample space for social events and cultural programs with a music room, conservatory, dining room, reception room, library and lounge. Visiting General Federation of Women's Clubs members could stay in bedrooms located on the third and fourth floors, where the organization's president also resided during her term of office.[49]

Despite the historical significance of many places connected with white women's clubs and associations, they have limited interpretive potential for the black women's club movement. Although a common concern for self-improvement, moral uplift, and service linked all women's clubs, pervasive racism divided black and white women into separate communities, led to the development of racially segregated club movements, and attached a special meaning to African American women's struggle for dignity.

Researchers have found examples of organized community activity among African American women reaching back to the late eighteenth and early nineteenth century. Dorothy Sterling, editor of a collection on *Black Women in the Nineteenth Century*, cites the Daughters of Africa, an 1821 organization of

Philadelphia washerwomen and domestics, and the Female Anti-Slavery Society, an 1832 organization of black women in Salem, Massachusetts, as early examples of mutual relief and social reform efforts organized by African American women in Northern cities.[50] Black women's literary societies that formed during the second quarter of the nineteenth century provided sources of philanthropic support and focal points for the debate of public issues in black communities, according to Howard University archivist Dorothy Porter.[51] In her history of the black women's club movement, *Lifting as They Climb*, Elizabeth Davis found early evidence of organized community activity among Boston's African American women in the 1848 efforts of a female benevolent society to secure shoes and clothing for runaway slaves.[52]

In an essay on "The Community Work of Black Club Women," which laid the foundation for later scholarship, historian Gerda Lerner explained the significance of African American women's voluntary activities. She observed that "the virtual absence of social welfare institutions," particularly in many Southern communities, combined with "the frequent exclusion of Blacks from those that existed, led women to found orphanages, old folks' homes, and similar institutions."[53] Some of these institutions, however, were originally founded and financed by white philanthropists, which made autonomous operation problematic.[54] Building on a long tradition of black women's activism in the church and benevolent organizations, it was Ida B. Wells's stirring campaign against lynching during the last decade of the nineteenth century that seeded the formation of black women's civic clubs nationwide, prompting them to coalesce as a movement and galvanizing them into action.

According to Wells's autobiography, in the wake of her 1893 British lecture tour she began speaking to New England audiences about the need for her black sisters "to become more active in the affairs of their community, city and nation, and to do these things through organized civic clubs."[55] The first black women's civic clubs were founded as a result of her influence. These included the Women's Loyal Union in Brooklyn and Manhattan, and the Woman's Era Club of Boston. After the founding of the Boston club, the team of Ida B. Wells and Josephine St. Pierre Ruffin organized other black women's clubs in towns throughout New England, including New Bedford, Massachusetts, and Providence and Newport in Rhode Island.[56] The Chicago civic club that Wells helped to organize was later named in her honor.[57]

An open letter published by the president of the Missouri Press Association that attacked Ida B. Wells's moral character, and by implication slandered black women generally, provided the impetus for the formation of the National Federation of Afro-American Women at an 1895 meeting called by Woman's Era Club president Josephine St. Pierre Ruffin. According to Paula Giddings's account, "one hundred women from ten states" met in Boston to formulate plans for a national federation that soon linked "thirty-six clubs in twelve states."[58] The National Federation merged with the National League of Colored Women the following year in 1896, creating the National Association of

Colored Women's Clubs with Mary Church Terrell as its first president. The Association boasted a membership of fifty thousand women in over one thousand clubs two decades later.[59]

The civil rights movement of the 1960s, and the subsequent creation of black studies programs at universities across the country, gave rise to myriad efforts to improve the presentation and interpretation of black history during the 1970s, particularly as the nation prepared to celebrate the Bicentennial. The designation of Mary Church Terrell's Washington, D.C., residence[60] and Ida B. Wells's Chicago residence[61] as National Historic Landmarks signaled growing appreciation in the 1970s of African American women's contributions to United States history.[62] However, the ubiquitous tendency to save only historic houses associated with notable individuals obscures creative possibilities for commemorating the history of African American women at sites of their collective accomplishment and activity. Recent histories of the African American women's club movement provide a solid intellectual foundation for the researcher who takes on the much-needed project of surveying the historic sites and buildings associated with the National Federation, National League, and National Association.[63]

A unit of the National Park System allows visitors to learn about the National Association of Colored Women's Clubs through its work in the area of historic preservation. Beginning in 1916, the National Association and its constituent clubs became involved in the preservation of African American history when they assumed responsibility for the restoration and preservation of Frederick Douglass's home in the Anacostia district of Washington, D.C. The association maintained the home for nearly fifty years as a memorial to the great abolitionist leader.[64] Authorized by Congress as a unit of the National Park System in 1962, it was donated to the National Park Service in 1964. This historic site provides opportunities for public interpretation of the contributions made not only by Douglass but also by organized African American women who saved and restored the site for the community. As well, it serves as a base for interpreting the history of the surrounding Anacostia Historic District.[65]

The historical record indicates that black women's clubs accomplished a substantial amount of institution-building in their own communities, despite the constraints of their economic resources. The Atlanta Women's Congress that met during the 1895 Cotton States and International Exposition encouraged black women's clubs to redouble their efforts "to establish reformatories, homes for the aged, [and] friendly shelters for girls."[66] Speakers at later meetings of the National Association of Colored Women, in 1899 and 1901, added kindergartens and day nurseries to the list of black community institutions that they urged women's clubs actively to support.[67] Their call was met with an overwhelming response. Elizabeth Davis's history of the National Association of Colored Women illustrates the variety of clubhouses, community centers, and group homes that African American women's clubs had purchased or erected by the mid-1930s. Some examples include: the Indianapolis Woman's

Improvement Club, purchased in the late 1920s;[68] the Oklahoma Community Center;[69] the Margaret Murray Washington Home for Delinquent Negro Youths, near Clinton, Mississippi, by that state's Federation of Colored Women's Clubs;[70] and the Chicago Phyllis Wheatley Home, purchased in 1906.[71]

The rapid spread of the club movement, particularly in cities with a substantial black population, testifies to the importance of community work among African American women. Yet the limited evidence from one local survey indicates that black women's clubs appear to have built and owned relatively fewer clubhouses than their white counterparts. Sharp contrasts between the economic and social resources of white and black communities, even within the same cities, had direct implications for the purchase and construction of women's clubhouses. Darlene Roth's 1980 study, "Feminine Marks on the Landscape," pointed out just this difference in the context of Atlanta:

> By 1940 at least half of the federated [white] women's clubs in the state of Georgia had their own clubhouses, including the Atlanta women's clubs and suburban clubs in the neighborhoods of West End, Grant Park and Capitol Hill, as well as nearby Decatur and College Park.[72]

In contrast, Roth observed,

> There were no clubhouses in the Atlanta black community until 1947, though there were many plans and ideas for them. . . . For a long time the only exclusively female meeting space in black Atlanta was the Phyllis Wheatley branch building of the YWCA; otherwise clubwomen met in homes, in churches, and in fraternal lodge buildings.[73]

Consequently, organized black women in Atlanta were more likely than white women to share meeting space with men's groups. This pattern may indicate a lesser degree of sex segregation in the black community, though more likely sex segregation in the black community was maintained through temporal barriers, whereby men and women alternated their use of space until such time as separate institutions could be maintained. It was 1947 before the Atlanta Federation of Colored Women's Clubs was able to purchase an existing residence and convert it into a clubhouse.

The joy of discovering tangible remains such as these, associated with groups that traditionally have been underrepresented in American history, however, is dampened by existing eligibility criteria for the National Register of Historic Places, which generally prohibits the designation of buildings constructed within the last fifty years. It poses special problems for preserving tangible resources of relatively recent vintage associated with groups whose organizational roots extend further back in history, as appears to be the case for many black women's clubs. Greater sensitivity is needed on the part of staff within preservation agencies to the distinctive social, economic, and political circumstances that have shaped the historical relationship of women and minorities to property. A clearer understanding of these issues might lead to the relaxation of eligibility criteria with less fear of compromising the integrity of the National Register program.[74]

Few examples of black women's clubhouses currently appear on the National Register of Historic Places. Their status on local registers of historic places remains to be determined. The identification of an extant clubhouse associated with the Sacramento Negro Women's Civic Improvement Club in a recent survey of ethnic sites in California, however, suggests that rich finds await discovery by future surveyors.[75]

Gender so powerfully organized and divided late nineteenth- and early twentieth-century American society that much of women's philanthropic and reform work remained independent of the male-dominated mainstream. As a consequence, the organizations that formed to provide housing and social services for low-income workers did so in spheres separated by sex. A significant number of middle- and upper-class women formed associations to plan, design, build, remodel, and operate group homes for working women. Both the headquarters of groups such as the Young Women's Christian Association and the organized homes that they founded merit greater attention in the landmark survey and designation process.

These female reformers recognized that housing was a formidable problem for working women who lived apart from the family in late nineteenth- and early twentieth-century American cities. The sexual wage differential, overt discrimination in the housing market, and social mores that favored chaperoned situations for "respectable" women narrowed the range of decent, affordable, and acceptable housing options for women "adrift," as they were called.[76] In her labor history, *From Working Girl to Working Mother,* Lynn Y. Weiner describes the origins and spread of work that women undertook in this area:

> The first boarding home that offered permanent residence to nondestitute women was established by the Ladies Christian Union in New York City in 1856. The Young Woman's Home contained sewing, laundry, meeting and dining rooms, two parlors, and sleeping rooms. . . . By 1877, at least twenty similar homes had been organized in cities including Boston, New York, Cincinnati, and Denver. Most of these were founded by women's organizations like the YWCA, WCA, and such church groups as the Sisters of Mercy. Some public-spirited individuals sponsored homes as well.[77]

The number of homes and boarders grew so rapidly, according to Weiner, that "by 1898, there were at least ninety boarding homes opened in forty-five cities," housing 4,500 women at a time and over 30,000 women annually.[78]

In Boston there were approximately seventy thousand working women by 1900, nearly 30 percent of whom were estimated to be living apart from their families.[79] In response to what they perceived as a crisis, wealthy patrons established at least eighteen separate group homes in Boston for working women between 1866 and 1915.[80] While the majority of women "adrift" lived in commercial boarding houses in turn-of-the-century Boston, one in ten lived in an organized (that is, nonprofit) residence.[81]

The first nonprofit boardinghouse in Boston was established in 1866 by the Young Women's Christian Association, which sought to alleviate the supposed moral perils and genuine economic hardships faced by white Christian working women living apart from their families. In its first years of operation, the YWCA's Beach Street residence had the capacity to house 180 women. The residents included seamstresses, milliners, store clerks, and office workers, among others.[82] But demand soon outstripped the capacity of the YWCA's initial residence, which was demolished to accommodate the widening of Beach Street, and two new homes were built, at 68 Warrenton and 40 Berkeley Street, with a combined capacity of more than three hundred residents.

The Young Women's Christian Association was a complex urban institution that provided more than just shelter. Rather, it successfully wedded housing with a vast array of social services. In addition to a library and reading room, similar to many other local branches, the Boston YWCA had formal educational facilities where women studied stenography, typewriting, bookkeeping, and the liberal arts. A well-equipped school of domestic science was intended to elevate middle-class homemakers to the level of professionals, and a school for domestic servants rationalized the process of training household labor. In one year alone, from 1896 to 1897, the YWCA employment bureau found work for over forty-five hundred women. A gymnasium provided physical exercise and training for over five hundred women during that same year.[83] At the beginning of the Great Depression the total value of YWCA property nationally was estimated to exceed seventy million dollars.[84] During the 1930s there were nearly three hundred YWCA residences nationally that accommodated between one quarter and one half million women per year and provided services to many more.[85]

Some surviving YWCA buildings, such as a 1914 example from Richmond, Virginia, are listed on the National Register of Historic Places. A 1983 call for information in the YWCA Interchange identified several other YWCAs in Fresno, California; Clinton, Iowa; Philadelphia and Lancaster, Pennsylvania; Mankato, Minnesota; Quincy, Illinois; and Zanesville, Ohio; each property benefiting from some measure of landmark protection on local, state or national registers of historic buildings.[86] Still, a great need remains for concerted action to identify and protect some of the most important examples of association headquarters and residence buildings.

The most appropriate place to commemorate the YWCA's contribution as an urban institution is at the oldest known surviving city association building, which is located at 7 East 15th Street in Manhattan. Built in 1885 by architect R. H. Robertson, the YWCA of the city of New York actually began its occupancy of the site a decade earlier in a previous building. This building and the surviving YWCA Margaret Louisa Residence, which is located on an adjacent site at 14–16 East 16th Street, are related to one another both architecturally

Young Women's Christian Association of the City of New York. (Photograph by Steven Senigo)

and programmatically. Together they merit consideration for National Historic Landmark designation as outstanding representative examples of the unique urban building types developed by the YWCA in the last quarter of the nineteenth century and as potent symbols of the YWCA's contribution to the development of the American city.[87]

A second aspect of the YWCA's history that merits recognition are sites associated with its National Board, which has coordinated local efforts and initiated national programs since 1906. Two facilities that were operated by the YWCA National Board and designed by architect Julia Morgan have survived to date. The Asilomar Conference Center, located in Pacific Grove, California, is a designated National Historic Landmark. It brought together thousands of YWCA members for formal training and informal exchange. The Hollywood Studio Club, a Los Angeles Historic-Cultural Monument that is also listed on the National Register, is nationally significant on account of its relationship to the rise of the motion picture industry and the women who worked within it. Established by the YWCA in 1916, it served over the years as a group residence for young women who came to Los Angeles seeking work in Hollywood. The

most significant building associated with the National Board, its historic headquarters at 600 Lexington Avenue in New York City was demolished in
1982.[88] The abundance of architectural relics salvaged by many long-term staff
members, who made the transition from the stunning old building to the rather
sterile new one, testifies to their passionate attachment to that elegant, but no
longer extant, historic place.

While the YWCA was the most sophisticated provider of low-cost housing
and services for working women, smaller independent institutions shared that
organization's concern for establishing homelike group residences for low-income women. In Boston, three-and-a-half to four-story row houses in the city's
South End proved quite adaptable as shelters for between sixteen and twenty-
one residents each. Surviving examples include the Home for Working Women
on Shawmut Street, which assisted its residents in finding employment and engaged unemployed residents in a work-exchange program in an on-site laundry
and sewing room;[89] and the Massachusetts Home for Intemperate Women on
Worcester Street, which treated 1,735 women to a program of detoxification,
rest, religion, industrial training, and employment assistance in its first ten
years of operation from 1879 to 1888. Like the Shawmut Street Home, this
facility also featured a sewing room and laundry, which generated two-thirds
of the home's income by taking in work from the Back Bay.[90] Parallel examples
of local significance probably survive in every major city in the United States
and these resources have important unexplored potential for interpreting not
only the history of the middle-class women who founded them and the working-class women who inhabited them, but also, significantly, the relationship
between these two classes of women.

One of the most significant sets of tangible resources that remain from the
black women's club movement are the group homes that local clubs established. The Home for the Aged that Harriet Tubman, the famous conductor of
the Underground Railroad, established in 1908 in Auburn, New York, appropriately was designated as a National Historic Landmark in 1974.[91] Research
is needed to identify the built remains of black branches associated with the
Young Women's Christian Association, which were established as segregated
subsidiaries of white locals, a practice that according to Paula Giddings
spanned from 1893, when the first black YWCA was established in Dayton,
Ohio, to 1946, when the YWCA adopted an "Interracial Charter" and embarked on an organizational commitment to achieving racial integration.[92] In
World War I, the YWCA's War Work Council established recreational facilities
for black soldiers and black women working in war industries in forty-five
communities, the tangible remains of which have yet to be surveyed. Sophonisba Breckinridge, in *Women in the Twentieth Century*, reported sixty-three
black branches of City Associations in 1933 serving approximately twenty-
eight thousand members.[93]

As well, representative examples of the group homes for working women
that were established by independent black women's groups merit serious con-

sideration for national, state, and local landmark designation. Significant examples of homes established by independent black women's groups for young black working women are known to have survived in Boston, Chicago, and Los Angeles. In 1904, a philanthropic group of African American female Bostonians founded the Harriet Tubman Home, which sheltered approximately sixteen working girls and students in a South End row house.[94] In Chicago the Melissia Ann Elam Home, which has served as a residence for black working women since the 1930s, has been designated a city landmark.[95] In Los Angeles, the Sojourner Truth Industrial Club has operated homes for young female students and workers for approximately eighty years. The first house that the club acquired at 1119 East Adams Boulevard still stands. When originally designed, it had fifteen rooms including nine bedrooms, two baths, a kitchen, a dining room, a reception hall, and a library. Besides serving as a group home, it was an important cultural center where the local black community went to meet prominent black visitors to the city.[96] Although the homes that this Los Angeles club established are likely candidates for being the oldest continuously operating homes for black working women in the nation, they have not yet been considered for landmark designation at the local, state, or national level. Many more homes that once met young women's needs for shelter and a social life apart from their families probably survive in cities whose population swelled as a result of northern and western black migration.

What can be learned from differences in the building programs undertaken by black and white women's groups, and what are their implications for historic preservation? Given the relative scarcity of women's clubhouses in the black community, surveyors should attempt to identify the variety of places where black women's groups held meetings, while preservationists should make special efforts to save extant clubhouses and community meeting places. Cautious deliberation is warranted as these building types come under consideration for landmark designation; particular effort should be made to avoid unfair comparisons between white and black women's club buildings in terms of their relative aesthetic significance.

Black women's clubs typically had to "make do" with more limited resources than their white counterparts, as the dearth of actual clubhouses indicates. Their awareness that black women were "a working class" led them to place a high priority on meeting basic needs for childcare and shelter by establishing day nurseries and boarding homes.[97] The Sojourner Truth Industrial Club of Los Angeles built its first home in 1908 with a "mile of pennies," which when computed at twenty cents a foot raised one thousand dollars.[98] Likewise, the Harriet Tubman Home of Boston hired an amateur draftsman to draw up its remodeling plans.[99] Grass-roots strategies to establish and build black community institutions often were reflected in the resultant architecture. In contrast, the class base of some white women's clubs in the late nineteenth century allowed them to pursue more grand building strategies. Fund-raising for expensive new buildings often was accomplished by combining the pro-

Sojourner Truth Industrial Club, Los Angeles, California. (Photograph by Gail Lee Dubrow)

ceeds from numerous small subscriptions with large donations from the wealthiest club members. As a result, many elegant architect-designed women's clubhouses have graced the urban landscape. Unfortunately, the association of important architects with the design of white women's clubhouses too often has led preservationists to place a disproportionate emphasis on their aesthetic merit, while overlooking the women's history connected with them.

As this review of the black and white women's community-building activities reveals, new scholarship in women's history now makes it possible to evaluate more fully the historical significance of extant tangible resources and to assess their relative merit for listing in the National Register of Historic Places and possible National Historic Landmark designation. The abundance of archival materials documenting the activities of national and state federations of women's clubs, as well as the work of local clubs and associations, promises to facilitate future efforts to identify, interpret, and preserve the tangible remains of these women's movements.[100]

Substantial tangible resources are likely to be revealed in future surveys by historic preservation planners, yet their architectural form and character may vary. Emerging scholarship on the history of women in Native American, Asian American, and Chicano/Latino communities will open other new possibilities for historic preservation. Multicultural understandings are likely to enrich on-site interpretations at the historic clubs and associations that enabled women to work so effectively in their own communities, and that served as springboards for their greater participation in the public spheres of American society and culture.

It is an accepted tenet of historical scholarship that social settlements, which were established primarily by college-educated women in the poorer districts of cities, are important institutions for interpreting late nineteenth- and early twentieth-century American urban history. The importance of the effort made by the social settlement movement to bridge sharp divisions in urban society and culture, with varying degrees of success, has been recognized as well. However, to the extent that women's obvious leadership and high levels of participation in the movement caught the attention of past scholars, in the estimation of historian Gerda Lerner, their scholarship minimized "Jane Addams' enormous contribution in creating a supporting female network and new structures for living,"[101] by labeling them, according to Dolores Hayden, " 'a group of frustrated college-trained women with no place to go.' "[102]

In recent years, with the rise of new scholarship in women's history, attention has turned to the meaning of the social settlements for the historical experiences of women: as leaders in the movement, as residents in the settlements, and as members of the communities served by them. Recent works by Helen Lefkowitz Horowitz, Dolores Hayden, Kathryn Kish Sklar, and others have contributed to the literature on social settlements, providing more complex and subtly nuanced interpretations of the gendered meaning of the subject.

Social settlements originated in London with the 1884 establishment of Toynbee Hall by Oxford University students. In turn, Toynbee Hall inspired the establishment of the social settlement movement in the United States. The first two American settlements were established in New York City. Women collectively entered the movement in September 1889, with the establishment of the first project of the College Settlements Association at 95 Rivington Street, which harnessed the considerable energies and talents of college graduates from Smith, Wellesley, Vassar, and Bryn Mawr.[103] A visit to Toynbee Hall prompted Jane Addams and Ellen Gates Starr, a week and a half after the founding of the College Settlement, to establish Hull House in Chicago, which was the most important social settlement established in the United States. The movement spread rapidly in the wake of the establishment of these first American settlements. Seventy-four separate institutions were listed in the *Handbook of Settlements* by 1897. By the turn of the century there were more than one hundred settlements, after which the number doubled approximately every five years, yielding more than four hundred settlements by 1911.[104]

A position at the helm of many settlements provided women with an independent institutional base for leadership in social reform. Hull House provided just such a platform for Jane Addams, as did New York City's Henry Street Settlement for Lillian Wald and Greenwich House for Mary Simkhovitch. The

Hull House, Chicago, Illinois. (Photograph from Allen Pond, "The Settlement House," *The Brickbuilder* 11:9 [September 1902]: 179)

political effectiveness of these female reformers, according to Kathryn Kish Sklar, is attributable both to the social settlement's existence as a community of women reformers, and the important links that they forged to male-dominated political culture.[105]

Although most settlements had some mix of male and female residents, distinguishing them from far more rigidly sex-segregated environments in other social spaces occupied by women in colleges and philanthropic homes for working women, both the leadership and rank-and-file of the movement were female-dominated. The evolution of the staff at Henry Street Settlement, founded in 1893, was typical in this respect. According to Lillian Wald's biographer R. L. Duffus:

> The household was at first feminine, but men were soon represented among the staff workers and in the membership and in time there were a few male residents.[106]

A 1922 survey of 250 major settlements showed that seventy percent of the nearly fifteen hundred residents identified were women.[107] Hull House alone nurtured the careers of a whole generation of female social reformers such as

Sophonisba Breckinridge, Dr. Alice Hamilton, Grace and Edith Abbott, Florence Kelley, Julia Lathrop, and Mary McDowell.

One consequence of women's leadership in the social settlements, and their preponderance among residents, was the high level of attention paid to the particular needs of immigrant and working-class women in the communities served by social settlements. According to Woods and Kennedy in *The Settlement Horizon*,

> the fact that women residents had found a large new field for their powers and were experiencing some of the adventure afforded by vocations out of the home, made them conscious that there was such a thing as economic solidarity among women. They hoped to have a hand in making conditions under which all women shall share in the varied work of the world.[108]

According to Kathryn Kish Sklar, women in the social settlement movement probably found that their claims to social scientific expertise on the subject of women, as opposed to men or humanity as a whole, were less likely to be contested by their male peers.[109]

The settlements' built form illustrates a variety of strategies that were deployed in the effort to synthesize seemingly disparate reform elements, which until that point had been brought together only in limited ways, such as in the complex social and architectural programs carried out by the YWCA. In this sense, it might be argued that the settlements were the culmination of a gradually evolving architecture of Progressive reform. An essay by Allen B. Pond in 1902 observed a pattern in the typical development of social settlements. The desire to blend into the surrounding community made it preferable to begin in an existing building, as a sign of "unostentatious neighborliness."[110] The settlement expanded gradually beyond these "small beginnings," creating

> a modicum of creature comfort for the "residents,"—that is, the members of the new community,—a certain relative spaciousness to adapt it to larger social uses, and a form, external and internal, expressing, or capable of being made to express, hospitality and homelikeness.[111]

A distinctive feature of settlements, as noted by Horowitz and Hayden, was their unique combination of residential and social spaces.[112] A cooperative living space, as well as a community center, the social settlement effectively

> lightened the burdens of the late nineteenth-century household. Unlike the single family house, it offered the larger sociability and fellowship of a female community—especially vital to women whose emotional world revolved around other women.[113]

For career-minded women, according to Dolores Hayden, Hull House meant a life enriched and sustained by close contact with dozens of others with similar goals. In this sense,

> domestic life in a settlement solved the logistical problems of spinsterhood, by providing a respectable, adult home life, autonomous yet collective. It was more independent than living with relatives and far more congenial than living alone.[114]

Helen Lefkowitz Horowitz, in a 1984 article titled "Hull-House as Women's Space," concluded that settlements offered active professionals "a haven," while promising "commitment and community."[115] Whereas, the union of work and life in traditional domestic arrangements was a fundamental source of oppression for women, the communal arrangements at Hull House unified the two in a way that was liberating. Hayden emphasizes the importance of a cooperative housekeeping arrangement for freeing female reformers from conventional domestic roles and enabling their participation in movements for social reform.[116]

An examination of the public or social spaces provided by settlements reveals a great deal about the various independent reform movements that coalesced under the shelter of the settlements' expansive wings. Kindergartens, day nurseries, public kitchens, playgrounds, and homes for working women numbered among the many domestic reform efforts incorporated into the social settlements and were a tangible expression of middle-class reformers' commitment to improving the quality of life for working-class women. Social settlements also widened the reach of the club movement into working-class and ethnic communities. As a cooperative living environment, the social settlements incorporated some of the ideals and forms associated with earlier communitarian experiments. Finally, the many public meeting spaces provided by social settlements, which supported social, political, labor, cultural, and recreational gatherings, reflected both the temperance movement's commitment to providing substitutes for the saloon and Progressive reformers' determination to create a public domain independent of commercial interests and corrupt political machines.

The vast array of social spaces provided by settlements meant that they were able in only some cases to carry out a gradually expanding program of activities from their original base, as did the College Settlement.[117] As some settlements matured, they moved into or expanded to include buildings specifically designed for them. Hull House, which began in 1889 with a portion of an existing mansion, expanded through new construction. By 1910 it included thirteen buildings on a city block. The University Settlement in New York City, Goodrich House in Cleveland, Chicago Commons and the Northwestern University Settlement all occupied buildings expressly designed for settlement work.[118]

A close examination of the decisions made about the preservation of Hull

House, when the University of Illinois chose the Harrison-Halsted neighborhood as the site for the new Chicago Circle campus, serves as a cautionary tale for others seeking to preserve the tangible remains of social settlements. While the massive complex, understandably, proved difficult to retain, the University of Illinois's decision to destroy eleven of the thirteen buildings that comprised Hull House overwhelmingly compromised the integrity of the most important social settlement in the United States. The expansive nature of social settlements often produced a complex array of associated sites, structures, and buildings that certainly complicated the process of planning for their preservation. Yet the full constellation of tangible resources is essential to the definition of what constituted social settlements, and therefore, especially in the case of the most significant examples, every effort should be made to preserve them. In the case of Hull House, however, the decision was made to save only the oldest structure, the Hull Mansion, and one of the twelve buildings designed by Irving and Allen Pond, the Hull House Residents' Dining Hall, which was reoriented to make room for the construction of the University Student Union.

The effort made by social settlements to adapt to changing community needs typically led them to undergo perpetual remodeling, a characteristic that complicates the process of setting a target date for restoration purposes. The 1960s demolition of the physical complex surrounding the Hull Mansion revealed the full extent of the mansion's alteration by Jane Addams and her associates. Shorn of its context, the mansion was left with doors to nowhere on the second floor and the imprint of staircases on newly revealed sections of the exterior that for decades had served as party walls. The decision to restore the Hull Mansion to its appearance when Jane Addams first found it in 1889 required extensive rebuilding. Its physical integrity was restored, however, at the expense of preserving evidence of the continual change that prevailed at the place during its single most significant period, Jane Addams's tenure, from 1889 to 1935.

In recognition of Addams's stature as a nationally significant figure, the interior of Hull House was restored to the period of her occupancy. Visitors, in fact, can see many original furnishings in the remaining buildings, which are open to the public. Yet, ironically, the archival management program for the Hull House papers may have overemphasized Addams to the exclusion of the other significant Hull House residents and the continuity of the institution's history, with some disastrous consequences. "Most of the papers and documents associated with the settlement were mistakenly hauled to the dump," according to historian Kathryn Kish Sklar, as a result of which, "only those with Jane's signature survived," which limits the ability of scholars to research the place as a site of collective accomplishment and activity.[119]

Open to the public, the surviving Hull House buildings are now home to special programs and exhibits that convey the social settlement's historical role in the surrounding community, as well as its national significance. Unfortunately, the scale of surrounding university development undermines the integrity of feeling and association at the few fragments of Hull House that remain.[120]

The Henry Street Settlement in New York City, also a National Historic Landmark, has survived to the present day with a greater degree of integrity than Hull House. The three-story house at 265 Henry Street is the original core of a series of three townhouses that together formed the Henry Street Settlement. In addition to the Henry Street complex, the Neighborhood Playhouse two blocks north on Grand Street was included in the National Historic Landmark designation. Yet even these remains misrepresent the full extent of the Henry Street Settlement's outreach into the city of New York. In 1913, for example,

> Instead of one house on Henry Street there were now seven; there was a house on Seventy-ninth Street and one, staffed by colored nurses, on Sixtieth Street; there were seven vacation homes in the country; there were three stores used for stock rooms, milk stations and clinics; the Henry Street classes and clubs alone had three thousand members; there were ninety-two nurses who were making two hundred thousand visits a year.[121]

The continuing presence of the Henry Street Settlement, in the midst of an urban context that has been transformed since Wald's day, suggests both the settlement's uncanny ability to adapt to changing community needs and the persistence of certain fundamental problems, especially urban poverty, that social settlements tried to address from the 1890s onward.

Some excellent sources are available to aid in conducting a nationwide survey of the physical remains of the social settlement movement, which is important since most of the scholarship to date has focused on only a few prominent examples with little awareness of broader patterns. Woods and Kennedy's *Handbook of Settlements*, which contains entries describing the programs, facilities, and staff of approximately four hundred settlements, is both a useful index of the scope of social settlement activity in 1911 and an invaluable source for conducting a systematic survey of historic sites and buildings associated with it. City directories and archival sources can be used to fill in local and chronological gaps once the *Handbook* has been used to frame the basic structure of the survey.

Although social settlements predominantly were urban institutions, the *Handbook* paints an intriguing picture of the ways that they sprung up in every part of the country, tailored to distinctive local conditions and the needs of particular social groups. The Calhoun Colored School and Settlement, for example, established in the cotton belt just three years after the founding of Hull House, served the needs of a large community of Afro-American tenant farmers.[122] The Pine Mountain Settlement School, established in eastern Kentucky in 1913 by Ethel de Long, Katharine Pettit, and William Creech, Sr., launched

Pine Mountain Settlement School, Harlan County, Kentucky. (Photograph courtesy of Pine Mountain Settlement School)

one of the most important efforts to adapt the urban settlement house to a rural community.[123] The Big Log House, which was the first building of the Pine Mountain Settlement School and the focus of its activities, was listed on the National Register of Historic Places in 1978. The Pine Mountain Settlement School was unique in the national, Southern, and Appalachian experience by virtue of the flexibility of its program, its longevity, and the scope of its work. These sites in rural areas balance the conventional urban portrait of the social settlement movement.

Emerging scholarship specifying the distinctive elements of African American, Jewish, and other ethnic and cultural group experiences in the settlements will open new possibilities for the interpretation and presentation of the past at the sites of their history.[124] It is vital to survey sites and buildings associated with the social settlement movement with an eye to what they reveal about the communities in which they were situated, and the lives of reformers who were associated with them.

Social settlements exemplify the conceptual and political challenges that the theme of community poses for historic preservation planning. Given that the meaning of social settlements is inextricably bound up with the fate of the communities in which they were located, the remaining settlements might best be treated as contributing resources within the larger context of historic district nominations. The issue of their preservation must also be firmly linked to a grass-roots neighborhood planning process that takes full stock of the social spaces in the community worth saving and creating; a model for which, ironically, can be found in the community surveys conducted so adeptly by the Hull House women as social scientists. With this documentation completed, a community's need for open space, low-income housing, public meeting places, and recreational facilities can be translated into a plan for the sensitive integration of preservation and new construction.

The social settlements, within the larger context of the Progressive movement, widened the dimensions of the public domain. In so doing, they claimed vital public space for those who, by virtue of their gender, class, ethnicity and race, otherwise numbered among the dispossessed. The need to preserve the community resources that were bequeathed to present and future generations by Progressive reformers takes on special significance when viewed from the vantage point of our current era, which has been characterized by a retreat from federal commitment to the cities, a decline in public support for social services, and a diminished public sector. In this sense, the social settlements might serve as potent symbols and sources of inspiration for those making renewed political claims for an expanded and equitable public domain.

As this chapter's review of the tangible resources associated with women's work as community-builders reveals, there remains a need not only for a fuller integration of this theme into historic preservation planning but also for the integration of women's historians with this area of expertise into the preservation planning process. Their insights are needed in the development of a historic context for inventories and surveys, and in all other phases of preservation planning.

NOTES

1. This essay on the tangible remains of women's work as community-builders borrows from material covered at greater length in the author's dissertation, *Preserving Her Heritage: American Landmarks of Women's History* (Graduate School of Architecture and Urban Planning, University of California, Los Angeles, 1991). The author wishes to thank the following individuals for their comments on this chapter in draft form: Carolyn Flynn, Neile Graham, John Hancock, Dolores Hayden, Nancy Matthews, Carrie Menkel-Meadow, Anne Vernez Moudon, Martin Wachs, Shirley Yee, and Lisa Yost.

2. Victor Azarza, "Community," *The Social Science Encyclopedia* (London: Routledge and Kegan Paul, 1985), 135.

3. Azarza, "Community," 136.

4. Sara M. Evans, *Born for Liberty: A History of Women in America* (New York: Free Press, 1989), 70. As an example of the differences between male and female values expressed in one community, Evans cites Susan Lebsock's findings in *The Free Women*

of *Petersburg: Status and Culture in a Southern Town, 1784–1860* (New York: W. W. Norton, 1984), chapter 2.

5. Ella Giles Ruddy, ed., *The Mother of Clubs: Caroline M. Seymour Severance* (Los Angeles: Baumgardt Pub. Co., 1906), 18, citing Severance's friend Mary Newberry Adams.

6. Ruddy, ed., *Mother of Clubs*, 18.

7. Robert Lewis Taylor's *Vessel of Wrath: The Life and Times of Carry Nation* (New York: New American Library, 1966) exemplifies both tendencies.

8. Summarizing the available literature, Jill K. Conway has written: "The history of the movement has not attracted the attention of scholars until very recently. Annie T. Wittenmyer's *History of the Woman's Temperance Crusade* (1878) is a partisan, eyewitness account. B. F. Austin's *The Prohibition Leaders of America* (1895) and *A History of the First Decade of the Department of Scientific Temperance Instruction in Schools and Colleges* (1891) are laudatory accounts written by participants. Gertrude Stevens Leavitt and M. L. Sargent, *Lillian M. N. Stevens, A Life Sketch* (1921) is a sympathetic biography of a major temperance leader. Elizabeth Putnam Gordon's *Women Torch Bearers: The Story of the W.C.T.U.* (1924) begins a slightly more objective narration of the history of the WCTU's foundation and leadership." Jill K. Conway, *The Female Experience in 18th and 19th Century America: A Guide to the History of American Women* (Princeton: Princeton University Press, 1985), 241–42. Immediately following the publication of Conway's guide, Joseph R. Gusfield reopened historical debate over the political implications of the American temperance movement with the publication of *Symbolic Crusade: Status Politics and the American Temperance Movement* (Urbana: University of Illinois Press, 1986).

9. Conway, *The Female Experience in 18th and 19th Century America*, 241–42.

10. Noted in Marion Tinling, *Women Remembered: A Guide to Landmarks of Women's History in the United States* (New York: Greenwood Press, 1986), 553.

11. Marion Tinling notes several other sites associated with Carry Nation, including: her birthplace in Lancaster, Kentucky; and Hatchet Hall in Eureka Springs, Arkansas, where she ran a school for young prohibitionists during the last years of her life, both of which are listed on the National Register; and a monument erected by the WCTU at Nation's grave in Belton Cemetery in Belton, Missouri. Tinling, *Women Remembered*, 121, 162, and 193–194.

12. Tinling notes several other sites associated with Frances Willard: a monument in North Danville, Vermont, at her mother's birthplace; a marker on the site of Willard's birthplace in Churchville, New York; and a schoolhouse were she taught in Janesville, Wisconsin, which is listed on the National Register. Because Willard without question was the most important woman of her era, numerous memorials and likenesses were commissioned in her honor, including a statue in the U.S. Capitol by sculptor Helen Farnsworth Mears, a bust in the Hall of Fame, and a memorial fountain in Chicago's Lincoln Park. Tinling, *Women Remembered*, 97, 371, and 559.

13. Ruth Bordin, *Woman and Temperance: The Quest for Power and Liberty, 1873–1900* (Philadelphia: Temple University Press, 1981), xviii.

14. Bordin, *Woman and Temperance*, 15.

15. Bordin, *Woman and Temperance*, 20; citing Matilda Gilruth Carpenter, *The Crusade: Its Origin and Development at Washington Court House and Its Results* (Columbus: W. G. Hubbard and Co., 1893), 43–44.

16. Bordin, *Woman and Temperance*, 20, 22; citing Jack Blocker, Jr., "Why Women Marched: The Temperance Crusade of 1873–74," paper read at the annual meeting of the American Historical Association (New York, 1977), 4.

17. Tinling, *Women Remembered*, 519. Also cited in Taylor, *Vessel of Wrath*, 340–41.

18. Bordin, *Woman and Temperance*, 143.

19. Financial panic and economic depression beginning in 1893, however, made it difficult to rent fully such a large office building and ultimately undermined the project. After years of fund-raising in support of the temple, which drained the local unions, the WCTU finally voted to sever all financial ties to it after Willard's death in 1898. Bordin, *Woman and Temperance*, 147–48.

20. Dorcas J. Spencer, *A History of the W.C.T.U. of Northern and Central California* (Oakland, Calif.: West Coast Printing Co., 1911). Upon reading this manuscript in draft form, one reader speculated rather grimly on the likely absence of rum raisin ice-cream from the Temperance Ice Cream Parlor's menu.

21. Details on the Los Angeles temperance temple are contained in: Emma Harriman, "Temperance Temple in Los Angeles," *The Woman's Journal* 20 (1889): 206; and the Woman's Christian Temperance Union of Southern California, *22nd Annual Report* (1904), Special Collections, University of California at Los Angeles.

22. Jennie Ray Thompson et al. *Victories of Four Decades: A History of the WCTU of Southern California* (State Executive Committee of the WCTU of SC, n.d., ca. 1964), 1–2.

23. State WCTU headquarters are located at 551 South Kingsley Drive in Los Angeles, California. Jennie Ray Thompson, *Victories of Four Decades*, iv.

24. This figure is cited by Mary Ryan in *Womanhood in America: From Colonial Times to the Present* (New York: Franklin Watts, 1983), 204.

25. Karen J. Blair, *The Clubwoman as Feminist: True Womanhood Redefined* (New York: Holmes & Meier Publishers, 1980).

26. Blair, *Clubwoman as Feminist*, 5.

27. Blair, *Clubwoman as Feminist*, 20.

28. The historic locations of these meetings and the current status of these sites merit further study.

29. According to Karen Blair, Sorosis never owned a clubhouse. While the historic Delmonico's building in which Sorosis held its formative meeting no longer stands, Marguerite Dawson Winant's *Century of Sorosis, 1868–1969* (Uniondale, N.Y.: Salisbury Printers, 1968), and the collection of Sorosis club papers held in the Smith College Library, Northampton, Massachusetts, potentially would be useful for identifying the succession of meeting places it occupied. In general, the commemorative brochures and pamphlets produced by most women's clubs, in combination with local fire insurance maps and city directories, are useful preliminary sources of information for inventory and survey purposes.

30. Sources useful for tracing sites associated with the New England Woman's Club and affiliated organizations include: Julia A. Sprague, *The History of the New England Women's Club, 1868–1893* (Boston, 1893); the Bromley and Sanborn atlases; the Boston City Directory; articles in *The Woman's Journal*; and records of the New England Woman's Club in the Schlesinger Library at Radcliffe College.

31. Historic locations for the New England Woman's Club, the offices of the *Woman's Journal*, the Massachusetts and New England Woman Suffrage Associations, and the Women's Educational and Industrial Union during this early period were 3 Tremont Place and 3–5 Park Street. An eleven-story bank subsequently was erected on the Tremont Place site. In 1918, the historic structure at 3 Park Street was replaced by new construction. The Catholic Information Center built at 4–6 Park Street replaced one of the most important late 19th century centers of woman's rights activity. As the contemporary headquarters for 9-to-5, dedicated to organizing office workers, this site has

continuing significance in women's history. The tight cluster of these historic sites around the Granary Burial Ground enhances the possibilities for public interpretation of the women's history that took place there.

32. Mrs. C. M. Severance, "Address Before the Woman's Club of Los Angeles, Soon After Her 80th Birthday, January 12, 1900," New England Woman's Club Papers, Schlesinger Library, Radcliffe College.

33. The Chauncy Hall Building is located at 585–91 Boylston Street. See Maud Wood Park, "Busy Bee Hive Full of Workers for Women," *The Boston American* (Sunday, February 23, 1913), Part IV, Suffrage Section.

34. Other occupants included the College Equal Suffrage League, the Boston Equal Suffrage Association for Good Government, the Massachusetts Woman Suffrage Association, the Massachusetts Men's League for Woman Suffrage, the New England Woman Suffrage Association, and the offices of the weekly *Woman's Journal*.

35. Blair, *Clubwoman as Feminist*, 62.

36. Sophonisba Breckinridge, *Women in the Twentieth Century: A Study in Their Political, Social and Economic Activities* (New York: McGraw-Hill, 1933), 82. According to the one report, the larger women's clubs that either rented or owned their own clubhouses before the 20th century were: the St. Cecelia and the Ladies' Literary Association, Grand Rapids, Michigan; the New Century Club, Philadelphia, Pennsylvania; the New Century, Wilmington, Delaware; the New Century, Utica, New York; the Athenaeum, Milwaukee, Wisconsin; the Athenaeum, Kansas City, Missouri; the Propoleum, Indianapolis, Indiana; the Women's Club of Central Kentucky, Lexington, Kentucky; the Ladies' Literary Club, Salt Lake City, Utah; the Washington Club, District of Columbia; and the Arundell, Baltimore, Maryland. Ellen Henrotin, "The Attitudes of Women's Clubs and Associations Towards Social Economics," *Bulletin of the Department of Labor* 23 (July 1899): 501–45; especially 518.

37. The Kalamazoo Ladies' Library Association Building, located at 333 South Park Street, was added to the National Register in 1970. The other two Michigan women's clubhouses on the National Register are the Ladies' Literary Club in Grand Rapids, listed in 1971, and the Ladies' Literary Club Building in Ypsilanti, added one year later. *Federal Register* 44:26 (1979), 7505 and 7507.

38. Lynn Sherr and Jurate Kazickas, *The American Woman's Gazetteer* (New York: Bantam, 1976), 118.

39. Blair, *Clubwoman as Feminist*, 100–101, citing Breckinridge, *Women in the Twentieth Century*, 93.

40. The Outdoor Art Club, located at 1 West Blithedale Avenue, was founded in 1902 by thirty-five local women. It was entered in the National Register in 1978. *Federal Register* 44:26 (1979), 7431. California Department of Parks and Recreation, *California Historical Landmarks*, (Sacramento, 1979; revised 1982), CHL No. 922.

41. "Woman's Club Homes," *Woman Citizen* (August 12, 1922): 8–9; 16 and 18.

42. "Woman's Club Homes," and "Clubs in Claifornia," *Woman Citizen* 7:12 (November 4, 1922): 4. Also noted in Sara Holmes Boutelle, *Julia Morgan, Architect* (New York: Abbeville Press, 1988), 83.

43. For a comprehensive treatment of Morgan's projects see Boutelle, *Julia Morgan, Architect*.

44. The Berkeley Women's City Club is located at 2315 Durant Avenue. *Federal Register* 44:26 (1979), 7428. Also see *California Historical Landmarks*, No. 908.

45. Los Angeles Cultural Heritage Commission. "Historic-Cultural Monuments 1 [through] 299 Listed by Address" (December 30, 1985).

46. The American Woman's League [AWL] was founded in 1908 by Edward Gardner Lewis, who used the League to promote his popular woman's magazine, which was

based in University City, Missouri. AWL chapter houses were built in fifteen states, some of which join the group of nine from Illinois on the National Register. See Pauline Meyer, *Keep Your Face in the Sunshine: A Lost Chapter in the History of Woman Suffrage* (Edwardsville, Illinois: Alcott Press, 1980); "The American Woman's League," *Historic Illinois* 4:2 (August 1981): 2–3 and 12–13; and "American Woman's League Chapter Houses in Illinois," National Register of Historic Places Inventory-Nomination Form (1980), by the same author. Also see Lewis Publishing Company, *Woman's National Daily* (University City, Missouri, 1907–1916).

47. Evans, *Born for Liberty*, 150. For the official history of the General Federation of Women's Clubs see Mildred White Wells, *Unity in Diversity: The History of the General Federation of Women's Clubs* (Washington, D.C.: General Federation of Women's Clubs, 1953). Karen J. Blair covers the period of confederation in *The Clubwoman as Feminist*, chapter 6.

48. In addition to the 1922 purchase at 1734 N Street, N.W., the General Federation of Women's Clubs owned and occupied two adjacent buildings: the 1951 purchase of the house next door at number 1738 N Street, and the 1959 purchase of a somewhat larger house at 1728 N Street. "Historical Facts About the Headquarters of the GFWC," Archives, General Federation of Women's Clubs (Washington, D.C., n.d.).

49. See Blair, *Clubwoman as Feminist*, and Wells, *Unity in Diversity*. Also see various General Federation of Women's Clubs [GFWC] sources including: "Historical Facts about the Headquarters of the G.F.W.C.," Archives, GFWC, Washington, D.C.; *General Federation News*; "General Federation Headquarters" (ca. 1952–53), Schlesinger Library, Radcliffe College; and "The G.F.W.C.'s Home-Center," *The Woman Citizen* (1924): 12.

50. Dorothy Sterling, ed., *We Are Your Sisters: Black Women in the Nineteenth Century* (New York: W. W. Norton, 1984), xii-xiii.

51. Dorothy Porter, "The Organized Educational Activities of Negro Literary Societies, 1828–1846," *Journal of Negro Education* 5:4 (October 1936): 572; cited by Paula Giddings, *When and Where I Enter: The Impact of Black Women on Race and Sex in America* (New York: Bantam, 1985), 49.

52. Elizabeth L. Davis, *Lifting as They Climb: The National Association of Colored Women* (n.p.: n.p., 1933), 5.

53. Gerda Lerner, "The Community Work of Black Club Women," in *The Majority Finds Its Past: Placing Women in History* (New York: Oxford University Press, 1979), 83–93; especially 84.

54. I am grateful to Shirley Yee, Assistant Professor of Women Studies at the University of Washington, for this observation.

55. Alfreda M. Duster, ed., *Crusade for Justice: The Autobiography of Ida B. Wells* (Chicago: University of Chicago Press, 1970), xix.

56. Duster, *Crusade for Justice*, 81.

57. Duster, *Crusade for Justice*, xix.

58. Paula Giddings, *When and Where I Enter: The Impact of Black Women on Race and Sex in America* (New York: Bantam, 1985), 93.

59. Giddings, *When and Where I Enter*, 95.

60. The Terrell residence, located at 326 T Street, was designated a National Historic Landmark in 1975. See the U.S. Department of the Interior, National Park Service, History Division, *Catalog of National Historic Landmarks 1987*, 50; and Tinling, *Women Remembered*, 335–36. Note: Tinling gives 326 U Street as Terrell's residence.

61. The Wells-Barnett residence, located at 3624 South Martin Luther King, Jr., Drive, was designated a national Historic Landmark in 1974, *Catalog of National His-*

toric Landmarks 1987, 75. Also cited in "Ida B. Wells Barnett Home," National Register of Historic Places Inventory-Nomination Form; and the *Federal Register* 44:26 (Tuesday, February 6, 1979), 7463. Also noted in Sherr and Kazickas, *American Woman's Gazetteer*, 60; and Tinling, *Women Remembered*, 472. The lack of public access to this private residence limits the interpretive possibilities there.

62. Although not specifically responsible for nominating these sites for the Landmark designation, the theme study conducted by the Afro-American Bicentennial Corporation during the 1970s resulted in a sharp increase in the coverage of black history in the National Historic Landmark Program. Black women's history, however, was under-represented in the AABC's research. Out of forty-four sites of national significance researched at the end of three years, only six women's names emerged: Charlotte Forten Grimke, Maria Baldwin, Madame C. J. Walker, Florence Mills, Frances E. W. Harper, and Mary Ann Shadd Cary. Afro-American Bicentennial Corporation, *Summary Report of a Three Year Study by the Afro-American Bicentennial Corporation of Sites Determined to be Significant in Illustrating the Role of Afro-Americans in United States History* (August 1976). Records of the History Division, National Park Service, U.S. Department of the Interior.

63. Although a systematic study needs to be done, two sites located in Washington, D.C., surfaced in my limited review of the literature: an earlier headquarters of the National Association of Colored Women's Clubs at 1114 O Street, N.W., and a later one at 1601 R. Street, N.W. See Davis, *Lifting as They Climb*, 91, and National Association of Colored Women's Clubs, "Its Purpose and Programs," Schlesinger Library, Radcliffe College.

64. Charles Harris Wesley, *The History of the National Association of Colored Women's Clubs: A Legacy of Service* (Washington, D.C.: NACWC, 1984), 177.

65. Antoinette J. Lee, "Discovering Old Cultures in the New World: The Role of Ethnicity," in Robert E. Stipe and Antoinette J. Lee, eds., *The American Mosaic: Preserving a Nation's Heritage* (Washington, D.C.: US/ICOMOS, 1987), 179–206; especially 193.

66. Davis, *Lifting as They Climb*, 25.

67. Davis, *Lifting as They Climb*, 47, 48.

68. Davis, *Lifting as They Climb*, 147.

69. Davis, *Lifting as They Climb* (photograph), n.p.

70. Davis, *Lifting as They Climb*, 344.

71. Davis, *Lifting as They Climb*, 138.

72. Darlene Roth, "Feminine Marks on the Landscape: An Atlanta Inventory," *Journal of American Culture* 3 (Winter 1980): 673–85; especially 680.

73. Roth, "Feminine Marks on the Landscape," 681.

74. The Afro-American Bicentennial Corporation, which contracted with the National Park Service to survey sites in the early 1970s significant in the history of African Americans, was among the first to question the consequences of the fifty-year rule for many African American sites with tangible remains, given the likelihood of their demolition in the interim. The Corporation also raised the issue of whether racial and other cultural biases might shape the very nature of what historians consider to be of "transcendent importance" in ways that indirectly make it nearly impossible for places associated with the history of minorities to qualify as exceptions to the fifty-year rule. Afro-American Bicentennial Corporation, *A Summary Report of Thirty Sites Determined to be Significant in Illustrating and Commemorating the Role of Black Americans in United States History* (December 1973), 62.

75. State of California, Department of Parks and Recreation, *Five Views: An Ethnic Sites Survey for California* (December 1988), 71, 97.

76. For a detailed study of this phenomenon see Joanne Meyerowitz, *Women Adrift: Independent Wage Earners in Chicago, 1880–1930* (Chicago: University of Chicago Press, 1988).

77. Lynn Y. Weiner, *From Working Girl to Working Mother: The Female Labor Force in the United States, 1820–1980* (Chapel Hill: University of North Carolina Press, 1985), 53–54.

78. Weiner, *Working Girl to Working Mother*.

79. U.S. Senate, *Report on the Condition of Women and Children Wage Earners in the United States*, vol. 5: Wage-Earning Women in Stores and Factories (Washington, D.C.: U.S.G.P.O., 1910), 85.

80. Women's Educational and Industrial Union, *The Food of Working Women in Boston* (Boston: WEIU, 1917), 108.

81. U.S. Senate, *Report on the Condition of Women and Children Wage Earners in the United States*, 52.

82. Elizabeth Wilson, *Fifty Years of Association Work Among Young Women* (New York: National Board of the YWCAs, 1916), 34–35.

83. Robert Stein, "Girls' Cooperative Boarding Homes," *The Arena* 19 (1898): 397–417; especially 403.

84. Breckinridge, *Women in the Twentieth Century*, 58.

85. The smaller figure is cited in the Young Women's Christian Association, National Board, National Services Division, "Residence Reflections: Statistical Findings of Residence Survey for Use of Residence Study Committee and National Staff Members Only," (March 1939). YWCA of the USA, Archives of the National Board, New York City. The larger estimate of half of a million women sheltered at the YWCA's three hundred residences in 1930 comes from Breckinridge, *Women in the Twentieth Century*, 56.

86. "More YWCAs Report Landmark Building Status Designation," *YWCA Interchange* 12:1 (January/February 1985): 3.

87. These buildings are contributing resources to the Ladies' Mile Historic District, which was designated by the New York City Landmarks Commission on June 29, 1989. See Christabel Gough, "The Side Streets of 'The Ladies' Mile': R. H. Robertson and the Early Days of the Young Women's Christian Association," *Village Views* 2:4 (Fall 1985): 3–20; Margaret Moore, *End of the Road for Ladies' Mile?* (New York: Drive to Protect the Ladies' Mile District, 1986), 55; and miscellaneous sources in the Archives of the YWCA of the City of New York.

88. Two adjacent YWCA buildings independently occupied this site. The National Board Headquarters, built in 1912, was demolished. Still remaining at 610 Lexington Avenue is the YWCA of the City of New York, which was constructed several years after the National Board building. Air rights were sold in order to save and remodel this historic building. Personal communication with Elizabeth Norris, Librarian, Archives of the National Board, YWCA of the USA (January 31, 1990), and *Photo Memories of "600"* (New York: National Board, YWCA of the USA, 1983).

89. The extant building is located at 453 Shawmut Street. See the Associated Charities of Boston, *A Directory of the Charitable and Beneficent Organizations of Boston; Together with Legal Suggestions, Laws Applying to Dwellings, etc.* (Boston: Old Corner Bookstore, 1907), 12–13; the WEIU, *Food of Working Women in Boston*, 107, "Temporary Home for Working Women," *The Woman's Journal* 8 (1877): 141; and "A Working Women's Home," *The Woman's Journal* 8 (1877): 100.

90. L. S. [Lucy Stone], "Save the Women," *The Woman's Journal* 12 (1881): 340; "Massachusetts Home for Intemperate Women," *The Woman's Journal* 12 (1881): 203; A. H. Fellows, "Homes for Intemperate Women," *The Woman's Journal* 19 (1888): 185; Marion McBride, "MHIW," *The Woman's Journal* 19 (1888): 10 and 131; and 20

(1889): 42–43. For an overview of the establishment of such homes by temperance groups, see Bordin, *Woman and Temperance*, especially chapter 6.

91. U.S. Department of the Interior, *Catalog of National Historic Landmarks 1987*, 190.

92. Giddings, *When and Where I Enter*, 155–58.

93. Breckinridge, *Women in the Twentieth Century*, 57.

94. A commemorative plaque on site at 25 Holyoke Street details the significance of the Tubman Home for the black heritage. Sources useful for documenting this site include: Associated Charities of Boston, *A Directory of the Charitable and Beneficent Organizations of Boston*, 88; and the Women's Educational and Industrial Union, *Food of Working Women in Boston*, 108.

95. It is located at 4726 South Martin Luther King, Jr., Drive, Chicago, Commission on Chicago Historical and Architectural Landmarks, "Chicago Landmarks" (1985).

96. The East Adams Boulevard Home currently is owned by the Tabernacle of Faith Unity Church. The current location of the Clubhouse and Home is at 1803 Crenshaw Boulevard. Sources useful for documenting the history of these homes include: Delilah L. Beasley, *The Negro Trailblazers of California* (Los Angeles: n.p., 1919), 132, 135, 227 and 230; and the Sojourner Truth Industrial Club, Inc., "Golden Anniversary, 1905–1954," [October 17–21, 1954] (Los Angeles, 1954). Also see Susan Wirka's unpublished paper, "Women's Clubs in Los Angeles, 1891–1927," Graduate School of Architecture and Urban Planning, University of California, Los Angeles (1987).

97. Davis, *Lifting as They Climb*, 86.

98. *Los Angeles Daily Times* (February 12, 1909).

99. This assessment is based on the quality of plans Frank Klaydd submitted to the Boston Building Department for the proposed removal of exterior stairs that led to a second floor entrance and its replacement with a street-level entry. Boston Building Department (May 1929), Boston Public Library, [P64–1257].

100. See, for example, the National Association of Colored Women's Clubs of the United States, *Directory* (n.p.: n.p., 1936); Rebecca Stiles Taylor, *Official Directory of the National Association of Colored Women, 1926–1928* (n.p.: n.p., ca. 1928); and state and local directories such as the California Federation of Women's Clubs, *Club Women of California: Official Directory and Register* (San Francisco: CFWC, 1907–1915); and California Federation of Women's Clubs, *Los Angeles District Directory* (Los Angeles, The District, 1917–1932).

101. Gerda Lerner, "Placing Women in History: Definitions and Challenges," *Feminist Studies* 3 (Fall 1975): 6.

102. Dolores Hayden, *Grand Domestic Revolution: A History of Feminist Designs for American Homes, Neighborhoods and Cities* (Cambridge: MIT Press, 1981), 164.

103. Judith Ann Trolander, "College Settlement," in *Handbook of American Women's History*, ed. Angela Howard Zophy with Frances M. Kavenik, associate editor (New York: Garland, 1990), 120.

104. Robert A. Woods and Albert J. Kennedy, *Handbook of Settlements* (New York: Charities Publication Committee, Russell Sage Foundation, 1911), vi.

105. Kathryn Kish Sklar, "Hull House in the 1890s: A Community of Women Reformers," *Signs* 10:4 (Summer 1985): 658–77.

106. R. L. Duffus, *Lillian Wald: Neighbor and Crusader* (1938), 119.

107. Robert A. Woods and Albert J. Kennedy, *The Settlement Horizon* (New York: Russell Sage Foundation, 1922), 430–31.

108. Woods and Kennedy, *Settlement Horizon*, 178.

109. Kathryn Kish Sklar, "Women Reformers and the Use of Social Science as a Ve-

hicle for Welfare Reform in the United States, 1890–1930." Unpublished paper presented at the Eighth Berkshire Conference on the History of Women (June 1990).

110. Allen B. Pond, "The 'Settlement House,' " *The Brickbuilder* 11:7 (July 1902): 140–45; especially 142.

111. Pond, " 'Settlement House,' " 142.

112. Hayden, *Grand Domestic Revolution*, 165.

113. Helen Lefkowitz Horowitz, "Hull-House as Women's Space," *Chicago History* 12:4 (1984): 40–49; especially 50.

114. Hayden, *Grand Domestic Revolution*, 174.

115. Lefkowitz Horowitz, "Hull-House as Women's Space," 50.

116. Hayden, *Grand Domestic Revolution*, 174.

117. Pond, " 'Settlement House,' " 142.

118. Pond, " 'Settlement House,' " 142.

119. Kathryn Kish Sklar, "[A Review of] The Jane Addams Papers," *Journal of American History* 76: 1337–38.

120. National Register of Historic Places, Inventory-Nomination Form, "Jane Addams' Hull-House," Item 7.

121. Duffus, *Lillian Wald*, 134.

122. Woods and Kennedy, *Handbook of Settlements*, 7.

123. See James S. Greene III, "Progressive in the Kentucky Mountains: The Formative Years of the Pine Mountain Settlement School, 1913–1930" (Ph.D. dissertation, The Ohio State University, 1982); Nancy K. Forderhase, "Eve Returns to the Garden: Women Reformers in Appalachian Kentucky in the Early Twentieth Century," *The Register of the Kentucky Historical Society* 85 (Summer 1987): 237–61; and *The History of the Pine Mountain Settlement School* (n.p.: n.p., January 1918).

124. Unpublished papers in a session titled "Moving into the Neighborhood: Blacks, Whites, Jews, and Protestants in the Settlement Houses," presented at the *8th Berkshire Conference on Women's History* (1990), provide important points of entry into this subject. See Elizabeth Rose, Rutgers University, "When Uptown Moved Downtown: Gender, Class and Ethnicity in a Jewish Settlement House"; Susan Traverse, University of Wisconsin, Madison, " 'A Watch upon the Road Going Down to Jerico': Denison House, 1892–1912"; and Elizabeth Lasch, University of Massachusetts, Amherst, "Female Vanguard in Race Relations: 'Mother Power' and Blacks in the American Settlement House Movement, 1900–1945."

5 ◆ Women and Education

HELEN LEFKOWITZ HOROWITZ

The story of American women and education is critical to an understanding of the unique position that American women have held in national social, intellectual, and cultural life. The relationship between women and education is no simple story of progress. It is, rather, a story of opportunity and restriction, of possibility and limitation. To educate women beyond traditional ways is a dangerous experiment that challenges basic notions of women's nature and seems to threaten the social order. Each new advance faces efforts to contain the threat that education poses. National Historic Landmarks (NHLs) that document and commemorate women's contributions to American education and education's contributions to American women can tell us much about this complex struggle and can deepen public understanding of the intricate processes that shape American culture.[1]

As we consider existing NHLs and nominations for landmark status, we will try to look at the broader historical context in which historical sites occur. Several major factors limit this effort. Up until this point, there has been no systematic effort to identify NHLs important to women and education. Thus, there are too few with which to work, and some of those that exist do so because of their importance to a sponsoring group or institution. Because the literature of the history of education has emphasized the experience of the Northern white Protestant middle class, we know far too little about the South and West and about non-English speaking groups. Finally, the history of women has not taken education below the college level as a major theme: we know much more about the relation to women's experience of the Socialist Party or the settlement house than of the high school.

The first sites important to the education of American women can only be imagined, the households in Spain, England, and France that nurtured the daughters who would venture to the New World. Unlike what would follow, the traditional education of women was a safe system that posed no risks to the natural order as it was typically perceived. From the women immediately around them, their mothers, aunts, and grandmothers, girls learned the tasks necessary to sustain life. In the agricultural economies that bred the first colonists, men took primary responsibility for the cultivation of the fields and for the external relations that linked household to community and state; men produced raw materials. Male education came largely through apprenticeship. Only the very few who prepared for learned professions went to grammar schools and universities.

Women turned raw materials into goods that the family consumed. The value of the wheat of the field could only be realized in the bread at the table. Women also sustained complex relations of households through networks of barter, the transmission of medical knowledge, gossip, and religious practice. For most of the work that women accomplished, the household served as principal school, and the women of the household the principal teachers. The ability to read and cipher were useful but not necessary accomplishments, and they, too, were passed from mother to daughter. In the seventeenth-century colonies, these modes of education continued.

The Puritan women who arrived on the shores of Massachusetts in 1630, however, came with a unique advantage that posed a great risk. England's patriarchal system survived the Atlantic crossing intact, but religious enthusiasm had already breached a critical barrier that traditionally divided the sexes. Puritan women may have been ruled by husbands and barred from political participation, but they were potentially saints. Women read scripture and participated fully in worship. Puritan law required parents to teach daughters as well as sons to read.

The education that enabled women to read (but fewer to write) remained rudimentary, more suitable for subordinate participants in the culture than for dominant members. Only one-third of the initial female settlers could sign their names; and that proportion would grow to slightly less than one-half by the end of the colonial era (in contrast to 80 percent of men). Many New England mothers taught their daughters at home or sent them to dame schools to learn their letters and numbers. The grammar schools, which taught the classical curriculum based on the study of the Greek and Latin languages to a small proportion of boys in preparation for college, were not open to girls. However, to an unusual degree, women participated in the intellectual life of their time. While no Puritan women became ministers, several of them published their religious meditations, and Anne Bradstreet presumed to write poetry. A woman who could read the Bible and write her thoughts might come to her own interpretation of the holy writ. That Puritan leaders were aware of the danger that such a new possibility for women posed is clear in the trial and banishment of Anne Hutchinson. Faced with a woman presuming to interpret sermons to mixed gatherings of men and women, Puritan judges reaffirmed their notions of the proper boundaries between men and women by casting her out.

Outside New England, provision for schooling for boys as well as girls varied greatly, depending upon locale, religion, race, and class. Household apprenticeship remained the dominant institution of education for most girls. In the middle colonies and to a lesser degree in the South, home learning was supplemented by primary schools for free young girls and boys. Older daughters of Quakers, Moravians, certain Southern slaveholding families, and prospering merchants in the emerging cities had particular, albeit limited, advantages. Quakers, who allowed women to preach to their own sex and to run their own meetings, began to establish schools for their education. In 1749 the Moravians began a boarding school for the daughters of their sect, which later, as the Moravian Seminary, opened to outsiders. In 1754 Anthony Benezet opened a girls' school in Philadelphia in the same building as the boys' Latin School. Some of the wealthy planters who employed tutors to teach their sons began to indulge their daughters as well in the rituals of polite learning. In the eighteenth century, privileged merchant daughters in seacoast cities and towns, North and South, went to private-venture schools where they might study music, dancing, and literature; perfect their penmanship; master the useful and decorative needle arts; and learn French. These accomplishments "finished" young ladies for aristocratic society and made them more suitable for an advantageous marriage.

In general, while significant numbers of women knew how to read and write in the American colonies, only unusual women learned more than the rudiments. The grammar schools and colleges that trained the small number of boys and young men designated for the learned professions were male preserves. The most important institution in the education of girls was the home. In the existing NHLs devoted to houses or plantation dwellings, efforts should be made to enhance the interpretation of education that girls received within their walls.

Although elite girls could study literature and French, because they were barred from ancient languages, they remained largely outside the realm of ideas in the classical world of the eighteenth century. However, Abigail Adams's letters to her husband and Mercy Otis Warren's political satires make clear that some women were rethinking their relation to the polity and beginning to find public voices.

The period of the American Revolution changed the nature of education for both sexes. Academies sprang up in cities and towns, especially in New England. In addition to classical departments offering Latin and Greek as preparation for college, the academies offered the English curriculum: history, philosophy, modern languages, the natural sciences, and certain practical arts, such as surveying. During the school years in which the college-bound studied the ancient languages, students who took the English course completed their more worldly education. Academies had many different forms and sponsors.

Towns organized and supported some academies; private endowments, religious groups, or combinations of the three sustained others. In many cases, provisions for boarding created opportunities for rural young people. What is significant is that alongside academies for boys there appeared academies offering the English curriculum to girls and to both sexes together.

The American Revolution had begun its work for women. As their lives changed during the tumultuous years following independence, a new appreciation of the value of women's traditional tasks elevated their sphere. American women ceased to be merely helpmeets or ornaments. They became "Mothers of the Republic." They nurtured the future electorate and representatives of the polity. Conservative educators, such as Benjamin Rush, argued that the keepers of the nurseries of the new nation needed not only the virtue necessary for moral guidance but also the ability to understand the world of political discourse. Independent voices, such as that of Judith Sargent Murray, asserted that women needed education to develop their powers of reasoning and judgment so that they would become self-respecting and able, if necessary, to support themselves.[2] Across the Atlantic, Mary Wollstonecraft's *A Vindication of the Rights of Woman* echoed and amplified these sentiments. Extraordinary American women, such as the transcendentalists Margaret Fuller and Elizabeth Peabody, would soon demonstrate that there were no limits on women's intellectual power.

As schools multiplied, they required teachers. Labor-scarce towns turned to older daughters who had guided younger siblings in the rudiments. Academies gave girls additional training to prepare them for teaching. Fires of religious enthusiasm intensified the calling of evangelical academicians, who saw their schools as accomplishing the Lord's work.

Republican motherhood and the academies founded in the years after the American Revolution ended completely the age-old division that had given men the world of culture and women the world of nature. American women became culture-bearers. Through them, sons imbibed the milk of citizenship and virtue. To women—not just unusual individuals, but potentially the sex as a whole—the entire world of thought and expression opened. Cast in terms of value to the nation, women's education gained wide acceptance without appearing to threaten the gendered order. While efforts to impose barriers along the way and to channel women's minds hardly ended at the turn of the century, American women reached a new watershed from which they never turned back. American women became "heiresses of the ages."

In the early nineteenth century the word "seminary" began to replace the word "academy." The new word connoted a certain seriousness. The seminary saw its task primarily as professional preparation. The male seminary prepared men for the ministry; the female seminary took as its earnest job the training of women for teaching and for Republican motherhood. The curriculum and the quality of female academies and seminaries varied enormously. Some specialized in polite accomplishments, others promised skills useful for housekeeping.

The female seminary never offered the classical options of the male academy—Greek and Latin—nor its extensions into the classical element of the liberal arts college curriculum. At its best, the female seminary offered the English curriculum of the academy—history, philosophy, modern languages, and natural sciences—designed to prepare women for teaching.

The development of the seminary went hand-in-hand with that of the growth of the common school. New England villages and towns had common schools almost from their foundings, and these were carried west with the Northwest Ordinance. The common school increasingly accepted girls. The Massachusetts census of 1850 found literacy to be universal, establishing that in Massachusetts the years 1780–1820 were critical, as pressure on towns forced them to open schooling to girls.[3] In the East, the sexes were taught in separate schools or in buildings divided by a girls' and boys' side. In the West, with scarcer resources, coeducation became the norm.

Pressure developed for publicly supported schools. In the early nineteenth century, a process began that led to a new and clear distinction between tax-supported schools run by towns and privately supported schools, financed by fees and endowments. Accompanying the vast economic change that industrialism precipitated were social and political concerns about growing class and ethnic differences in American cities. New England reformers set out to bring all children under the public schools' aegis for longer periods of each year and to extend public schools to the West.

The school also took on a new task. In addition to the rudiments, it taught pupils the requirements of an urban and industrial order. Clocks and the school bell divided the day; rigid rows of desks divided the space. Students learned to work silently under the rule of the teacher. By the nineteenth century, girls attended common schools alongside boys and thus confronted the new discipline.

Who were the new teachers of the common school? In an earlier era, young men had often spent the first years after college serving a kind of apprenticeship as teachers. Now, males had more lucrative opportunities. As necessary as schools were, towns sought to operate them as cheaply as possible. In labor-scarce, economy-minded New England and Western towns the advantage of female schoolteachers quickly became apparent. They were plentiful. And they were cheap, because a woman teacher could command only one-third to one-half the salary of a man. A new argument for female teachers arose: as the natural guardians of the young, women were the best teachers. The demand was so great that many females were pulled into teaching when hardly more than children—and only semi-educated themselves. The feminization of teaching in Massachusetts happened quickly. By 1837, three out of five teachers were female; by 1850, two out of three.[4] At a time when some of women's traditional occupations—such as innkeeping and midwifery—were losing caste, teaching emerged as respectable and important work for middle-class women. Although the factory, with its higher wages was a competitor to the school during its

Prudence Crandall House, Canterbury, Connecticut. (Photograph courtesy of Prudence Crandall Museum, Connecticut Historical Commission)

early decades, school-keeping had strong appeal. In the years before the Civil War, it is estimated that one-fifth of New England women born in the United States taught school.[5] Schoolhouses that remain from the early nineteenth century are mute testimonials to schoolmarms and schoolgirls. Designated NHLs that dramatize and interpret these processes are essential.

The female academy and seminary, in the years before the normal school, were the leading educators of future teachers. Yet the academies and seminaries had a potentially threatening edge. The most important of these institutions carried work to early college level. Not surprisingly, the female academy and seminary were also the principal educators of future writers, reformers, and pioneer professional women, many of whom had to break with conventional expectations and strike out on paths no women had traveled before. Of the women born in the early nineteenth century who are listed in *Notable American Women*, 74 percent were academy-trained.[6]

As important as the academy was to the history of education for women, it was designed for some, not for all. African-American women in slavery in the South were denied access not only to schools but to literacy. That a few learned their letters testifies to courageous women, black and white, who dared violate Southern codes. In New England, Prudence Crandall learned the dangers of defying custom. In January 1832, she opened a school in Canterbury, Connecticut, at the invitation of town citizens. She acquired the Luther Paine house on the Canterbury Green. In the fall of 1832, after she admitted Sarah Harris, an African-American, Crandall was told that she must have Harris leave or lose the support of the town. Crandall turned for advice to William Lloyd Garrison, the noted abolitionist. Supported by him, she converted her enterprise into a school for black girls and admitted twenty students. The townspeople refused to sell her food and secured passage of a law in the Connecticut Assembly that made her school illegal. Crandall countered by seeking additional students. Harrassed, arrested, jailed for a night, tried, convicted, and ultimately acquitted on a technicality, Crandall bent to pressure only after men smashed the windows of the front rooms of her school. Unable to protect her students, Crandall, then the wife of Calvin Philleo, sent them home and closed the school. To remember both the bravery of teacher and pupils and the opposition that she faced, the Prudence Crandall House in Canterbury, Connecticut, is a state-supported museum. The house demonstrates the flexible planning of many early educational institutions. It had no rooms devoted solely to classroom use; all were used for living and learning. Domestic arts were taught in the rooms of the main level, furnished as a dwelling. Upstairs rooms gave living space for students, expanded by an ell at the rear of the house.

Four female seminaries, founded in the 1820s and 1830s, offered unusual opportunities to young women for intellectual development. Each was the creation of a remarkable educator working in a receptive environment: Emma Willard, in Troy, New York; Catharine Beecher, in Hartford, Connecticut; Zilpah Grant, in Ipswich, Massachusetts; and Mary Lyon, in South Hadley, Massachusetts. Each school upheld high standards and demanded original thought. While Catharine Beecher left an important legacy in her writings on education and household economy, her seminary declined after her departure in 1833.[7] Emma Willard's influence remained profound, shaping the lives of generations of graduates. The institution today remains a vital, independent preparatory school. The Emma Willard House in Middlebury, Vermont, a NHL, commemorates the school she established in her home in 1814, a forerunner of her great seminary. In that house, in 1818, Willard wrote her important address to the New York state legislature in which she sought state aid for permanent public female seminaries. She argued for women's education not only in terms of its usefulness to men and to society but also for its intrinsic importance to women.[8]

The combined impact of Zilpah Grant and Mary Lyon, however, was unique.[9] Ipswich and Mount Holyoke, their joint creations, became the models for many other female seminaries, for the female departments of coeducational colleges such as Oberlin and Knox, and for the earliest women's colleges.

Mary Lyon had developed her ideas with Zilpah Grant in a series of schools under their joint supervision.[10] She saw the seminary as offering far more than the English curriculum: the seminary was to change the consciousness of women students. She sought to encourage students to bring order into their lives and to move outside the private claims of the family circle. As she put it, she would take the "daughters of fairest promise," draw forth their talents, "to give them a new direction, and to enlist them permanently in the cause of benevolence."[11]

Lyon was influenced by the emerging mental asylum, which sought, through a system of order in an isolated setting, to create internal order in the minds of its inmates. Nineteenth-century reformers believed that if those who were disordered in their minds were placed in a separate environment of external order, they would internalize the rules to create an inner psychic order. The system of the seminary carries the same assumptions. The rules were strict. Between the bell that awakened students at 5 A.M. and required their lights to be out at 9 P.M., students followed a prescribed schedule of recitations, study, prayer, and housework in which they changed direction every fifteen minutes. They lived along a corridor with their teachers, and each week at "section meeting," the students monitored their own behavior in a required public confessional where they testified to a specific teacher as to how they had abided or broken the rules.

As an early nineteenth-century woman, Mary Lyon also drew instinctively on the strength of the the mother-daughter bond and applied it to the relationship between teacher and student. Mary Lyon was deeply devoted to her former teacher, Zilpah Grant, and she formed intense, loving relationships with her own students who became her assistants and teachers. She encouraged her teachers, women transformed by her system into agents of nineteenth-century order, to develop close ties to their students to better serve their students as appropriate objects of imitation.

The Mount Holyoke Seminary building, erected in 1837, both expressed and enforced rules and strengthened the bonds between teacher and student. Everything happened in a single building, designed as an enormous house for more than one hundred students and teachers. With its central entrance and stairwell, its complete provision for living, learning, and working, Mount Holyoke held no places for retreat, no interstices for freedom. The relationship between teachers and students blurred the distinction between external and internal authority. Love joined principal, assistant, and former students who served as teachers; and they formed new bonds with their students. Neither space, time, nor will allowed a separate student culture to emerge in the seminary.

In alumnae records, there is firm evidence that Mary Lyon changed the consciousness of her pupils: to a striking degree they entered public life as teachers and missionaries. They also became internal missionaries for education, bringing the seminary system to countless other academies and to the female departments of the pioneer coeducational colleges. Mount Holyoke holds a pivotal place in women's higher education. Although the original building burned in the late nineteenth century, the gravesite of Mary Lyon remains. The institution's later importance as a college can be fully traced in its buildings on the site. Fine examples of seminary buildings exist in settings as far-flung as Mills College in Oakland, California, and Peace College in Raleigh, North Carolina.

Oberlin opened as a coeducational institution for whites and blacks in 1833, but did not accept its first women for college, as opposed to preparatory work, until 1837. Female students lived under seminary governance under the supervision of a lady principal, brought from Lyon's and Grant's Ipswich Academy. The domestic work of the female students in kitchen and dairy complemented the manual labor of the male students in the fields. Most of the women took the Ladies' Course with lower entrance requirements and a curriculum similar to upper-level work of the best seminaries, but classes in common were truly coeducational. Beginning in 1837, four women entered the regular collegiate course, and, in time, the curricular distinction between the two sexes disappeared. Oberlin College is an important NHL because of its commitment both to women and to African-American students. No initial buildings survive, but Tappan Square in downtown Oberlin, the site, has an elm tree from the earliest years.

In 1861, a Poughkeepsie brewer named Matthew Vassar decided to create the first real college for women. He followed the advice of Milo Jewett, the former head of The Judson Female Seminary, who assumed the seminary system was the best way to protect the young women who would learn the liberal arts through Vassar's benevolence. Thus the first women who went to college did so in buildings and landscapes that had little to do with the forms of male colleges. By the early nineteenth century, men's colleges, whether formed piecemeal as at Yale or as a comprehensive plan as at the University of Virginia, were "academical villages." Men recited, studied, prayed, slept, and ate in a variety of structures. The buildings now called dormitories, represented on the Yale campus by Connecticut Hall, were generally three-to-four story stretches of rooms, reached through four entries, two on a side. There were rather strenuous rules on the books, enforced by a faculty of tutors and professors; but because men could enter their rooms through stairways without passing a central observation point and could move around from college to village, from residence hall to chapel, free from supervision, they had the freedom to develop a separate and powerful subculture—"college life."

Women had no such freedom. The design of women's colleges was initially intended to seclude them and keep them within a single building, where their every movement could be observed and controlled. To offer women the liberal arts was considered dangerous. At the most basic level, educators feared that higher education might unhinge women. As they imagined it, the rigors of Greek, Latin, mathematics—and life away from the familial circle—would turn women away from traditional femininity. Women might either imitate men or lose their innocence and virtue, both abominations to right-thinking Americans in the mid-nineteenth century.

Thus in 1861, when Matthew Vassar endowed Vassar College for women, "to be to them, what Harvard and Yale are to young men,"[12] he hedged his bets by taking away with one hand what he was giving with the other. He founded a real college, with an undiluted liberal arts course and a full college faculty; but he linked to it the plan of governance and built environment of the female seminary, quite a different institution.

Vassar College therefore was built as an immense seminary building, designed by one of America's foremost asylum architects, James Renwick, in Second Empire style. In keeping with the newest approaches of asylum planners, Vassar College was placed on a picturesque site in the country. Renwick essentially copied the plan of Mount Holyoke to accommodate four hundred students and faculty. The largest building in America when it was built, Vassar College was one fifth of a mile long, with sections four and five stories high. The central pavilion housed all the public spaces. Beyond the ceremonial entrance staircase were the reception hall, parlor, dining room, chapel, museums for science and art, library, president's quarters, and classrooms. The male college faculty lived with their families in apartments in the end pavilions. Students lived with their teachers, the young female assistants of the professors, along the corridor. These assistants supervised their charges under the direction of a lady principal, who was responsible for creating and maintaining the seminary system that attempted to control students as firmly as Mount Holyoke. Vassar's Main Building, which is a NHL, is a fitting testimonial to the hopes and fears of offering higher learning to women.

Vassar's system and its building seemed initially to solve the problem of offering women the higher learning, while keeping them within the protective bonds of womanhood. Without really looking closely at its workings or considering alternatives, Henry Fowle Durant planned Wellesley College as a close copy of Vassar. In 1875, when Wellesley opened, it, too, offered women the liberal arts linked to the seminary system of governance and building.

The shapers of Smith College, however, decided that the seminary system failed to protect the femininity of young female collegians. Vassar in 1865 was not Mount Holyoke in 1837. Students who came to Vassar from all over the divided nation and were of varying ages had no intention of submitting their wills to a lady principal. In their corridors, they developed a collective culture that had much in common with their brothers at Yale. They saw the rules as external and sought to evade them. They reveled in their private friendships in the suites along the corridor. They formed alliances with those professors who also rebelled against the administration's authority. And they developed the curious customs and traditions that gave collective expression to their lives and suggested a questioning of conventional notions of femininity.

Although Sophia Smith endowed the women's college, its plan was the combined work of her minister and advisor, John Morton Greene, and the Amherst professors who aided him.[13] From the outset of Greene's conversations with Sophia Smith, the minister made it clear that Smith College should differ from Vassar and Mount Holyoke in several critical ways. Smith would not put its students into one large building, but rather in several "cottages." And instead of the isolated village or rural site, Smith would be located in the town of Northampton. Together these two features would mean that students would remain in touch with the social life of the town and would remain, as Greene put it, "free from the affected, unsocial, visionary notions which fill the minds of some who graduate at our girls' schools."[14]

Women's colleges were breeding their own dangers. The all-female world did not serve to protect women and conventional femininity. Instead it fostered intense female friendship and generated strong-minded women. The solution Smith's shapers found was to educate women in college but keep them symbolically at home. In 1875 Smith opened with an impressive Victorian Gothic main building for instruction, close to the center of Northampton; an ample house for the president; and a cottage, soon to be followed by others, where the students lived in quasi-familial settings. Female students were brought into daily contact with men as president and faculty. They were encouraged to enter into the life of the town, as the college provided no chapel or library.

In 1879, unable to convince Harvard to accept women, a new venture opened in Cambridge, Massachusetts, known as the Harvard Annex. In 1882 it became incorporated as the Society for the Collegiate Instruction of Women, and in 1894, with an endowment and a formal relation to Harvard, it emerged as Radcliffe College, a coordinate college. From the outset, Harvard professors taught women students the same courses offered to men in the Yard. The annex's founders so disliked the seminary system as they had seen it at Wellesley that they went beyond Smith. Radcliffe's initial plan had no provision for living quarters. Young women taught by Harvard professors attended classes in rented rooms in a house in Cambridge. The students lived at home, if they were from the area; if they lived farther away, they boarded with Cambridge families. This eliminated the possibility that they would be affected by living together in a closed "seminary" environment. It also rendered the annex less visible, which initially seemed all to the good. Despite these modest beginnings, Radcliffe graduated generations of women important in national intellectual and cultural life. The institutional approach that Radcliffe represented, the coordinate women's college, was imitated by Barnard College of Columbia University, Flora Mather College of Western Reserve, and Pembroke College of Brown University, among others.

In 1885 when Bryn Mawr arose in a suburb outside Philadelphia, it initially copied Smith's plan of academic building and cottages exactly. But Bryn Mawr had a second birth. The original design for Bryn Mawr came from its Quaker founder, Joseph Wright Taylor, and the group of conservative Quaker men whom he made trustees. One of their daughters, M. (Martha) Carey Thomas, had different ideas. She had a proper Quaker childhood in Baltimore, but from early on had the aspiration to achieve and to be an inspiration to women. After getting her B.A. from Cornell, she went to Europe, and in 1883 received her Ph.D. *summa cum laude* from the University of Zurich. She wrote to the Bryn

Mawr board suggesting herself as president of the new college; they made her dean instead, but essentially allowed her to create a college of the very highest standard for women. She gathered an extraordinary faculty largely trained in Germany, set a curriculum modeled after the Johns Hopkins' plan of the group system, and established a graduate school. In 1894 M. Carey Thomas became Bryn Mawr's second president, a position she held until 1922.[15]

M. Carey Thomas was trying quite consciously at Bryn Mawr to inspire women students to break away from the patterns of domesticity and to achieve in the male arena. She wanted a college that had nothing to do with cottages that looked like home, and she wanted buildings that carried no suggestion about the gender of the student body. She did not believe in a separate female culture, but rather thought that the life of the mind was neuter: "Science and literature and philology are what they are and inalterable," she announced. "Given two bridge-builders, a man and a woman, given a certain bridge to be built, and given as always the unchangeable laws of mechanics . . . it is simply inconceivable that the preliminary instruction given to the two bridge-builders should differ" because one was a man and the other a woman, or, as she put it, one wore "knickerbockers and the other a rainy-day skirt."[16] Thomas admired Oxford and Cambridge Universities and loved the theatrical style of Jacobean architecture. When Bryn Mawr was built under her influence, it took form as quadrangles, one of the earliest and most elegant compositions of what has come to be called College Gothic. Bryn Mawr influenced male and coeducational colleges and universities, and it was the critical breakthrough in the building history of women's colleges. Before M. Carey Thomas at Bryn Mawr, women's colleges were distinctive structures designed to protect young women as they received higher learning. With the quadrangles at Bryn Mawr, buildings at women's colleges entered into the mainstream of collegiate architecture, at least in their facades.

The M. Carey Thomas Library, completed in 1907, designed with Wadham and Oriel Colleges of Oxford University in mind, is Bryn Mawr's crowning symbol. Its ornate reading room, seminar rooms, and enclosed cloister captures Thomas' vision of the dignity of scholarship. Bryn Mawr's design innovations paralleled its unique role in insisting that a women's college match or top the highest standards in male higher education. Bryn Mawr College is one of the nation's most important monuments to women's higher education.

Thomas turned Bryn Mawr into a women's college in a feminist mode, but other women's colleges attempted to moderate and contain the possibilities of higher education for women by stressing ladylike gentility or religious tradition.

Many Southern women's colleges, as dedicated crusaders such as Elizabeth Colton, professor of English at Meredith College in Raleigh, North Carolina, pointed out, were often only preparatory schools. Even the best of the white and black schools, such as Agnes Scott College in Georgia or Bennett College in North Carolina gave mixed messages to students. At one level these schools

Interior of M. Carey Thomas Library, Bryn Mawr, Pennsylvania, ca. 1940s.
(Photograph courtesy of Bryn Mawr College Archives)

offered high-level training and served to educate women who became important teachers and civic leaders in the South; on the other they emphasized feminine skills and social graces that underlay conventional marriage.

Catholic women's colleges found it necessary to blend higher education
with church teaching. In a deeply divided religious community, advocates of
women's higher education and of full opportunity for women had to counter

conservative opposition in both the church hierarchy and the laity. Some colleges saw their mission as preparing women for traditional roles as wives and mothers or for woman-identified work, such as nursing, and limited their curriculum. Others, such as Emmanuel College in Massachusetts or St. Mary's College in Indiana, insisted that women partake fully in the liberal arts and prepare themselves, if they chose, for unconventional vocations.

While one important tradition can be traced through women's colleges, a second begins with the efforts by states to educate future teachers. Public higher education for women began with the normal school. In 1838, the Massachusetts state legislature matched a donor's gift of $10,000 to establish the first state-supported female teacher-training institutions. Coeducational and women's normal schools quickly followed elsewhere in Massachusetts, New York, Pennsylvania, Connecticut, and Michigan. By 1872, there were fifty-seven publicly supported normal schools and forty-four that were linked to other institutions.

Following the movement to create public secondary education for boys, which began in Boston in 1821, the first public high school for girls was established in 1824 in Worcester, Massachusetts. Although a good number of female and coeducational high schools were established in New England and the West in the first half of the nineteenth century, it was not until the Civil War era that significant numbers of high schools were founded. The great growth of the high school came at the turn of the century. In 1920, there were ten times the number of high school students as in 1890, while the population in the United States as a whole had grown less than 60 percent. Female incentives for finishing high school were stronger than male, since a diploma was a necessary credential for white-collar work and teaching, both fields dominated by women workers. More than 60 percent of students graduating from high school in 1920 were girls. A late nineteenth- or early twentieth-century high school structure should be designated an NHL and an extensive effort made to interpret its significance in women's history.

Across the country independent women pioneered schools to meet the different needs of different regions, groups, and ages. Reform-minded women created the American kindergarten movement. Margarethe Meyer had studied early childhood education with Friedrich Froebel in Hamburg, Germany. As the wife of Carl Schurz, she brought Froebel's ideas to Watertown, Wisconsin, where she established an informal kindergarten in her house. The small house, a simple one and one-half story frame structure, has been moved to the grounds of the Octogon House in Watertown, and restored to its original state. In Boston the transcendentalist Elizabeth Peabody learned of Meyer's work and, in 1860, began her own famed kindergarten. Peabody traveled to Europe to study kindergartens and devoted a good part of her energies to their promotion, establishing and editing the *Kindergarten Messenger* and the American Froebel Union. Boston philanthropist Pauline Agassiz Shaw expanded Peabody's work. By 1883 Shaw established thirty-one kindergartens; in 1888 she turned fourteen of them over to the city, insuring their public support.

With the growth in education at all levels, women increasingly dominated teaching. By 1880, slightly more than half of all teachers in the United States were women. By 1910, the proportion had risen to almost 80 percent. The femininization of teaching had a double edge, for with opportunity came restriction and limits. The assumption that teachers were female brought low pay and low status to the profession. (A good contrast is engineering, which brought high pay and status: its practitioners were presumed to be men.[17]) Women were particularly concentrated at the kindergarten and elementary levels. And just as female factory workers were generally supervised by male foremen, so, too, female teachers were generally directed by male principals and school superintendents. An unusual exception was Maria Louise Baldwin, principal and later master of the Agassiz School, also in Cambridge, Massachusetts. Her distinguished career as educator, civic leader, and lecturer is recalled in the Maria Baldwin House in Cambridge. It was into this house that Baldwin, an African-American leader, welcomed W. E. B. DuBois and other black Harvard students for weekly literary readings.

The desperate needs of blacks inspired some of the most dedicated efforts of women, white and black, for their education. As slaves were freed during the Civil War, Northern women ventured south to organize schools and to teach. In 1862, a school was established at Beaufort on St. Helena Island in South Carolina, by Laura Towne of Philadelphia, and Ellen Murray, who had come with a group of Northern missionaries and abolitionists to the sea islands. Named the Penn School, it used the Brick Church, built in 1855, for classrooms for eighty students. In 1864, it moved to a prefabricated structure sent by the Pennsylvania Freedmen's Association. Laura Towne supervised the school until her death in 1901. It later evolved into the Penn Normal, Industrial, and Agricultural School and served as a health, welfare, and cultural center for the community. With the closing of the school, community functions continue in Penn Center, a designated historic district.

The Mary McLeod Bethune House, a NHL, on the campus of Bethune-Cookman College in Daytona Beach, Florida, is dedicated to the memory of the noted African-American educator and public figure who, in 1904, created out of sheer determination the Daytona Normal and Industrial Institute for Negro Girls.[18] Supported by Northern philanthropy, Bethune established her school on a solid base. It has evolved, through steady stages, merger, and development into Bethune-Cookman College, an accredited, coeducational, four-year Methodist college. Mary McLeod Bethune was also the founder of the United Negro Women of America, director of the Division of Negro Affairs in the National Youth Administration, and consultant on interracial affairs to the first United Nations General Assembly in San Francisco.

State-supported universities followed a somewhat different path from that

of the private colleges. The Morrill Land Grant Act of 1862 strengthened public responsibility for higher education by making public lands available to
states as endowment for colleges in agriculture and mechanical arts. In some
states, such as Iowa, new branches joined existing state universities; in others,
state universities were created. Although the measure did not explicitly include
women, it was normally assumed that they were part of the "industrial classes"
who were, under the act, to receive "liberal and practical education . . . in the
several pursuits and professions of life." While many coeducational colleges
drew on the tradition of the female seminary, as state universities began to include women they thought of them largely in terms of normal schools. Although coeducational institutions were to be found in all regions, the movement for coeducational universities was centered in the West. Some
Midwestern universities, such as the University of Wisconsin in its early years,
made obvious efforts to limit the work of women to normal departments; others tolerated them in liberal arts programs and professional schools. A few advocates of coeducation enthusiastically welcomed female students into all aspects of the university's academic life. Women took full advantage of the new
opportunities. In 1875, there were 9,572 students in women's colleges to 3,044
female students in coeducational institutions, but by 1900, the women's colleges counted 15,977 students to 19,959 female enrollees in coeducational
schools. In 1900 the 81,084 men in coeducational schools still far outnum-
bered the women, but women were entering in increasing proportions. By
1920, women constituted roughly 37 percent of the students in 354 coeducational colleges and universities.

Coeducational institutions offered women a range of curricular choices.
Some great universities, such as the University of Chicago, opened the highest
level work in important fields to women. In many places, women had access to
the liberal arts but were barred from studies such as engineering or law. Even
when schools were technically open, women tended to be tracked into education programs or domestic economy.

Outside the classroom, women's experience varied widely. Denominational
schools felt a commitment to guide the moral life of female as well as male
students and bounded undergraduate lives accordingly. Public universities, by
contrast, initially presumed to regulate neither the men nor the women. At the
University of Michigan and at Cornell in the initial years of coeducation, for
example, no formal codes or rules separated the sexes. In time, however, public
pressure, reform efforts by faculty wives, philanthropy, and the desire to convince parents of their daughters' safety led universities to build residential halls
for women and to regulate their lives. Significant women's buildings on a number of university campuses, such as the Michigan League at the University of
Michigan, demonstrate these concerns in brick and mortar.

The pioneer generation of women college students found themselves outside the social stream dominated by college men. This mattered little, for they
were in college for its formal education. Later, as more conventional and afflu-

ent young women entered universities, they found themselves dissatisfied with the limitations on their social and extracurricular opportunities. In many places they were barred from campus government, the newspaper, honor societies, and athletics. Unwilling to remain outside, they—supported by women deans—developed their own extracurricular world. As sororities joined fraternities on campus, new pressures toward conventional attitudes and behavior limited some women's aspirations and blunted the potential impact of higher education on some female students' lives. Yet even on the most conservative university campuses, some women continued to challenge prevailing notions of gender both inside and outside the classroom.[19]

As college education became a more conventional choice for American women, many entered with only vague or undefined notions of what they wanted from an education. Seeing their future as one of marriage and children, they found the new offerings in home economics particularly appealing. They had little awareness that such courses had arisen out of the reform mission of pioneer women educators such as Ellen Swallow Richards and Marion Talbot to make household technology rational and scientific and to broaden the social, economic, and political concerns of the home to the larger community. As the movement grew, colleges and universities broadened their home economics offerings to include courses, majors, and schools. Home economics is a prime example of the tension between opportunity and containment that has characterized the relationship of American women to education. For many undergraduate women it became a way of getting through college with the least possible intellectual or personal challenge. But for others, it became a route to a career. Home economics provided a major source of employment to female high school teachers and university professors. Yet opportunity also meant limitations, as brilliant women physical and social scientists were often sidetracked in home economics departments and schools.

For African-American women, home economics became part of a larger educational mission that emphasized vocational training within a program of race advancement. The Virginia Randolph Museum in Virginia honors the work of the pioneer black educator for whom it is named, a promoter of vocational training for rural African-Americans. Appropriately, the museum was originally the home economics building of the Virginia Randolph Training School. The Nannie Burroughs School in Washington, D.C., carries the name of its founder, who sought through the Baptist Women's Convention to create a national school for African-American women to prepare them for economic self-sufficiency and domestic efficiency. Unlike many vocational institutions, it insisted on the importance of academic subjects and required that all students take a course given by its department of Negro history. The Trades Hall, built in 1927–1928, served as its main classroom building. This carefully designed structure with Renaissance motifs housed twelve classrooms, offices, a print shop, and an assembly area. It is currently the headquarters of the Progressive National Baptist Convention.

In the nineteenth century it was almost as likely that a female college graduate remain single as marry (and for graduates of Northern women's colleges far more likely). Marriage and career seemed for most an either/or choice. A significant percentage of those who chose a career turned to teaching. A study by the Association of Collegiate Alumnae found that 72.4 percent of roughly thirty-five hundred graduates in the late nineteenth century became teachers. Teaching, especially at the lower levels of the educational ladder, was open to women, but as they sought to enter the learned professions of law and medicine, they found the door only slightly ajar.

In medicine, as in law, the informal system of apprenticeship had given way to professional schools. Several antebellum female medical schools were established, but women were excluded from hospitals. In 1857 Elizabeth Blackwell and Marie Zakrzewska established the New York Infirmary for Women and Children.[20] After the Civil War, seventeen female medical colleges offered higher quality training. Opening in 1872, Zakrzewska's New England Hospital for Women and Children trained some of the most able female doctors in America.[21] One of the most talented, Susan Dimock, became a resident physician at the New England Hospital. After her early death on a trip abroad, her parents endowed a bed at the hospital. The old historic hospital is now the Dimock Community Center and has been nominated as a NHL. Its eight buildings on nine acres were constructed between 1872 and 1930 and offer a delightful range of architectural styles ranging from the Stick Style of the nineteenth century to the Georgian Revival of the early twentieth. The major buildings comprised a maternity cottage, a large medical building, an additional maternity structure, a surgical building, a facility for children, a residence for nurses, and structures for laundry and power. They reflect the scientific approaches of their era—the importance of ventilation and sunshine—as well as their founder's commitment to serve women patients and to educate women as nurses and doctors. Their scale and decoration suggest the power of women's institutions at the turn of the century.

Beginning with the University of Michigan in 1869, a number of male medical schools took women students, and by the turn of the century, at certain schools, women were an impressive proportion of the student body: at the University of Michigan, 19 percent; at Tufts, 42 percent. By 1880, there were 2,432 registered women doctors; by 1910, over 9,000—6 percent of all doctors and 14 percent of Boston doctors. Interestingly enough, one-quarter to one-half of these female doctors were married. This was the high point. Decline came as women's medical schools closed and as the coeducational schools began to discriminate sharply against women, establishing in a number of cases a 5 percent quota on female students.[22]

In 1869, the law school at St. Louis University opened its doors to women, and some important schools gradually followed. Only at Howard University could black as well as white women study law. Prestigious schools that barred women were Harvard, Columbia, and the University of Virginia. In 1896 two

New England Hospital for Women and Children, Zakrzewska Building, Roxbury,
Massachusetts, ca. 1870s.

New England Hospital for Women and Children, Zakrzewska Building, Roxbury,
Massachusetts, 1990. (Photograph by Gail Lee Dubrow)

Washington, D.C., attorneys, Ellen Spencer Mussey and Emma M. Gillett, founded the Women's Law Class, which two years later became the Washington College of Law. A coeducational institution since its 1898 incorporation, it hailed itself as "the first law school in the world to be established primarily for women." For twenty-eight years the Washington College of Law was housed in an older residence, the former home of Alabama's Senator Underwood, at 2000 G Street in the nation's capital. Its spacious hall, elegant reception room, and winding mahogany and ivory staircase added a gracious touch to a building that also contained the three large classrooms, a kitchen, and a ladies' tearoom.[23] Among its graduates are important women judges and public officials. In 1915 Portia Law School opened as a night school in Boston for women students.

Many educated women faced the dilemma expressed by a turn-of-the-century pamphlet: *After College, What?* Beginning in 1889, an answer emerged, with the creation of the two pioneer settlement houses, Chicago's Hull-House and New York's College Settlement Association. Women came to live in these settlements in immigrant neighborhoods and brought to these new community institutions a wide range of skills: child care, arts education, club work, medicine and nursing, and political organization. The power of the concept was so great that by 1910, over four hundred settlement houses existed. The settlement idea spread beyond its urban origins, and settlement schools were established in the Appalachian region. In 1913 Katherine Pettit and Ethel de Long, who had been involved in rural education in Kentucky, established a settlement school in Harlan County, Kentucky, on the north side of Pine Mountain on 136 acres of land. The school taught furniture making, weaving, nursing, and dairy farming, as well as academic subjects. Out of respect for the mountain heritage of its pupils it preserved the folksongs and dances of the region. Many of the structures on the grounds were built between 1913 and 1928 by students and local labor. The Big Log House, its initial building dating from 1913, was originally Pettit's residence. Later it housed twenty-five children and staff members, and then became the director's dwelling. Many of its furnishings were made by Pine Mountain students. Beginning with a boarding grade school, in the 1920s it established a high school. In the 1930s, as more public grammar schools entered the region, the grade school was closed. The Pine Mountain Settlement School, currently an environment education center, has been nominated as a NHL.

Only a small number of sites that document the story of American women in education have achieved NHL status. There are far too few historic buildings with interpretive programs that aid a visitor in understanding the cultural context of the structure. Existing sites only begin to establish the material record of the critical relationship between women and education in the United States.

A systematic effort must be made to encourage the nomination of potential NHLs that will more fully document women in education. NHLs focused on women in education can play an important role in broadening knowledge of women in American society and thereby deepening public understanding of American culture.

Education has been a critical lever that has enabled women to move into American economic, intellectual, and cultural life. Education opens essential doors for women. But at the same time, because the education of women challenges the basic gender structure of society, it calls forth an array of attempts to contain the threat to the existing order that it poses. This is the story that carefully chosen and imaginatively interpreted NHLs can tell.

NOTES

1. This essay depends significantly on two heavily documented works: Thomas Woody, *A History of Women's Education in the United States*, 2 vols. (New York: The Science Press, 1929); and Barbara Miller Solomon, *In the Company of Educated Women: A History of Women and Higher Education in America* (New Haven: Yale University Press, 1985). In addition, some of the material is adapted from or draws on the author's *Alma Mater: Design and Experience in the Women's Colleges from Their Nineteenth-Century Beginnings to the 1930s* (New York: Alfred A. Knopf, 1984), which provides full documentation. Important additional information came from *Notable American Women*, 4 vols. (Cambridge, Mass.: Belknap Press of Harvard University Press, 1971 and 1980) and NHL nomination forms. Unless otherwise cited, all the specific information, including statistics, comes from these sources.

2. Linda K. Kerber, *Women of the Republic: Intellect and Ideology in Revolutionary America* (Chapel Hill: University of North Carolina Press for the Institute of Early American History and Culture, 1980); and Mary Beth Norton, *Liberty's Daughters: The Revolutionary Experience of American Women, 1750–1800* (Boston: Little, Brown, 1980).

3. Kathryn Kish Sklar, "The Founding of Mount Holyoke College," in *Women of America: A History*, ed. Carol Ruth Berkin and Mary Beth Norton (Boston: Houghton Mifflin, 1979), 180.

4. Redding S. Sugg, Jr., *Motherteacher: The Feminization of American Education* (Charlottesville: University Press of Virginia, 1978), 76.

5. Richard M. Bernard and Maris A. Vinovskis, "The Female School Teacher in Ante-Bellum Masachusetts," *Journal of Social History* 10 (1977) : 333.

6. Norton, *Liberty's Daughters*, 288.

7. On Beecher, see Kathryn Kish Sklar, *Catharine Beecher: A Study in American Domesticity* (New Haven: Yale University Press, 1973).

8. On Willard, see Alma Lutz, *Emma Willard* (Boston: Houghton Mifflin, 1929); and Anne Firor Scott, "The Ever Widening Circle: The Diffusion of Feminist Values from the Troy Female Seminary, 1822-1872," *History of Education Quarterly* 19 (1979): 3–25.

9. On Grant, see Linda Thayer Guilford, *The Use of a Life: Memorials of Mrs. Z. P. Grant Banister* (New York: American Tract Society, 1885).

10. On Lyon, see Elizabeth Alden Green, *Mary Lyon and Mount Holyoke: Opening the Gates* (Hanover, N.H.: University Press of New England, 1979).

11. M. L., *Mount Holyoke Female Seminary*, South Hadley, Sept. 1835, 2. Copy in the Huntington Library, San Marino, California.

12. Milo P. Jewett, "Origin of Vassar College," March 1879, typed copy, 5, Vassar

College Library, Poughkeepsie, New York. The underlinings in the original have been deleted.

13. On Sophia Smith, see Elizabeth Deering Hanscom and Helen French Greene, *Sophia Smith and the Beginnings of Smith College* (Northampton: Smith College, 1925).

14. John M. Greene to Sophia Smith, April 28, 1869, quoted in ibid., 70–71.

15. On Thomas, see Edith Finch, *Carey Thomas of Bryn Mawr* (New York: Harper Brothers, 1947); Marjorie Houspian Dobkin, ed., *The Making of a Feminist: Early Journals and Letters of M. Carey Thomas* (Kent, Oh.: The Kent State University Press, 1979); and forthcoming biography by Helen Lefkowitz Horowitz to be published by Alfred A. Knopf.

16. M. Carey Thomas, "Education for Women and for Men," printed in Barbara M. Cross, *The Educated Woman in America*, Classics in Education no. 25 (New York: Teachers College Press, 1965), 151, 147–48.

17. Jill K. Conway, "Politics, Pedagogy, and Gender," in *Learning About Women: Gender, Politics, and Power*, ed. Jill K. Conway, Susan C. Bourque, and Joan W. Scott (Ann Arbor: The University of Michigan Press, 1989), 137–55.

18. On Bethune, see Rackham Holt, *Mary McLeod Bethune* (Garden City, N.J.: Doubleday, 1964).

19. Helen Lefkowitz Horowitz, *Campus Life: Undergraduate Cultures from the End of the Eighteenth Century to the Present* (New York: Alfred A. Knopf, 1987), chapter 9, 193–219, provides a full discussion.

20. On Blackwell, see Ishbel Ross, *Child of Destiny* (New York: Harper, 1949).

21. On Zakrzewska, see Virginia G. Drachman, *Hospital with a Heart: Women Doctors and the Paradox of Separatism at the New England Hospital, 1862–1969* (Ithaca: Cornell University Press, 1984).

22. Mary Roth Walsh, *"Doctors Wanted: No Women Need Apply": Sexual Barriers in the Medical Profession, 1835–1975* (New Haven: Yale University Press, 1977), 178–206, 224.

23. "Building the Washington College of Law," *The Advocate: Magazine of the Washington College of Law, American University* (Fall 1984): 15.

6 ◆ Women and Politics

JOAN HOFF

Throughout U.S. history, women's participation in the country's political system has been as frustrating as it has been rewarding. Unfortunately, the American Revolution did little to further the legal or political status of women in the United States. In fact, the Constitution of 1787 completely ignored them, thus implicitly making women second-class citizens. Over two hundred years later women are still trying to overcome the legal and political disabilities inherited from English common law and U.S. constitutionalism following the American Revolution. Since 1789, for example, some ten thousand individuals have served in Congress, but only a little over one hundred have been women.

Obviously, until women could vote, they could not directly participate in the electoral process. Ironically, their efforts to change American society through membership in such reform movements as temperance, abolition, suffrage, Progressivism, and the New Deal from the 1830s and 1840s through the first three decades of the twentieth century proved more impressive than any similar attempts by women reformers since they were belatedly granted the right to vote in 1920.

After a seventy-two-year struggle, the Nineteenth Amendment enfranchised women, but their ability to influence directly the course of political events did not dramatically increase since they seldom voted as a bloc. Contrary to the fervent hopes of the suffragists, who fought so long and hard for the vote, "no identifiable 'women's vote' emerged . . . following the extension of the suffrage in 1920." In the 1920 election, just a few months after ratification of the Nineteenth Amendment, only approximately one-third of the eligible women voted for president. Three factors limited initial female participation in the electoral process. First, there were administrative difficulties of trying to register newly enfranchised women in the short amount of time before the 1920 November election. Second, black females in the South remained disenfranchised. Finally, since most women obviously were not in the "habit" of voting, many of them in 1920 could easily be discouraged from exercising this newly conferred right of citizenship in the face of hostile prevailing social and political mores.[1]

Therefore, until recently, there was little talk of a "gender gap" with respect to voting patterns because the interests and ideas of women were not considered distinct from those of men. From 1920 though the 1950s political commentators, for example, assumed that married women in particular simply voted the way their husbands did. In fact, however, in the decade following their enfranchisement, a number of individual women carried on with their reform activity in the social justice tradition of the Progressive Era. Female political activism continued in the 1920s, in the face of postwar conservatism under the guise of President Warren G. Harding's call for a return to "normalcy" with a wide variety of programs, ranging from voter education and social welfare legislation directed toward the needs of women and children to the promotion of international peace in the 1920s. Many of these activities culminated in the 1930s when, with the help of First Lady Eleanor Roosevelt, an elite group of black and white women became largely responsible for giving the New Deal a more humane and egalitarian image than otherwise might have been the case. This tradition of social reform on the part of women dated back to the second quarter of the nineteenth century—long before they could vote.

Women cut their first political teeth in the temperance movement beginning at the local levels across the country in the 1830s and 1840s. This marked the beginning of a century of female reform activity that continued through the Great Depression. The temperance movement has been variously interpreted by historians. Some have ridiculed it because of such direct-action tactics as physically attacking with hatchets saloons in general and liquor barrels in particular (known in the nineteenth century as "hatchetation"). The temperance movement has also fallen into disrepute among historians because its major symbolic success, the Prohibition Amendment to the U.S. Constitution passed in January 1919, is now considered a failure because it attempted to legislate morality. Others, usually WCTU members, have praised it and its most famous leaders—Eliza Thompson, Carry A. Nation, and Francis Willard—indiscriminately. Most recently, historians have positively analyzed it as one of the finest and largest American grass-roots movements that "converted female moral authority in the home into a vehicle for increasing women's power in the public sphere."[2] Another important and still neglected aspect of temperance activism, however, is that ultimately it represented "one of the first expressions of organized feminism in the United States."[3]

In the beginning, under the leadership of "Mother" Thompson, the temperance movement was little more than largely private attempts by individual women to change the drinking habits of the men in their lives. This one-on-one conversion approach was not only too labor intensive to give rise to a mass, grass-roots movement, it also kept women isolated and separated from each other in their private domestic spheres. Only after the Civil War did the temperance movement become a collective, and radical, activity among thousands of average women with societal, rather than individual, reform as its goal.

Even in its earlier, personal conversion stage, however, the temperance movement served as a training ground for future female leaders of both abolitionism and women's rights. Susan B. Anthony, for example, made her first public speech in 1849 on behalf of the Daughters of Temperance. It is fitting that the home of Frances Willard, in Evanston, Illinois, which served as the longtime headquarters of the Woman's Christian Temperance Union (WCTU), is a National Historic Landmark (NHL). Built by her father, Joseph Willard, in 1865 based on designs of English cottages, it was known among WCTU women as "Rest Cottage," although it really was a beehive of political activity during the thirty-five years Frances Willard occupied it. Originally L-shaped, it remains a good example of the early experimental use of concrete in foundation walls. Subsequent additions in 1878, 1890, and 1893 turned it into a two-story, seventeen-room example of Carpenter Gothic architecture, painted pearl gray with white trim.

The WCTU has carefully preserved both the exterior and interior with all the furnishings in it at the time of Frances Willard's death in 1898. A building at the rear of this historic house still serves as both the national and international headquarters of the WCTU. It is now divided into two parts—the north side serving as a museum and the remainder a testament to the private home-life of Willard who lived there, first with her mother and then with Anna Gordon, her companion and private secretary, from 1877 until her death. Gordon remained in the house and became president of the WCTU in 1914. Beyond any doubt the heart of the Willard house is "The Den" in which Willard and Gordon wrote about and coordinated WCTU national and local activities. Its desk, couch, books, and especially three quilts—representative of those that Willard encouraged women to make with squares on the back inscribed with the names of those donating money for the temperance crusade—capture the grass-roots, woman-centered nature of the WCTU. Just as Anthony was to give grass-roots organization and direction to the suffrage movement, Willard did the same for temperance. Both recognized the importance of organized political action on the part of disfranchised women, and the two women cooperated in making sure that the early suffrage and temperance movements supported one another, especially after the Civil War.

Before the Civil War, however, women also engaged in another major reform movement: abolitionism. Initially symbolized as early as the 1830s by the individual courage of such early Southern abolitionist pioneers as Sarah and Angelina Grimke, abolitionism soon became a Northern phenomenon. One of the abolitionist movement's most charismatic leaders was Harriet Tubman, the black woman who personally led more than three hundred slaves through the Underground Railroad to freedom as far north as Canada. At one point in the

Harriet Tubman Home for the Aged, Auburn, New York. (Photograph courtesy of National Park Service)

1850s, Southerners offered rewards for her capture totaling $40,000. One NHL consists of twenty-four acres of land and a house in Auburn, New York, that Tubman purchased at an auction in 1908 to establish a home for aged and destitute African-Americans. Unfortunately, this two-and-one-half-story building, which is rectangular with a shingled, gabled roof and chimneys at each end, conveys little of the drama and hardship of Tubman's early life as an abolitionist, an underground African-American activist, and Northern military adviser to Col. James Montgomery during the Civil War. It is a fitting monument, however, to her personal success and enduring concern for African Americans. It was refurbished in 1947 and serves as both her museum and the Harriet Tubman Home for the Aged.

By the middle of the nineteenth century most of the major female abolitionists in the United States, such as Lucy Stone, Sojourner Truth, Antoinette Brown, Susan B. Anthony, and Elizabeth Cady Stanton, were simultaneously working for the emancipation of African-Americans and of themselves as women. (As noted above, many of them had begun their reform activity as members of the temperance movement.) By 1850 women constituted a majority in Northern abolition societies and were the leading organizers of antislavery petition drives. Unfortunately, but not too surprisingly, most male abolitionists both before and after the Civil War opposed women taking up their own cause along with that of African-Americans. Such sexism was to reveal itself in full force after the Civil War when the leaders of the first women's movement, who subordinated the cause of women to supporting the Northern war at the behest of their male colleagues in the abolitionist movement, tried to return to the work of their own emancipation.

While their oratorical and organizational skills may have been honed by participation in temperance and abolitionist work, it should not be assumed that the first feminists took up their own cause as an afterthought or simply to emulate other groups. The political and civil disabilities of U.S. women were such that they would have spoken out in any case, as they slowly awakened from the deep sleep that decades of privatized morality as virtuous republican wives and mothers and their constitutional neglect following the American Revolution had induced. Before and after the American Revolution, women such as Abigail Adams may have occasionally urged better legal treatment of married women, but there was no organized attempt by women to improve their legal or political status. The Founding Fathers had no reason to heed the isolated voices of even the likes of Abigail Adams. From the compact saltbox cottage in Quincy, Massachusetts, which was the first home of John and Abigail Adams, she conducted an intelligent, but entirely private, assessment of the American Revolution through an extensive correspondence. This cottage now contains period furniture from the 1760s reflecting Abigail's living conditions, including the bed that she and John shared as newlyweds (whose mattress was made of ropes instead of springs), the 1767 cradle that held the newly born later-to-be president of the United States, John Quincy Adams, and one of her size-seven silk dresses. But if the American Revolution did not prompt women to organize politically on behalf of themselves—what did?

As it turns out, religious revivalism in the form of the Second Great Awakening, improvements in female education, debates in state legislatures over married women's property rights, and participation in temperance and abolitionist crusades all hastened the awakening of the first generation of U.S. feminists in the 1830s and 40s to the possibility of improving and moving out of their private spheres by playing more public political roles as reformers. This metamorphosis had been gradual and was not complete by the time the Civil War started in 1861—not because women's reform activities were weak or their needs unsubstantiated but because male political opposition to public roles for females was so intransigent and male domination of the legal system so pervasive.

Prior to the Civil War, however, this small group of women political activists finally overcame the one-on-one approach to reform that had characterized their early temperance and abolitionist work and asserted their own collective right, as well as that of slaves, to equal and humane treatment under natural law. The famous Declaration of Sentiments and resolutions passed in 1848 at the Seneca Falls (New York) Convention held in the Wesleyan Methodist

Chapel represented, therefore, not a sudden beginning but the thoughtful product of several decades of individual reform work at the state level on the part of women reformers, especially in New York. Female and male reformers coalesced in 1848 with a vision for women and society that transcended their individual self-interest on particular issues.

The historical importance of the legal document produced at Seneca Falls remains unique. Physically, it is the first example of a legal text becoming part of the material culture of women's history. Moreover, this text's major emphasis was not primarily about obtaining the individual rights then held by white males; rather, it was about the general subordination of all women and married women in particular in mid-nineteenth-century American society. Later generations of women activists settled for the single individual right to vote in the name of traditional motherhood and the patriarchal family. Participants in the Seneca Falls Convention did not.

In many ways Seneca Falls (and the surrounding area) was ripe for such a historic meeting, situated as it was in the religious revival and reform area of central New York State known as the "Burned-over District."[4] All that was missing from the mills, factories, and three thousand inhabitants living in approximately four hundred houses of Seneca Falls near the "psychic highway" of the Erie Canal was a strong woman leader to produce a feminist synergism of momentous proportions. When Elizabeth Cady Stanton and her husband moved to Seneca Falls in 1847, they settled in a wood-frame house that their son Gerrit Smith Stanton remembered as one "with its wings had many bedrooms, and . . . was . . . just the place for 'advanced thinkers' to gather without being disturbed, express their views while partaking of the Stanton viands by day and calmly reposing in the Stanton beds at night."[5]

Although designated an NHL in 1965, it was not until the 1980s that Congress authorized and funded the Women's Rights National Park at Seneca Falls, New York, and included the Stanton house within its boundaries. By then, the residence had fallen upon hard times and the interior had been extensively altered by successive owners. The extant portion of the house has been restored to its 1848 appearance and is now open to the public. It has an unusual number of oddly placed and spaced windows which are purported to have been put in by Stanton so that she could more easily watch her children at play outside without having to move her increasingly portly body up and down stairs. Unlike the Susan B. Anthony residence described below, however, almost none of the original furniture or personal memorabilia from the time Elizabeth Cady Stanton lived there has been preserved—a reflection in part of her rather disorganized, but nonetheless often brilliant, mode of operation as a founder of the first women's movement.

By the late 1840s, social and economic ferment already prevailed in the area around Seneca Falls, with its newly constructed Wesleyan Methodist Chapel serving as a free-speech haven for female activists, abolitionists, and opponents of alcohol. Despite its historic significance for both abolitionism and the first women's movement, little is known about how the original chapel looked. No photograph or sketch of the original 1843 structure or of its appearance in 1848 exists. Over the years it was modified several times, incongruously serving as a church, meetinghouse, opera house, skating rink, auto dealership, and rental apartments. Until the 1987 decision by the National Park Service to place a memorial design on the site, this famous historic structure was ignominiously last utilized as a combination laundromat and movie house.

All that remains of the 1843 chapel are a partial roof and two side walls. These convey nothing of the singular importance of this structure in the political history of U.S. women. As a result of the National Park Service's design competition, a memorial consisting of a simple sanctuary (preserving the historic remains of the original chapel), with a courtyard sloping into an amphitheater and ending in a granite waterfall wall with the 1848 Declaration of Sentiments engraved on it, is now under construction. With this memorial, over a hundred years of historical neglect of one of the most important occasions in U.S. women's history has finally been rectified.

Stanton's and Lucretia Mott's choice of this chapel for their 1848 meeting was not unusual, nor was their concern for sex equality a sudden or whimsical idea. They had been thinking along these lines since at least 1840 and 1841 as they discussed the refusal of a majority of both British and American representatives to the World Anti-Slavery Convention in London to seat the U.S. women who had been sent as official delegates. In the intervening years, Mott had continued to devote most of her time to abolitionism and Stanton to raising a family in Boston, where she was in contact with radical abolitionists and other reformers of the day. Compared to her life in Boston where "all my immediate friends were reformers," Stanton became bored and depressed on the outskirts of Seneca Falls with her husband absent for long periods of time and without "modern conveniences and well-trained servants." In July 1848, Stanton took advantage of an invitation to meet with Mott and a few other women in Waterloo, New York. "I poured out the torrent of my long-accumulated discontent with such a vehemence and indignation," Stanton later recalled, "that I stirred myself, as well as the rest of the party, to do and dare anything." The result was a notice in several local newspapers calling for a "WOMAN'S RIGHTS CONVENTION. . . . to discuss the social, civil, and religious condition and rights of woman. . . ."[6]

Uppermost in the minds of women who gathered at Seneca Falls in response to this advertisement was the general Enlightenment pursuit of "true and substantial happiness" for themselves, within the private sphere of marriage, *not* individual political rights identified with the public sphere of men up to that time. After rejecting several reform documents by their male contemporaries that proved "too tame . . . for the inauguration of a Rebellion such as the world had never seen before," the women decided at a planning meeting a few days before the Seneca Falls Convention literally to go back to the words of the Founding Fathers, by using the Declaration of Independence as a model.[7]

Wesleyan Chapel, Seneca Falls, New York. Site of the 1848 Women's Rights Convention. (Photograph by Gail Lee Dubrow)

National Park Service's winning conceptual design for development of Wesleyan Chapel block. (Photograph by Joan Harkness Hantz, courtesy of National Park Service)

What is important about the Seneca Falls meeting *is not* simply that the major statement was patterned after the Declaration of Independence and became the first postrevolutionary female legal text, or that one of the resolutions called for the enfranchisement of women. (This was, by the way, the only resolution that was not passed unanimously because almost half of the one hundred men and women attending feared that a demand for the right to vote would defeat the other resolutions by making the convention look ridiculous.) While the right to vote may have been the most emotionally controversial and tactically radical resolution passed at this 1848 meeting, it did not specifically address the basic purposes of the gathering: the legal disabilities of most married women, and the religious and educational discrimination suffered by all women. This was a collective, natural-rights vision of equality that called for far more than specific individual rights; it called for the long-overdue reconciliation of republican theory with republican practice.

The lasting historical significance of the Seneca Falls Declaration of Sentiments lay in its frontal attack on the institutions of religion and modern marriage. This first generation of U.S. feminists was demanding the complete and collective emancipation of married women in their churches and homes in the name of God, justice, and humanity. Disfranchisement is mentioned three times in the declaration segment of the 1848 document, but it did not become the central focus of the twelve resolutions or of women's political activity before the Civil War.[8] As an example of material culture, this document representing the collective demands of mid-nineteenth-century women is as important as the butter churns, quilts, romantic novels, and other material objects that also documented the lives and interests of American women at that time.

Although the first women's movement in the United States is usually said to have begun with the Seneca Falls Convention of 1848, in retrospect, there is no doubt that the Civil War effectively killed the political collectivity behind the broadly based humanitarian goals of the Seneca Falls Convention. By 1869 the first women's movement had split into two wings represented by the National Woman's Suffrage Association (NWSA) and the American Woman's Suffrage Association (AWSA). Ostensibly this division, which remained for twenty years, was caused by the dispute over whether or not women, as well as black males, should be granted the right to vote. However, it involved much more: strategy, socioeconomic tensions within the movement, commitment to a visionary feminism, and the conflict between radical and mainstream reform of American society.

Having supported the Civil War at the expense of their own movement and other reforms, leading feminists, such as Anthony, Stanton, and Lucy Stone, unlike their sisters during the American Revolution almost a century earlier, were politically conscious of the collective significance of their contributions to the war effort. Not until the introduction of two Reconstruction amendments (beginning in 1865 with the Fourteenth and ending in 1870 with the Fifteenth), however, did the vote replace all other possible modes of recognition for their patriotic actions. Only passage of these amendments finally convinced the most politically radical women that the conclusion of the war preserved the union and freed the slaves, but did nothing to enhance women's rights.

As Anthony viewed the battlefield of the first women's movement in the wake of the Civil War, she found the old enthusiasm and collectivity had waned. The 1860s and 1870s would probably have been typical years of post-war conservatism for women and for men, had it not been for the passage of these two Reconstruction amendments to the U.S. Constitution. It would have been difficult, if not impossible, to resurrect the first women's movement (as it proved impossible in the first decades after the First and Second World Wars) had it not been for the passage of the Fourteenth and Fifteenth Amendments. Because these amendments rallied the most radical of the first feminists, they also separated such women from their more moderate sisters. Hence, these Reconstruction amendments simultaneously acted *both* as a catalyst and as a check on postwar feminist political activity. They provided organizational motivation, but at the same time they first split and then skewed the goals of the revitalized movement more and more in the direction of individual litigation and single-issue politics.

The Fourteenth and Fifteenth Amendments forced the first feminists into temporarily developing some hastily conceived political and legal tactics known as the New Departure—most of whose tactics were designed to obtain the right to vote during the first years of Reconstruction and little of which can be documented by specific references to historical buildings or monuments. Like so much of politics and law, legal texts, rather than architecture, constitute the material milestones by which we trace the momentous decisions and actions taken by women following the Civil War.

When a small group of postwar feminists headed by Anthony and Stanton were told by Republicans to accept voting rights for black men as part of the Fourteenth and Fifteenth Amendments because it was "the [male] Negroes' hour," they expressed shock, anger, and dismay. Elizabeth Cady Stanton repeatedly and eloquently denied the justice of this partisan claim, because before the war radical reformers had talked about universal, not gender-specific, suffrage. By the end of 1865 it was clear to Anthony and Stanton that the proposed Fourteenth Amendment would have to be opposed politically if it ever was approved by Congress and sent to the states for ratification. This meant, however, that they would have to enter into political alliances of a much more formal nature than those they had experienced when supporting Married Women's Property Acts, child custody, or divorce reform legislation at the state level before the Civil War. This time they would be entering into a national coalition with the male-led American Anti-Slavery Society (later the American Equal Rights Association). When in December 1865 Theodore Tilton proposed a National Equal Rights Society, Anthony decided the time was right to consolidate the American Anti-Slavery Society with various state women's rights groups into this new organization, even though its first president would be Wendell Phillips—a supporter of the Fourteenth Amendment.

The New Departure began, therefore, with a conscious, but dangerous political decision on the part of Anthony and Stanton—dangerous because of the possibility of co-optation. Nonetheless, they decided to ally formally with men in order to keep universal suffrage (not simply the vote for black males) a goal of postwar politics. After becoming president of the American Anti-Slavery Society, Wendell Phillips killed this consolidation idea and went on to propose that the women should simply be content with the "intellectual theory" of women's suffrage and actively fight to remove "white," but not "male" from the New York and other state constitutions to insure the vote for all men. While Anthony understood the deviousness of this ploy before Stanton did, they both realized that women would have to continue to fight for their own enfranchisement with or without the support of former male abolitionists.

Their next foray into postwar politics proved even more discouraging, as they battled in vain from June 1866 through July 1867 to alter the wording of the Fourteenth Amendment. Female activists of the late 1860s interpreted the legal meanings of the text of the Fourteenth Amendment in two distinct ways. They initiated litigation on their own behalf under Section One in the hope that its emphasis and broad wording would aid them in their postwar campaign for constitutional equality. At the same time they reacted negatively to Section Two, in which the states were specifically informed that if they denied the right to vote to any *male* citizen over twenty-one, the basis of their representation in the electoral college, in the House of Representatives, among state executive and judicial offices and legislatures would be "reduced in the proportion which the number of such male citizens shall bear to the whole number of male citizens twenty-one years of age."

Women political activists could not anticipate in the late 1860s that the Republicans would never use federal power to ensure the civil rights of African-Americans or that they would use *both* the state and federal power of courts and legislatures to keep women from exercising civil rights during the Reconstruction decades. But this is exactly what happened. Republican commitment to federalism was exercised in contradictory, but equally negative ways when dealing with the individual rights of these two powerless groups: African-Americans and women. In other words, fear that radical Republicans would exercise arbitrary national power over the defeated South proved unfounded. Instead, they exercised it over those women who were staunch abolitionists and who had remained loyal during the Civil War; namely, Northern feminists.

Differing feminist responses to such overt discrimination produced a split in the first women's movement, represented by the National Woman Suffrage Association (NWSA) and the American Woman Suffrage Association (AWSA). Their differences lasted until 1890 when these two groups came together in the National American Woman Suffrage Association (NAWSA).[9] Male opposition

to female rights following the Civil War remains one of the major reasons behind the still incompletely explained split in the first women's movement of
1869, because most married feminists refused to oppose the views of their liberal husbands and male friends during the turbulent Reconstruction years. Of
the leading male abolitionists before the war, only four—Samuel J. May, Robert Purvis, Parker Pillsbury, and Stephen S. Foster—remained even minimally
loyal to women's rights after the war by insisting on their enfranchisement. All
the rest, including Wendell Phillips, George William Curtis, Thomas Went-
worth Higginson, Horace Greeley, William Lloyd Garrison, Gerrit Smith,
Theodore Tilton, Frederick Douglass, and the brothers Samuel and Henry
Blackwell, did not want any aspect of the "Women's Question" to complicate
their work of putting the country back together. Ultimately, Tilton and Henry
Blackwell headed moderate suffrage associations designed to diffuse female
opposition to the Fourteenth and Fifteenth Amendments that the Republican
party had made keystones of their Reconstruction program for the nation.[10]

Another reason for disagreement among postwar female activists was the
degree to which they personally felt legally humiliated by the Fourteenth and
Fifteenth Amendments.[11] After failing to change the wording of these two Reconstruction Amendments, Anthony and Stanton bravely but unsuccessfully
campaigned against their passage by the Kansas legislature in the summer of
1868. This failure convinced them that a national suffrage amendment was
needed to overcome the negative legal and political impact of the legal texts of
the Fourteenth and Fifteenth Amendments on women. Many of their former
female allies in the fight for abolitionism disagreed, arguing instead that the
right to vote for women should be obtained through widespread, but low-pro-
file, state-level political activity. The AWSA women preferred this more moderate form of activity compared to controversial court battles and confronta-
tional agitation for a federal suffrage amendment. In contrast, the more
militant women of NWSA, led by Anthony and Stanton, rejected most male
politicians as turncoats when it came to the rights of women in their continuing
battle for a broad range of collective female rights in the courts and specifically
for women's suffrage at the state and national levels. As Anthony and Matilda
Gage so bitterly noted in *The History of Women Suffrage*:

> It was not from ignorance of the unequal laws and false public sentiment against
> woman that our best men stood silent in this Kansas campaign; . . . it was not from
> lack of money and power, of eloquence of pen and tongue, nor of an intellectual
> conviction that our cause was just, that they came not to the rescue, but because in
> their heart of hearts they did not grasp the imperative necessity of woman's demand
> for that protection which the ballot alone can give; they did not feel for *her* the deg-
> radation of disfranchisement. . . .
> Our liberal men counseled us to silence during the war, and we were silent on our
> own wrongs. They counseled us again to silence in Kansas and New York, lest we
> should defeat "Negro suffrage," and threatened [that] if we were not, we might
> fight the battle alone. We chose the latter, and were defeated. *But standing alone we*

learned our power. We repudiated man's counsels forevermore; and solemnly [we] vowed that there should never be another season of silence until woman had the same rights everywhere on this green earth as man. [emphasis added]

Because NWSA leaders opposed these two Reconstruction amendments and the presumably radical Republicans who supported them, they left themselves open to the charge of racism. (More recently, the same charge was made against those white women who turned from the male-dominated civil rights and antiwar activities of the late 1960s to begin organizing the second women's movement.) The more moderate post–Civil War female reformers, and most of their male colleagues, on the other hand, were more than willing to place the vote for black men ahead of the vote for women—black or white. This charge of racism against Anthony and Stanton reeked of hypocrisy. Their uncompromising stand was grounded in principle and received support by several prominent black leaders such as Sojourner Truth and Robert Purvis.

Sadly, however, few Americans could rise above the prevailing racism of the day, and this included the former male abolitionists who became radical Republicans, most suffragists, and the legal profession. In retrospect, historians have noted that both Reconstruction amendments were predicated more on political expediency than any belief in the equality of the races. Most simply stated, the Northern-based Republican party saw the political potential of two million black male votes in the South and had no intention of letting the controversial women's question stand in the way of creating a power base in the formerly rebellious states. More tragically for the civil rights of African-Americans, while making proclamations implying an expansion of national power, the radical Republicans "intended to keep that expansion to a minimum" when it came to enforcing voting standards or any other "sweeping alterations in national-state relations." Apparently, they unrealistically hoped that the enforcement clause of the Fourteenth Amendment and the other conditions they set for the restoration of statehood would somehow be "self-enforcing."[12]

Ultimately, therefore, the radical Republicans not only failed to support the political rights of women with the Fourteenth and Fifteenth Amendments, but they also did not enforce voting rights for African-American men. Thus, from the early 1870s until the end of the century, women reformers systematically tried to obtain constitutional equality of treatment in the courts that would have removed their second-class citizenship status by allowing them to vote and to take their rightful positions with men in such professions as law and medicine. Such litigation largely failed, and as a result women increasingly turned to mainstream politics for redress of their legal and political grievances. One of the most notable unsuccessful trials during this period involved one of the best known feminists of the time—Susan B. Anthony.

After reading an editorial in her hometown newspaper on November 1, 1872, encouraging voters to register, Anthony left her two-story brick house, now an NHL, on Madison Street in Rochester, New York, and walked down to

Interior, Susan B. Anthony House, Rochester, New York, ca. 1900. Susan B. Anthony in her second-floor bedroom and study. (Photograph by Frances Benjamin Johnston, courtesy of Library of Congress Prints and Photographs Division)

the local registration office. She had lived in this gable-roofed house since 1866 and would die there in 1906. From her second-floor bedroom and study, which still contains her desk, typewriter, and other original spartan furnishings, including her lace curtains, Anthony directed and organized the first women's movement in U.S. history following the Civil War. This house, but especially these two private, sparsely furnished rooms, reflect as much about Anthony's determined personality and career as a feminist as her public political activity. Like her private account books, everything in this home is in order and practically functional. When she left the house she would occupy for forty years, on that fall day in November 1872, Anthony was determined to carry out only one task—that of exercising her political right to vote as a citizen of the United States.

After considerable argument, Anthony convinced three inexperienced male inspectors at the Rochester polling place that she should be allowed to register as a Republican, in part by threatening to sue each of them "personally for large, exemplary damages!"[13] Her bold and well-publicized action prompted approximately fifty other women to register to vote in Rochester, and on November 5, fifteen of them, including Anthony, actually did cast ballots. Within two weeks all were arrested on criminal, not civil, charges under a provision of the federal Civil Rights Act of 1870 that was designed to prevent white voters from canceling out black male votes by voting more than once. Obviously the 1870 law was never intended to apply to women trying to vote only once. Its enforcement against these Rochester women was a clear indication of the partisan nature of their arrests. Another suspicious political aspect of Anthony's subsequent trial in June 1873 was the presence of President Ulysses S. Grant's political aide and senator from New York, Roscoe Conkling, an avowed opponent of women's suffrage.

Between the time of her release on bail in November 1872, and her trial on June 18, 1873, Susan B. Anthony made numerous speeches on her own behalf in Monroe and Ontario counties, trying to influence prospective jurors. It was perspicacious of her to have done this because, as it turned out, she was not allowed to testify in her own defense. These speeches constitute the legal text she was not able to create as part of the court record— another example of the importance of texts as part of material culture so necessary for understanding U.S. women's history. In approximately fifty pretrial talks her theme remained the same: "Is it a crime for a United States citizen to vote?" This and most of the other legal questions that Anthony raised before her trial were not considered by the United States Circuit Court of New York that heard her case, nor were they dealt with by any American court in a gender-neutral fashion until a hundred years later during the last quarter of this century. The circuit court ignored questions such as whether the Fourteenth Amendment included women as citizens and therefore as persons; whether women had the right to a jury of their peers; and whether women should continue to submit to taxation without representation.

On June 18, 1873, Anthony could not repeat her pretrial statements in court because Judge Ward Hunt refused her the right to testify on her own behalf. Moreover, Hunt, described in the *History of Woman Suffrage* as "small-brained," delivered a previously prepared written opinion immediately following three hours of argument by her attorney; and, finally, summarily instructed the all-male jury to bring in a verdict of guilty, along with a fine of $100 plus court costs. When Anthony's lawyer questioned the constitutionality of this directed verdict in what was, after all, a criminal case, Judge Hunt simply discharged the jurors and denied a motion for retrial.

In the opinion he had written *before* hearing the defendant's case, Judge Hunt ruled that the Fourteenth Amendment could not be used as a basis for defense because of the recent Supreme Court rulings in the *Slaughter-House Cases* and *Bradwell v. Illinois* cases, which had determined that "the rights referred to in the Fourteenth Amendment are those belonging to a person as a citizen of the United States and not as a citizen of a state. . . ." He further argued that when Anthony voted on November 5, 1872, "she was a woman. I suppose there will be no question about that." Therefore, being "a person of the female sex," the act of voting was automatically "against the peace of the United States of America and their dignity."

In a final attempt to defend herself Anthony tried to speak in court before being sentenced. Although her remarks were ultimately cut short by Judge Hunt, she did manage to question whether she indeed had been tried by her peers and to express her defiance of the entire male-dominated legal system. Anthony's words continue to ring in the ears of generations of American feminists down to the present. They were uttered in a courthouse like so many of the past and present that do not reflect the history that is often made in them. While courthouses across the country may be physically interchangeable, the decisions emanating from them are not. As such courthouses stand as mute testaments to the legal and material text created inside their often nondescript interiors. Such was the case in this instance.

Although Anthony never paid the $100 fine, she was not sentenced to jail. So the case of U.S. v. Anthony ended anticlimactically for a number of reasons. Most important was the fact that it never reached the United States Supreme Court because of two legal technicalities—both beyond her control. First, she would have been able to take her case directly to the Supreme Court by writ of habeas corpus if her counsel had not independently decided, over her protests, to pay her bail of $1,000 to prevent her from actually being imprisoned before her trial. Likewise, presiding Judge Hunt later refused to enforce his judgment against her, which would have been to sentence her to a jail term for refusing to pay the fine. Prevented in this manner from going to jail a second time, she could not seek direct Supreme Court review of the adverse decision.

No doubt this inability to appeal the circuit court decision was a great disappointment to Anthony. She appealed to Congress instead. On January 22, 1874, Anthony petitioned Congress for remission of the fine imposed by the New York court. On June 20, 1874, the Senate Committee on the Judiciary turned down her request. And so ended U.S. v. Anthony. In retrospect it is saddening to realize the enormous significance of her defeat. After losing this case the tactical and strategic views of Anthony and of the entire first women's movement naturally began to focus more narrowly on the single issue of obtaining suffrage. In part this was inevitable because the New Departure of the early postwar years dictated that women activists play the established political and legal game by petitioning Congress and state legislatures, and litigating in court. Once they entered this all-male atmosphere, however, they began to sound less feminist and more like men than they had before the Civil War. Their anger over the Fourteenth and Fifteenth Amendments was justifiable, but these women could not have anticipated how quickly co-opting male constitutional language can be; how quickly collective demands on behalf of womanhood could deteriorate into individualistic legal pursuits and political fragmentation.

Anthony's personal testimony about the negative precedent her case and others like it had set was memorialized when she composed the Declaration of Rights in 1876. In this legal document, written on the occasion of the hundredth anniversary of American Independence, she stated that the trials of women who had tried to vote under the Fourteenth Amendment added up to the same thing: "making sex [that is being female] a crime in the eye of United States laws." By that time, however, suffrage was beginning to assume a life of its own—something that the first feminists had not anticipated in 1848.

The Philadelphia Centennial Celebration of the American Revolution in 1876 symbolized a turning point in the theoretical and tactical realignment of the priorities of the first women's movement. After being refused a place on the Philadelphia commemorative program, Anthony and four other NWSA women insisted on formally presenting a Women's Declaration of Rights during the official proceedings and passing out copies to the centennial audience. Beginning with the words: "The history of our country the past 100 years has been a series of assumptions and usurpations of power over women, in the direct opposition to the principles of just government," this 1876 Declaration of Rights called for the impeachment of all American leaders. With this declaration, the original generation of women reformers and their younger followers turned more and more to the single political activity of achieving the right to vote—in part out of the realization that they had failed to improve their post--Civil War legal status through the courts, and in part to cope with postwar political conservatism.

Thus, the Declaration of Rights of 1876 is more like the Bill of Rights in its listings of desired legal protections against the power of the state than it is like the Constitution. It tried to balance a limited notion of individual rights with natural rights collectivity in an uneasy tension that was more than a century old. Some of the most general basic rights demanded in 1848 had been obtained by women by 1876. For example, they no longer had to insist upon the right to speak in public or to participate in most religious and educational institutions. The difference between the original 1848 Seneca Falls Declaration of Sentiments and the 1876 Declaration of Rights symbolizes most clearly not only the initial defeats that women had suffered at the hands of the courts following the Civil War, but also the gains women as a group had made in their nonconstitutional status since the original 1848 Declaration of Sentiments.

More than half of the Declaration of Rights deals with issues from 1776. The only references to issues reflecting nineteenth-century legal or political conditions were those that mentioned married women's statutes, certain nativist remarks against Asian immigrants, and criticism of universal *manhood* suffrage that established an "aristocracy of sex," which was described as worse than European aristocracy in which at least upper class women held some authority and power. Other social and cultural issues representing women's continued subordination in society, such as the double standard of morality, male dominance in marriage, inequitable divorce and child-custody settlements, were given passing notice in the 1876 Declaration of Rights, but not the prominence they had been accorded in the 1848 Declaration of Sentiments. Nonetheless, this legal text is another important example of female material culture. Additionally, it ended with a rhetorical flourish reminiscent of 1848 that has never been accorded its rightful recognition as representative of the best nineteenth-century political oratory:

> And now, at the close of a hundred years, as the hour-hand of the great clock that marks the centuries points to 1876, we declare our faith in the principles of self-government; our full equality with man in natural rights; that woman was made first for her own happiness, with the absolute right to herself—to all the opportunities and advantages life affords for her complete development; and we deny that dogma of the centuries, incorporated in the codes of all nations—that woman was made for man—her best interests . . . to be sacrificed to his will. We ask of our rulers, at this hour, no special privileges, no special legislation. We ask justice, we ask equality, we ask that all the civil and political rights that belong to citizens of the United States be guaranteed to us and our daughters forever.[14]

In summary, the political and litigious experiences of the New Departure retarded, rather than enhanced, the original radical militancy of the first women's movement. Clearly this was a sign of post–Civil War times. It was becoming increasingly evident, especially to the most militant female reformers, that women could not oppose the prevailing male Victorian standards of morality and socioeconomic mores, particularly those associated with industrialization, the modern nuclear family, and sexuality. Feminist radicalism was slowly being eased out of the first women's movement and replaced by male mainstream political organization with all its compromising liberal overtones. This liberal, rather than radical, reorientation meant, among other things, that by 1900 married and single women reformers alike emphasized their private roles as mothers or supporters of Victorian morals and traditional family values that subordinated the private roles of women to those of men.

Because the Supreme Court overtly discriminated against the professional and political desires of post–Civil War women, by the turn of the century many female reformers joined the Progressive movement at state and local levels. Some of these female reform leaders consciously attempted to link the social welfare wing of progressivism with suffrage. They were the same women, like Jane Addams, Alice Hamilton, Lillian Wald, Grace and Edith Abbott, and Florence Kelley, who kept avenues of communication open between working- and middle-class women and who resisted the anti-immigrant ethos so prevalent in American society at the turn of the century. An unusually high proportion of them were single, well-educated, and independently wealthy. For these reasons, they were more able than many of their married counterparts to devote themselves to the public sphere of political work. At the same time they often received private support and encouragement from a closely knit network of single and married women friends.

Moving logically from individual urban reform projects like settlement houses, such women soon realized that they needed political power to build better neighborhoods and to improve the deplorable working conditions of the urban masses. And so, along with suffrage for women, they formed or supported numerous national organizations dedicated to securing state legislation to make modern society more livable for all U.S. workers. In particular, the National Consumers League (NCL) became the major lobbying force behind protective legislation. Florence Kelley, as NCL general secretary, with the legal expertise of Josephine Goldmark, laid the ground work for creating a favorable judicial climate for protecting factory workers through government regulation of contracts. Previously the courts had held that such protective measures interfered with workers' constitutional right of freedom of contract.

Initially, these women progressives in the NCL and other organizations supported protective labor legislation for all workers—women, men, and children. But in the long run they obtained such legislation only for working women. Although they were also the most class-conscious of all middle-class suffrage leaders, the militancy of the first-generation feminists was gone, as this generation of female reformers became assimilated into mainstream politics during the Progressive Era. Their success was represented by several major Supreme Court decisions (originating with *Muller v. Oregon* in 1908) and a variety of state legislation aimed primarily at protecting lower-class, working women. These decisions and statutes were based on what are considered today to be debilitating stereotypical views of all women, regardless of class. Ironically, the legal and political successes of these progressive female politicians in addressing the plight of working women with the passage of protective legislation[15] led to a fifty-year battle line between those female reformers who thought lower-class working women needed protection, that is, special treatment, and those who thought that all women would be better off if they simply obtained equal rights with men.[16]

Beginning in 1895 the NCL headquarters was located in the United Charities Building (UCB) on Park Avenue and 22nd Street in New York City. At that time this seven-story building housed four charity organization societies all devoted to aiding the poor. While the building's main lobby was remodeled (ca. 1930s) the foyer retains original oak and glass doors with decorative metal grillwork. The lobby features a marble plaque framed in a Scottish thistle motif, dedicated to the United Charities founder J. S. Kennedy, on an entrance wall. Throughout the United Charities Building, a substantial amount of original woodwork is in place in public corridors and offices. The original marble stairways with iron railings in the form of Ionic colonnettes and ornate newel posts grace most of the building. One of the most striking features of the building's interior is the assembly hall on the ground floor. It is composed of a rectangular space, defined by four complex piers with Ionic pilasters, surrounded by four quarter-arched coffered vaults. An elaborately detailed metal ceiling incorporates its own lighting system. Clerestory windows with the original

United Charities Building, New York, New York. (Photograph by Andrew Dolkart)

leaded panes of stained glass grace the room's north elevation. In addition, the assembly hall retains its richly carved wood wainscotting and trim, fine marble mosaic entrance floor, and terra-cotta cheek walls.

This description does not do justice to the part that the building played in providing space during the entire Progressive Era for female and male social reformers to exchange ideas and plan effective political action. As such the UCB architecturally represents a material base from which fundamental change for American workers and the poor emanated, with the NCL being but one of the most famous and influential occupants of this historic building. It has recently been designated an NHL.

The most interesting aspect of the NCL's success in *Muller* was the indirect impact it had on the first women's movement, as represented in 1908 by the National American Woman Suffrage Association (NAWSA). Most NAWSA women had concentrated their political efforts in the first two decades of the twentieth century on obtaining suffrage. NAWSA in general, and the more militant National Woman's Party (NWP) in particular, had not attempted to influence state or federal court decisions on protective legislation, although individual members of both these suffrage groups supported such legislation through other organizations. After its political triumph in 1920 with the passage of the Nineteenth Amendment, the first women's movement rapidly began to fragment. Some divisions were already evident before and during the First World War, as disagreements arose within the NAWSA during the final years of the battle for suffrage under the leadership of Carrie Chapman Catt.

Anthony named Catt, who had been an effective suffrage organizer in Iowa, her successor to head NAWSA in 1900. For four years until the illnesses of both her mother and her husband forced her to resign in favor of Anna Howard Shaw, Catt demonstrated a "great genius" as a national suffrage organizer. Catt returned to head NAWSA in 1915, after complaints about Shaw's lack of organizational strategy forced her to resign.[17] Catt's Upper West Side apartment overlooking Central Park in New York City is proposed for designation as an NHL. Following her husband's death, Catt moved into this twelve-story, Beaux-Arts style apartment building known as the Orwell House on West 86th Street. From 1907 to 1917 she lived there with her domestic partner and political ally Mary Garrett Hay. These were years for which she was best known, because during that time she organized the International Woman Suffrage Alliance and resumed leadership of NAWSA. Nothing, however, in the existing building reflects its importance to the history of American women.

With the passage of the Nineteenth Amendment in 1920, the first women's movement succumbed to internal divisions which, this time, proved terminal. For example, Alice Paul, a militant suffragist and Quaker pacifist, informally broke with NAWSA in 1913 to form the militant Congressional Union. This organization ultimately became the National Woman's Party (NWP). After 1917 the split within suffrage ranks became official with the formation of the NWP under Paul's leadership. At first she ran the NWP from a bare basement office on 14th Street and several other locations which have not survived.

Then, in 1929 the Sewall-Belmont House, a block from the Capitol building in the northeastern section of Washington, D.C., became the national headquarters of the NWP, largely as the result of the support of socialite and suf-

Sewall-Belmont National Historic Site. Washington, D.C. (Photograph by Vernon Horn)

fragist Alva Erskine Smith Vanderbilt Belmont who contributed $146,000 to purchase it. Fittingly, the property on which it stands was once administered by Margaret Brent in the late seventeenth century when she owned enough property to be one of the few colonial women to request voting privileges in the Maryland General Assembly. As one of the oldest houses in the nation's capital, whose construction began in the 1750s as a colonial farmhouse, it represents a patchwork example of "sequential architecture" added and subtracted to over the years for practical rather than aesthetic reasons. The main house was built by Robert Sewall in 1800. However haphazard its subsequent construction, inside its contents faithfully commemorate the history of the struggle for suffrage and its most famous leaders.

Most of the historic furniture and busts in the Sewall-Belmont House are the result of the forty-five years that Alice Paul spent in residence there fighting for passage of the Equal Rights Amendment which she first drafted in the early 1920s. From the entry way, with its busts of Paul, Anthony, Stanton, and Lucretia Mott, to the 1917 NWP suffrage banner in the stairwell, to the picture of Abigail Adams in a second-floor study hanging above a desk once used by Anthony, this house brings the history of both the suffrage and ERA battles to life.

Paul lived there from 1929 until 1974 when the Sewall-Belmont House was designated an NHL. The staff of the NWP literally became her family during this time—taking care of her personal and professional needs. One can almost imagine Paul working in her upstairs bedroom at her cluttered desk with her most-used dress hanging, not in the closet, but on the fireplace mantel for quick dressing. With the exception of the library, purportedly the oldest feminist collection in the United States founded by Florence Bayard Hilles in 1943, the Sewall-Belmont House is open to the public and remains the official headquarters of the National Woman's Party. Alice Paul's birthplace in Mt. Laurel Township, Burlington County, New Jersey, where she spent the first twenty-five years of her life growing up in a Quaker family, is also under consideration as a possible NHL.

The final disintegration of the first women's movement occurred in large measure over the Equal Rights Amendment (ERA)—first introduced in Congress by the National Woman's Party in 1923. As revised in 1943, in twenty-four words this historic legal document simply stated: "Equality of rights under the law shall not be denied or abridged by the United States or by any State on account of sex." The ERA battle was fought not only in the United States, but also at international conferences in the 1920s and 1930s in which opposing factions of U.S. women participated. Although Emily Greene Balch and Jane Addams won Nobel Peace Prizes, the American women's peace movement did not present a united front to the world in the interwar years. This was in part because of the differences provoked by the ERA. Perhaps the most significant aspect of the disagreement between those who supported the Equal Rights Amendment to the U.S. Constitution in the early 1920s and those who did not was the fact that it created a division among women reformers that lasted more than a half century. None of the original participants in this internecine struggle over the ERA anticipated how enduring and personally embittering their dispute would be. After all, most of them had worked together to obtain passage and ratification of the Nineteenth Amendment.

Prior to experiencing these debilitating divisions at home and abroad, women of the first women's movement remained united enough to obtain their major constitutional goal; namely, the Nineteenth Amendment. When women finally achieved the right to vote in 1920, little else of significance had been done to improve their constitutional status. Questions of full citizenship, property and fiduciary rights, personhood, credit, wages, domicile, divorce settlements, child custody—even the right of married women to a birth name—all remained largely neglected or subject to statutes that varied drastically from state to state. Not until the late 1960s did a second women's movement emerge to raise these matters in litigation and legislation. Once again, however, as with suffrage, the sweeping attack on the general subordination of women in society made by the radical feminists of the late 1960s would subsequently take a back seat to another narrow, single-issue crusade—the Equal Rights Amendment—thus repeating the experience of the drive for suffrage.

By 1920, U.S. women had more political, legal, educational, and economic opportunities than they had in 1865. But they still had not achieved constitutional equality before the law with men. As in the past, only the more far-sighted feminists of the 1920s realized that full emancipation still lay ahead and that certain political successes like the vote had been too little, too late. Unfortunately, the militant leaders of the National Woman's Party, like the first feminists of the 1870s, narrowed their initial collective approach to equal rights by focusing primarily on the ERA, while moderate reformers fragmented their energies into a variety of male-dominated liberal causes that at best could only marginally improve the socioeconomic and legal status of women. As a result of these divisions, the first women's movement faded and faltered until it disappeared as a national phenomenon during the interwar years. Consequently, from the 1930s to the 1960s, there was no congressional legislation that made gender a central issue, and the *Nineteenth Amendment remains the only successful attempt to include women by gender in the Constitution.*

In the 1920s the equal rights followers of Alice Paul viewed suffrage as only the beginning, not the end, of woman's battle to obtain the same legal status enjoyed by white males. Thus, they no longer thought of the Nineteenth Amendment as a panacea for women's or society's problems. In addition, members of the NWP continued to fight the sexist implications of protective legislation that applied only to women, and to urge women to run for public office as independents or members of third parties. Initially their voices had been drowned out before the First World War by a sea of moderate suffragists and female social welfare progressives, representing special treatment of working women. So it fell to a handful of feminists in the 1920s like Alice Paul, Anne Henrietta Martin, and Burnita Shelton Matthews to take a militant stand. These members of the NWP clearly saw that the vote was at best an inefficient tool and that all inequalities in the law pertaining to jury service, property rights, marriage, divorce, and work had to be eradicated before women could truly exercise the right to vote in any meaningful manner. Above all, they realized that the vote had not eliminated sex discrimination in American life, nor had protective legislation eliminated discrimination in the work place.

Even after such women as Jeannette Rankin, Edith Nourse Rogers, and Mary Norton successfully used their enfranchisement to participate in two-party politics on a par with men, most women found that their attempts at direct partisan participation were not welcomed by men within the Republican or Democratic parties. Although Rankin did not hold national public office as long as Rogers and Norton, she is better known because during her two widely separated terms in the U.S. House of Representatives (1916–1918 and 1940–1942), she acquired the unique distinction of having been the only person to vote against American entrance into *both* world wars. From 1917 until her death fifty-six years later, Rankin campaigned against United States involvement in all wars. The Rankin ranch outside of Helena, Montana, where she maintained her voting residence and often spent her summers, is now an

NHL. The property consists of ninety of the original two thousand acres, on which stands the original one-story, white frame ranch house and eight out-buildings built in 1923. There are no original furnishings in the house itself.

Rankin's family wealth did not make it all that easy for her to run for office. Many of the reasons for the difficulties Rankin and other newly enfranchised women faced in trying to obtain elective office still plague female candidates today. They are: (1) women's lack of traditional political experience; (2) their inability to raise as much money as male candidates; (3) the reluctance of male politicians to agree that women should have prominent roles in government and political parties; and (4) a dearth of successful female politicians for younger women to emulate as role models.

Consequently, when such women as Maud Wood Park, Belle Sherwin, and Marguerite Wells formed the League of Women Voters as a successor to NAWSA in 1920, it was not to support more female candidates but primarily to educate new voters, and also to obtain social welfare legislation on behalf of women and children. They were joined in this latter cause by the National Federation of Business and Professional Women, as well as by women involved in the labor union movement, especially those represented by the Women's Bureau created within the Department of Labor in 1920. In fact, this form of indirect (and often nonpartisan) political participation constituted the major form of political activity on the part of most women reformers in the interwar years.

This momentous decision to dissolve NAWSA and form the League of Women Voters took place in the Congress Hotel in Chicago on February 13, 1920, during what was billed as a NAWSA "Victory Convention" on the eve of passage of the Nineteenth Amendment. Intended to be a temporary organization to educate women on how to exercise their newly won right to vote, it became a permanent political organization devoted to issues of concern to women and children and a major force in the American political system. The League of Women Voters is credited, among other things, with initiating in 1960 the now traditional nationally televised presidential debates and with motivating more and more women to run for office in the 1970s and 1980s. Although the League of Women Voters moved from Chicago to Washington, D.C., in 1923, none of the existing Washington structures which housed it at various times reflects both the simplicity and multiplicity of the League as well as the Chicago Congress Hotel on Michigan Avenue between Congress and Harrison Avenues. Originally eleven stories constructed in 1893 and called the Auditorium Annex Hotel, the building is appropriate for designation as an NHL because of the continuing importance of the League of Women Voters in the political history of twentieth-century U.S. women.[18]

Because women did not vote as a bloc to produce the utopian society often promised by both groups of suffragists in the last years of their long battle for the right to vote, the suffrage victory came to be unfairly regarded as a hollow one even by some of the Nineteenth Amendment's staunchest supporters. Even

Congress Hotel, Chicago, Illinois. (Photograph by Jill S. Topolski)

more regrettably, during the course of the 1920s, suffrage came to be looked upon in many circles as a political victory but as a major moral failure, not unlike that of Prohibition. It would be unfair, however, to fault women of the 1920s for not voting as a bloc or for falling victim to divisions. Gender-gap politics based on political unity among women, unfortunately, was not much more a reality in the 1980s than it was in the 1920s. For example, Progressive suffragists such as Jane Addams and Florence Kelley, who had worked so hard for protective legislation for women, naturally refused to support the ERA. In their minds, support of complete legal equality with men would negate the recently hard-won victories in the courts and state legislatures protecting women. It also would force them to reconsider the crucial question of the limitations of working within established capitalist and liberal political parameters to reform society. Women favoring protective legislation were not prepared to do so.

The interwar years were indeed a confusing time for women. They still did not have true economic independence, equal social expectations, political experience, or even the educational and professional training necessary for obtaining leadership in politics. At the same time they were faced with postwar reaction against socioeconomic change disguised under the superficially liberating glitter of the Jazz Age and Freudian theories on sexuality. Finally, women were confronted by the Great Depression of 1929, which turned Flappers back into Gibson Girls overnight, as traditional values were once more reasserted and men given preference for jobs. The first women's movement would scarcely have survived even had it not been plagued by disputes over strategy, tactics, and personality conflicts between the militant supporters of equal rights and the moderate defenders of protective legislation. In the 1920s, the supporters of the ERA tended to be identified with the Republican party, while those in favor of protective legislation were more nonpartisan. In the 1930s, these protectionists increasingly became associated with the Democratic party. In the 1930s, there was also an increasing tendency for older professional and business women (often Republicans) to support the ERA.

While both Republican and Democratic women worked side by side for reform in the Progressive Era, by the time of the Great Depression and the New Deal, reform activity (except for some very prominent and wealthy Republican women supporting Alice Paul and the ERA) increasingly became identified with the Democratic women who followed first Florence Kelley and Jane Addams, and later, Eleanor Roosevelt. Thus, the division over the ERA was, in part, perpetuated before and after the Second World War by partisanship (with more Democrats against it and more Republicans for it), even though both parties endorsed the amendment in the 1940s. Until the early 1970s working-class women and union leaders (usually Democrats) opposed it, as did the aging generation of Progressive women reformers who had originally supported protective legislation. These partisan positions were reversed in the course of the fight for the Twenty-seventh Amendment after 1972 when Democrats replaced Republicans as champions of the ERA.

Although the split in the 1920s appeared very similar to the one that had plagued the original generation of female reformers after the Civil War, in fact, the two groups—those representing individual and collective rights—had switched positions. In the 1870s the women who single-mindedly focused on obtaining the individual right to vote were not strategically or philosophically as radical as members of the NWP became in the 1920s when they took up a broad spectrum of individual rights, pointing to the arbitrary diversity of state laws affecting women. Conversely, social justice Progressives representing the successors to women like Anthony and Stanton, who had continued to advocate collective improvements in status for women in the 1870s, found themselves tactically on the defensive in the 1920s because they had narrowed their sights to concentrate on protective legislation for women exclusively. By either standard, however, the first women's movement ended on a less emancipatory and hence "deradicalized" phase in the 1920s than it had started in the mid-nineteenth century. In part this was because the seventy-two years it took to win suffrage made it seem like an overblown and much less significant issue by the time it was achieved than when it was first proposed. The same would have been true of the ERA had it been ratified in 1982 — fifty-nine years after it was first introduced in Congress.

Having discovered that they could not easily win political office in the face of male indifference or outright opposition, some women, within both the Democratic and Republican parties, began to exercise effective behind-the-scenes influence in the 1920s and 1930s by becoming active in their respective parties' governing bodies. Initially, the best known were Democrats. Two women besides Frances Perkins and Eleanor Roosevelt, who became public figures in their own right, were Belle Moskowitz and Molly Dewson. Both practiced what has been called "feminine" rather than "feminist" politics and, like Perkins and Roosevelt, neither entered politics to advance their own careers.[19]

In the tradition of the Progressive Era, these women, and others like them, entered the political fray to promote certain social ideas or economic programs. Moskowitz, for example, served behind the scenes as one of Al Smith's closest political advisers when he was governor of New York in the 1920s and when he ran for the presidency in 1928. Molly Dewson, who was to become an even more powerful behind-the-scenes force in Democratic patronage politics as head of the Women's Division of the Democratic National Committee in the 1930s, once described Moskowitz as "Al Smith's tent pole." Dewson was also a member of FDR's Commission on Economic Security and is credited with writing the Social Security Act of 1935. While Dewson herself came to be thought of as the "first female American political boss," she shared with Moskowitz, Perkins, and Eleanor Roosevelt an early interest and career in social work, a personal denial of any "careerism" ambitions, and the ability to promote causes, rather than herself.[20]

Like so many other single, professional women at the turn of the century, Dewson devoted herself to the public work of liberal politics from the Progressive movement through the New Deal. This "strand of liberal feminism," according to her biographer, "stretched from Carrie Chapman Catt to Molly Dewson and Eleanor Roosevelt and eventually to Betty Friedan." In 1910 Dewson began a fifty-two year relationship with Mary (Polly) Porter, and in 1922 they bought a two-bedroom cooperative in a six-story apartment building in New York's Greenwich Village. For the next thirty years of Dewson's active political life they occupied this "small but attractive" apartment with its oriental rugs and "menagerie of dogs or cats" to which they gave "whimsical names such as Solemn Sister and Bad Girl."[21] While the original furnishings and animals are long gone, descriptions of their apartment indicate that they created a physical space and atmosphere that reflected not only their enduring relationship but also a haven from Dewson's hectic political career. The Perkins' home in Washington, D.C., has recently been designated as an NHL. As secretary of labor during the New Deal, Frances Perkins became the first woman member of a U.S. cabinet. She previously had advised Franklin Roosevelt privately and through official appointments on labor matters when he was governor of New York.

No other female political activist of this era in either party, however, achieved the indirect power, influence, and international recognition of Eleanor Roosevelt. A small cottage called Val-Kill, two miles east of the main Roosevelt estate at Hyde Park, New York, is an NHL and a Historic Site in the National Park System. It was built in 1925 on the advice and plans of two close friends of Eleanor Roosevelt's, Nancy Cook and Marion Dickerman, to serve as both residence for them and haven for her "when neither Franklin nor the children were at the Big House."[22] This intimate dwelling with its tiny, second-floor bedroom whose doorway opened on to a balcony overlooking a sunny living space below, provided all three women with a privacy and opportunity to explore female friendship that Roosevelt, orphaned at the age of ten, had not experienced since boarding school in England as a teenager. The building of this cottage with Cook and Dickerman, combined with her burgeoning political and social network of other women reformers, marked the beginning of the transfer of Eleanor Roosevelt's emotional and reform activities away from her family, husband, and always present mother-in-law in the 1920s and 1930s. Only at Val-Kill, however, was she able to physically create her own sense of space away from the "Big House" at Hyde Park occupied by FDR, their children, and his mother. According to historian William H. Chafe, Eleanor Roosevelt seldom returned from the Val-Kill cottage to her husband's estate and world before the outbreak of the Second World War "without resentment and regret," because she felt that her emotional "family" was at Val-Kill.[23]

Close to the cottage, a "shop" was built in which Cook and Dickerman and a mutual friend Caroline O'Day made furniture under the name Val-Kill Industries. In actuality the "shop" constituted an experimental, cooperative furniture craft factory that these women hoped would teach local farm workers additional skills as makers of early American furniture, pewter pieces, and weavings. The linen and towels they manufactured there bear the monogram "EMN"—for Eleanor, Marion, and Nancy. Their enterprise failed in 1936—a victim of the Great Depression. Cook and Dickerman continued to live at Val-Kill until 1947, and Eleanor Roosevelt joined them frequently on weekends, holidays, and during the summer for two decades. Her sons remodeled the cottage in the 1950s, adding bedrooms with dormers indiscriminately, in addition to other suburban facades popular in that decade. It is this post–World War II version of Val-Kill that has been restored by the National Park Service rather than the very personal retreat cottage that had been utilized by Eleanor Roosevelt and her two friends during the interwar years.

In the end, it was Eleanor Roosevelt who, as First Lady, determined that the Democratic party would not support the ERA until the late 1940s, and she was the only woman with enough national stature and charisma to force an end to the continuing split between ERA supporters and proponents of protective legislation following the Second World War. But her own protectionist convictions and advice from the powerful member of FDR's political team, Molly Dewson, prevented Roosevelt from taking action to resolve this long-standing division among women reformers.

During the decades of the 1920s and 1930s, it was difficult to argue that there was a clear-cut class, generational, or racial division among pro- and anti-ERA forces, since the leaders on both sides were middle- and upper-middle-class women who claimed that they were acting on behalf of all women. Alice Paul's followers tended to be younger than the antiratification women during the interwar years, because young women, especially those who were career-oriented and/or enjoying the sexual revolution of the 1920s, gravitated toward the ERA as a symbol of the new individual opportunities they were experiencing. For them, equal rights became a very personal, individualistic goal as well as the major focus of the NWP.

To confuse matters more, the National Association of Colored Women (NACW), led by Mary Church Terrell, a wealthy black suffragist, endorsed the ERA, while the National Council of Negro Women (NCNW), founded by Mary McLeod Bethune, did not. Terrell's residence, an NHL in the northwest area of Washington, D.C., served as her personal headquarters for fighting all forms of racial discrimination in the work place, public accommodations, and education. Modest by contemporary standards, the Terrell House is typical of turn-of-the-century "simplified" Richardsonian row houses that can be found in the District of Columbia, with its red brick exterior sandwiched between two similar two-story dwellings on U Street. Its narrow, cramped appearance belies the far-flung antidiscrimination activities of its famous resident.

In addition to obvious partisan politics, along with some generational and class-conflict overtones, it is clear in retrospect that the philosophical differences between these two groups of interwar feminists led to legal, political, and rhetorical battles not only at home over protective legislation and the ERA, but also at international conferences, the League of Nations, and later, the United Nations. They fought over treaties that included broad guarantees for the equal treatment of men and women, especially with regard to independent nationality status and naturalization procedures. Again, Eleanor Roosevelt played a role in keeping this division alive, because her views on peace were not those of the National Woman's Party.

As the author of the first Equal Rights Amendment submitted to Congress in 1923, Alice Paul and her followers insisted that the ERA be on the agenda at all international conferences. Until the late 1930s they successfully argued for equal rights at Pan-American conferences. As a former progressive reformer, Roosevelt believed that working women had special needs recognized in existing legislation protecting them in the work place. Thus, she opposed the activities of the National Woman's Party on domestic and foreign affairs between the wars, out of the conviction that endorsement of a blanket Equal Rights Amendment would endanger working women around the world. However, in 1948 she finally accepted a compromise with NWP and Third World women representatives in the wording of the United Nations Declaration of Human Rights—accepting the term "all people" in place of "all men." Nonetheless, the divisiveness that the debate over equal rights created among American women activists continued at home long after it had been settled at the UN.

Not until 1972, when Congress finally approved the proposed Twenty-seventh Amendment to the Constitution and sent it to the states for ratification, did mainstream and radical feminists begin to coalesce behind the ERA. However, postwar conservatism soon set in following the end of the Vietnam War in 1973. This conservatism combined with Watergate and "stagflation" to create a national cultural and political backlash not equaled since the 1920s. Despite these adverse conditions, the newly organized second women's movement experienced a number of political and juridical successes from the late 1960s to the present, but passage of the ERA was not one of them.[24]

Since the Second World War women's impact on national politics has remained erratic, symbolized by the fact that seventy years after winning the right to vote and representing over half of the total population of the United States, only 5 percent, or 27 of the 535 members of Congress, are women. In 1974 former UN Ambassador Jeane Kirkpatrick lamented:

> Half a century after the ratification of the nineteenth amendment, no woman has been nominated to be president or vice-president, no woman has served on the Supreme Court. Today, there is no woman in the cabinet, no woman in the Senate, no woman serving as governor of a major state, no woman mayor of a major city, no woman in the top leadership of either party.[25]

In the intervening years, things have improved considerably, ranging from the 1984 nomination of Geraldine Ferraro as the Democratic vice-presidential nominee to the appointment of Sandra Day O'Connor to the Supreme Court. Likewise Elizabeth Dole served in the Reagan cabinet as secretary of transportation—along with two other women, Margaret Heckler (secretary of health and human services) and Ann McLaughlin (secretary of labor)—before going on to serve two years in the Bush cabinet as secretary of labor. Dole left the Bush administration in 1990 to become head of the American Red Cross, and another woman, Lynn Martin, succeeded her. Kirkpatrick herself became ambassador to the UN under the Reagan administration until she resigned in 1984. As of 1991, two women hold seats in the U.S. Senate: Nancy Kassebaum

(R-KS) and Barbara Mikulski (D-MD). Ann Richards (D-TX), Barbara Roberts (D-OR), and Joan Finney (D-KS) serve as state governors.

Moreover, women have made impressive political inroads in recent years, particularly at the state and local levels, despite the fact that it remains more difficult for them to project a credible public image and to raise money than for their male counterparts. By the middle of the 1980s, for example, women constituted 9.6 percent of all U.S. mayors (including the mayors of some very large cities like San Francisco and Houston) and almost 15 percent of all state legislators. In 1986 alone, 26 out of 52 women running for statewide executive positions won, and the number of the female state legislators grew to 1,120 nationwide. Eighty-five women ran for state offices in 1990, and 51 were elected. They included 6 women lieutenant governors, 10 secretaries of state, 3 attorneys general, and 12 state treasurers. The number of women attorneys appointed to state and federal judgeships has also increased significantly in the 1970s and 1980s, as have the number of law degrees awarded to women.

Even more encouraging is the fact that a real, as opposed to a mythical, gender gap seems to be developing in American politics that may give women more leverage, at least in national elections, than they have had since first voting in 1920. While Gallup polls found no significant gender preferences for presidential candidates between 1960 and 1972, in every presidential election in the 1980s more women have voted than men. In the 1988 presidential election, for example, 6.8 million more women than men exercised their franchise. This is particularly true among Democrats, where women voted 6 to 8 percentage points more than their male counterparts. It is conceivable as the percentage of women in the total population continues to rise well above half for the remainder of the 1990s that women's issues will be given more consideration by both female and male candidates for national office.[26] Moreover, despite the defeat of the Equal Rights Amendment in 1982, in the last twenty-five years the legal status of women has changed more dramatically than in the previous two hundred years, largely due to the lobbying and litigation efforts of such organizations as the National Organization for Women (NOW), the Women's Equity Action League (WEAL), the National Women's Political Caucus (NWPC), and National Abortion Rights Action League (NARAL).

At the end of the 1980s the political potential of feminist politics remains alive and strong, despite the defeat of the ERA. It has not yet produced, however, the number of recognized national leaders equivalent in power and influence to those women who emerged at the turn of the century. Nor has any subsequent First Lady exercised the power and influence of Eleanor Roosevelt.[27] Nonetheless, the second women's movement still remains a strong force for general political reform in the country in the last decade of the twentieth century. Most importantly, unlike the first women's movement one hundred years ago, its agenda has widened to include all Americans, not simply women and children.

NOTES

1. Susan J. Carroll, *Women as Candidates in American Politics* (Bloomington: Indiana University Press, 1985), 3 (quotation); Bella Abzug with Mim Kelber, *Gender Gap* (Boston: Houghton Mifflin Co., 1984), 109; see John J. Stucker, "Women's Political Role," for an elaboration of the three factors in 1920 limiting female voting turnout in *Current History* (May 1976): 212–13.

2. See Gail Dubrow's essay in this collection.

3. Kathleen Barry, *Susan B. Anthony: A Biography of a Singular Feminist* (New York: New York University Press, 1988), 51.

4. For details about the intellectual and economic ferment in the Seneca Falls area, see Whitney R. Cross, *The Burned-Over District: The Social and Intellectual History of Enthusiastic Religion in Western New York 1800–1850* (New York: Harper & Row, 1950), 3–6, 55–56, 237. Cross coined the phrase "psychic highway" in referring to those people in this area of New York who were "devoted to the crusades aimed at the perfection of mankind and the attainment of millennial happiness." The term "Burned-over" or "Burnt" district refers to the analogy between forest fires and fires of the spirit. The evangelist Charles Grandison Finney first applied the term to this region of New York State. The Erie Canal, completed in 1825, aided economic development in the area. Its completion also marked the beginning of major religious revivals.

5. Quoted in National Park Service, U.S. Department of Interior, *Women's Rights Trail: Seneca Falls and Waterloo, New York* (Boston: Eastern National Parks and Monuments Association), 11.

6. Quotations in Theodore Stanton and Harriot Blalch, eds., *Elizabeth Cady Stanton as Revealed in Her Letters, Diary and Reminiscences*, 2 vols. (New York: Harper & Brothers, 1922), 1:142–43, 145. The segment of this essay about the participants in the Seneca Falls Conference relies heavily on the published and unpublished works of historian Judith Wellman, "Women's Rights, Republicanism and Revolutionary Rhetoric in Antebellum New York State," *New York History* (July 1988): 353–84; *idem,* "The Mystery of the Seneca Falls Women's Rights Convention: Who Came and Why?" May 31, 1985 (unpublished manuscript), 13–26, referred to in chapter 1 of the U.S. Department of Interior, National Park Service, *Special History Study: Women's Rights National Historical Park, New York,* prepared by Sandra S. Weber (Denver: Denver Service Center, 1985); and *idem,* "The Seneca Falls Women's Rights Convention: A Study in Social Networks," *Journal of Women's History* 3 (Spring 1991): 9–37. Also see: Glenn C. Altschuler and Jan M. Saltzgaber, *Revivalism, Social Conscience and Community in the Burned-Over District, The Trial of Rhoda Bement* (Ithaca, New York: Cornell University Press, 1983), 89–140; and Ross Evans Paulson, *Women's Suffrage and Prohibition: A Comparative Study of Equality and Social Control* (Glenview, Ill.: Scott, Foresman, 1973), 37.

7. Elizabeth Cady Stanton, Susan B. Anthony, and Matilda Joslyn Gage, eds., *History of Woman Suffrage,* 6 vols. (Rochester, N.Y.: Susan B. Anthony, 1889; reprint ed., New York: Source Book Press, 1970), 1: 50 (first quotation), 68 (second quotation). When compared word for word with the Declaration of Independence only 152 of the 1,071 words in the original were duplicated exactly in 1848. Although the format is that of the Declaration of Independence, it is the general Enlightenment natural law theories that the first feminists borrowed more than the precise Jeffersonian wording or phraseology. For a discussion of what the Enlightenment meant to Stanton and Anthony, see Barry, *Anthony,* 114–45, especially 126–33.

8. The complete text of the 1848 Declaration of Sentiments (including the resolutions) can be found in Stanton, Anthony, and Gage, eds., *History of Woman Suffrage,* 1:

67–74; or in Joan Hoff, *Law, Gender, and Injustice: A Legal History of U.S. Women* (New York: New York University Press, 1991), 383–87.

9. For various descriptions of this schism and its resolution see Stanton, Anthony, and Gage, eds., *History of Woman Suffrage*, 2: 91–151, and 3: 158–74; Harper, *Anthony*, 241–94; Barry, *Anthony*, 195–224; and Ellen Carol DuBois, *Feminism and Suffrage: The Emergence of an Independent Women's Movement in America, 1848–1869* (Ithaca, N.Y.: Cornell University Press, 1978), 53–125; and Israel Kugler, *From Ladies to Women: The Organized Struggle for Women's Rights in the Reconstruction Era* (New York: Greenwood Press, 1987), 135–72.

10. For details, see Barry, *Anthony*, 146–94.

11. For details of post-Civil War litigation see Hoff, *Law, Gender, and Injustice*, 151–87.

12. Michael Les Benedict, "Preserving the Constitution: The Conservative Basis of Radical Reconstruction," *Journal of American History* 61 (June 1974): 85, 86 (quotations). For the general political, legal, and racial conservatism of the radical Republicans, also see Michael Kammen, *A Machine that Would Go of Itself: The Constitution in American Culture* (New York: Alfred Knopf, 1986), 119; and Hendrik Hartog, "The Constitution of Aspiration and 'Rights that Belong to Us All,' " *Journal of American History* 74 (December 1987): 1016–25.

13. Barry, *Anthony*, 250.

14. The complete text of the 1876 Declaration of Rights can be found in Stanton, Anthony, and Gage, eds., *History of Woman Suffrage*, 3:28–34; or in Hoff, *Law, Gender, and Injustice*, 388–92.

15. For a review of women workers during the Progressive Era, see: Margery W. Davies, *Woman's Place Is at the Typewriter: Office Work and Office Workers, 1870–1930* (Philadelphia: Temple University Press, 1983); Nancy Schrom Dye, *As Equals and As Sisters: The Labor Movement and the Women's Trade Union League of New York* (Columbia, Mo.: University of Missouri Press, 1980); Maurine Weiner Greenwald, *Women, War and Work: The Impact of World War I on Women Workers in the United States* (Westport, Conn.: Greenwood Press, 1980); Jacqueline Jones, *Labor of Love, Labor of Sorrow; Black Women, Work and the Family from Slavery to the Present* (New York: Basic Book, 1985); Meredith Tax, *The Rising of the Women: Feminist Solidarity and Class Conflict, 1880–1917* (New York: Monthly Review Press, 1980); and Leslie Woodcock Tentler, *Wage-Earning Women: Industrial Work and Family Life in the United States, 1900–1930* (New York: Oxford University Press, 1979).

16. For details upon which portions of this section are based, see: Nancy Cott, *The Grounding of Modern Feminism* (New Haven: Yale University Press, 1987); Christine A. Lunardini, *From Equal Suffrage to Equal Rights: Alice Paul and the National Woman's Party, 1910–1928* (New York: New York University Press, 1986); Steven M. Buechler, *The Transformation of the Woman Suffrage Movement: The Case of Illinois 1850–1920* (New Brunswick, N.J.: Rutgers University Press, 1986); and Felice D. Gordon, *After Winning: The Legacy of the New Jersey Suffragists, 1920–1947* (New Brunswick, N.J.: Rutgers University Press, 1986).

17. Robert Booth Fowler, *Carrie Catt: Feminist Politician* (Boston: Northeastern University Press, 1986), 16–20, passim.

18. Naomi Black, *Social Feminism* (Ithaca: Cornell University Press, 1989), 290–91.

19. For details about the public and private careers of all these women, see: Susan Ware, *Partner and I: Molly Dewson, Feminism, and New Deal Politics* (New Haven: Yale University Press, 1987); *idem, Beyond Suffrage: Women in the New Deal* (Cambridge: Harvard University Press, 1981); Elisabeth Israels Perry, *Belle Moskowitz: Feminine Politics and the Exercise of Power in the Age of Al Smith* (New York: Oxford University Press, 1987); *The Reminiscences of Frances Perkins* (1955) in the Oral History

Collection of Columbia University; Joseph P. Lash, *Love, Eleanor: Eleanor Roosevelt and Her Friends* (Garden City, N.Y.: Doubleday, 1982); and Joan Hoff-Wilson and Marjorie Lightman, eds., *Without Precedent: The Life and Career of Eleanor Roosevelt* (Bloomington: Indiana University Press, 1984).

20. For quotations, see: Perry, *Moskowitz*, xii, 160; and Ware, *Partner and I*, xiii.

21. Ware, *Partner and I*, xvii, 134.

22. Lash, *Love, Eleanor*, 103.

23. William H. Chafe, "Biographical Sketch" in Hoff-Wilson and Lightman, eds., *Without Precedent*, 3–14.

24. For a review of the legislative and litigious successes and failures of the Second Women's Movement, see: Hoff, *Law, Gender, and Injustice*, chapters 7, 8, and 9; Winifred D. Wandersee, *On The Move: American Women in the 1970s* (Boston: Twayne Publishers, 1988); Ellen Boneparth and Emily Stoper, eds., *Women, Power and Policy: Toward the Year 2000* (New York: Pergamon Press, 2nd edition, 1988); and NOW/ Legal Defense and Education Fund and Renée Cherow-O'Leary, *The State-By-State Guide to Women's Legal Rights* (New York: McGraw-Hill, 1987).

25. Jeane Kirkpatrick, *Political Women* (New York: Basic Books, 1974), 3.

26. Abzug, *Gender Gap*, 80–90; and Paul Taylor, "Politics of Gender 1990: Shift in Issues May Benefit Women," *Washington Post*, June 10, 1990, 16.

27. For reasons why, see Joan Hoff-Wilson, "Did Eleanor Roosevelt Make a Difference?" *Texas Humanist* 7, no. 2 (November-December 1984): 33–37.

7 ✦ Women and Religion

JEAN R. SODERLUND

The history of women and religion in America is marked by a series of ironies. While women comprised the majority of the faithful in many denominations, they lacked access to leadership and authority. In gender ideology they were the "moral guardians" of the nation, but they were denied opportunities to become pastors of mainstream congregations. Even in the Society of Friends, the one organized European religion that has recognized female ministers throughout its history, women exerted less authority than men in church affairs. Over the centuries since Anne Hutchinson challenged the Puritan magistrates of early Massachusetts, women who have accepted the call to preach have experienced banishment and excommunication. For spiritually motivated women, the choice has been either to accept the limits of their gender-defined roles, sometimes extending those limits to some degree, or to quit traditional denominations and establish their own. Just a few remarkable individuals have chosen the latter course, including Ann Lee, Rebecca Cox Jackson, Ellen White, Mary Baker Eddy, and Aimee Semple McPherson.

The convoluted relationship of women and religion complicates our understanding of the significance of religious buildings in women's history. For the vast majority of women, the church or synagogue was the only acceptable forum for social interaction outside the home. For women who were devoted to God and their faith, their house of worship was a place of spiritual fulfillment. For large numbers of women, especially those living in rural areas, the church was the primary site of companionship with neighbors and friends, regardless of spiritual commitment. But beyond the importance of religious buildings as social and spiritual centers, what meaning have they held in the history of American women? How did their architecture and interior design reflect the accepted gender roles of each denomination? Have women participated in their design or construction? In what ways did the women who founded new denominations reconfigure, or fail to reconfigure, the use of symbolism and space in constructing their own places of worship?

While much investigation remains to be done to answer these questions fully, it is clear that close study of extant buildings can enhance our understanding of women and religion in American history. To provide a conceptual framework for such study, this chapter will first discuss the experience of women in mainstream denominations and then examine the work of women who moved outside established religions.

For most American women, religious experience has encompassed activities within denominations which are based on the patriarchal model of the Judeo-Christian tradition. Gender ideology is central to this tradition. God and Jesus Christ are male, as have been the chief executors of earthly authority, the church hierarchy and ministry. During the colonial period, women of the Puritan, Presbyterian, and Anglican churches, the dominant groups of the period, exerted only informal influence; they had no formal voice in their congregations. And while the role of women increased by the early nineteenth century, it remained more circumscribed than that of men.

The spatial organization of church buildings represented accepted hierarchical relationships. In the spare Puritan meetinghouses of early New England, men and women sat on opposite sides of the room, each sex ranked by social status. The center of attention was the pulpit, from which the minister presented his sermons of about two hours each on Sunday morning and afternoon. Elders inspected the behavior of the congregation from their seat beneath the pulpit. At the end of the service, men left the meetinghouse first. In Anglican churches the pulpit, from which priests delivered sermons of only about twenty minutes, was also visually dominant, though it shared prominence with the altar and cross. The congregation sat in family pews, with the wealthiest at the front. The male gentry, many of whom were vestrymen, confirmed their authority by entering the worship service as a group after everyone else had arrived and then leaving en masse before the others. While theological differences over the significance of the sermon versus the sacraments and liturgy influenced specific forms within these churches, in both denominations (as in other mainstream churches except the Society of Friends) the male minister and the most substantial laymen held the focus of attention and power.[1]

Like many other seventeenth- and eighteenth-century Protestants, Puritans and Anglicans placed restrictions on women's activities and authority. They believed Saint Paul had set down rules on how the church should be governed. In 1 Corinthians Paul wrote, "Let your women keep silence in the Churches: for it is not permitted unto them to speak: but they ought to be subject, as also the Law saith. And if they will learn any thing, let them ask their husbands at home: for it is a shame for a woman to speak in the Church" (14:34). Such Protestants believed that women had equal access to salvation and thus could attain full membership in the church, but they should have no voice or vote in church governance. They rejected the cult of Mary and the nunneries that were part of Roman Catholicism, thus removing both a source of inspiration for women in religion and the location of significant female authority in the church.[2]

Among New England Puritans, women's status improved little over the colonial period, and in fact, possibly deteriorated as they became an increasing proportion of members. In the few New England churches where women had a vote during the early colonial period, laymen and ministers came to fear female domination and stripped women of their vote.[3] Over the course of the seventeenth century, women were a growing proportion of church members. By 1650, women in Massachusetts and Connecticut comprised 60 percent of church admissions and in some congregations made up as much as three-fourths of new admissions. Why did this occur? One explanation is that as New England society developed economically and attracted new settlers who did not share the founders' vision of a "city on the hill," the gulf widened between church and society. Men, who had authority in matters outside the household, became more interested in trade and commerce and left the church to women and ministers. Puritan society experienced role differentiation by gender: business affairs and politics were dominant and attracted the interest of men. Religion had less influence and thus was delegated to ministers and women. The male ministry took powers that were formerly held by laymen; women became guardians of religion and morality in their families, even though they still had no formal public role in the church.[4]

It is important to specify that Puritan women generally lacked *formal* authority in their church, because evidence demonstrates that they wielded influence informally on ministers and laymen. While men filled public roles—signed petitions for new churches and cast votes—women often supplied the energy for establishing new congregations. The primary reason for setting up churches was that as settlements grew, families in new areas found themselves miles from the closest meetinghouse. Older women and men and mothers with young children found it difficult to walk three or four miles to meeting. Thus, women convinced their husbands to support new churches. In 1677, the women of one Massachusetts town, Chebacco, went so far as to have a church built before their husbands had received authorization from the county court. They were fined by the court for contempt of authority. In other cases women used their influence with their husbands and the power of gossip to undercut the position of ministers who caused them trouble. In 1674 in Rowley, Massachusetts, a young minister, Jeremiah Shepard, was not given a pulpit because the community's women opposed him, apparently because he showed them disrespect.[5]

Less is known about the status of women in Anglican, Presbyterian, Baptist, Lutheran, Roman Catholic, and Jewish congregations in colonial British America. Yet in all, it seems clear, women were expected to accept a subordinate role. In the Anglican (later Episcopalian) church only men could preach, administer the sacraments, and serve on the vestries that were in charge of all parish business, including aid to the poor, sick, and elderly. Like their Puritan sisters, though, Anglican women had a measure of informal authority that proceeded from their duty to maintain family religious practice. In eighteenth-century Virginia, most burials and marriages took place at home, where women supervised preparations. Even some baptisms were conducted in the mother's house, despite the firm pressure by clergy to hold them at church.[6]

After the turn of the nineteenth century, women in major denominations carved out new institutional roles for themselves by establishing church societies for aiding the impoverished, distributing Bibles, and supporting ministerial training, Sunday schools, and mission work. Often they obtained a building, separate from the church, to serve as an orphan asylum or house of employment. The first known women's benevolent organization was the Female Society for the Relief of the Distressed, established in 1795 by Philadelphia Quaker women, but soon such groups sprang up throughout New England, the Middle States, and in some parts of the South. Women, who dominated most churches in numbers but lacked a formal voice in their governance, joined together to take responsibility for specific religious and benevolent purposes.

Evangelicalism swept the country during the Second Great Awakening, which lasted from about 1795 to 1830, and obligated women to reach out to the poor, the uneducated, and the unchurched. In Petersburg, Virginia, for example, women recognized the need for an orphanage for girls and in 1812 petitioned the state legislature for legal incorporation. They successfully raised funds and in 1814 opened the asylum in a rented house. The women of Petersburg took over responsibility for orphan girls from the town fathers: they cared for younger children in the asylum and bound out older girls as apprentices. Poverty was worsening in Petersburg in the early nineteenth century, and women hoped to remedy the lack of public schools and apprenticeships for girls. They feared that without education and financial assistance, orphaned girls would quickly turn to prostitution. Women managed the asylum until the 1850s when, as happened elsewhere throughout the United States, men infiltrated the organization, further institutionalized its operation, and took control.[7]

In Philadelphia in 1814, Sarah Ralston inspired women of the Second Presbyterian Church to found an Orphan Society, and within three months they had raised enough money to rent a house and hire a matron. By 1820, the Philadelphia Orphan Society had built a three-story brick building, no longer extant, and cared for ninety children. In addition, Ralston led women's church groups that distributed Bibles and built an asylum for indigent widows. All of these activities required significant amounts of money and managerial skills. In group after group, women raised money for their chosen projects by selling needlework, flowers, and specially-prepared foods, and by convincing wealthy benefactors to donate to the cause. The church women claimed new roles in society by establishing new institutions; in their churches they gained some new respect by providing funds to educate ministers and support missionaries.[8] Nevertheless, in the formal authority structure of their churches, Congregational, Presbyterian, and Anglican women remained voteless and voiceless. Indeed, as women increased as a proportion of the membership and found autonomous sources of funds, the clergy and male laity were ever more defensive of their power.

Among the earliest congregations of American Jews, comprising a total of about three thousand persons and located in urban areas, a parallel expansion occurred in women's role during the early nineteenth century. Judaic law and custom held that a woman could reach heaven only through her husband's piety, that her duties lay in helping him to achieve godliness by meeting his bodily needs. Women should observe dietary laws, have children as soon as possible to enable men to fulfill their duty to procreate, sit separately from the men in synagogue to avoid distracting them from worship, and visit the *mikveh*, or ritual bath, to cleanse themselves after menstruation. Following a Protestant model that went beyond Jewish tradition, Rebecca Gratz of Philadelphia established a Jewish Sunday school. And, in 1826, a mixed choir sang at the dedication of the new synagogue of Philadelphia's Mikveh Israel Congregation. Reform Judaism, the modern movement accepted by German Jews who immigrated to the United States between about 1820 and 1880, initiated further changes in women's status. Most fundamentally, the Reform Synod of 1846 held that women were the religious equals of men and should have the same educational opportunity. Seating in the synagogue was integrated, and women now counted as part of the *minyan*, or quorum, of ten necessary for public prayer. Opposition to the reforms was intense, however, especially among women who valued such rituals as the *mikveh* and dietary laws.[9]

Other women engaged in religious activities that took them beyond the bounds of their congregations: missionaries and the founders of schools and female seminaries. Among the first missionaries to Native Americans in the far Northwest were Narcissa Prentiss Whitman and Eliza Hart Spalding, who embarked in 1836 with their husbands, Dr. Marcus Whitman and Henry Spalding, on a mission in the Oregon Territory. The mission was sponsored by the American Board of Commissioners for Foreign Missions, a joint venture of the Presbyterian, Dutch Reformed, and Congregational churches. Narcissa Whitman had volunteered for the mission as a single woman but was permitted to participate only after her marriage. Despite the hostility of Cayuse Indians who lived in the area, the Whitmans established their mission at Waiilatpu (also the name by which the Cayuse called themselves), near Fort Walla Walla. There they built a large adobe house, sawmill, gristmill, smithy, and an emigrant house serving travelers on the Oregon Trail, which passed by the mission site. None of the buildings remain, but the ground on which the mission stood is now a National Historic Site. The Spaldings established their mission among the Nez Perces, at Lapwai, about 125 miles away.

Both missions grew over the next few years, but ultimately neither the Whitmans nor the Spaldings gained the trust or acceptance of the Native Americans. Narcissa Whitman flung herself into missionary duties, teaching school, supervising domestic work at the mission, and taking in foster children. But after her two-year-old daughter was drowned in 1839 and her eyesight began to fail, and as it became clear that the Cayuse were resistant to Christianity, she became increasingly despondent. In November 1847, after the outbreak of an epidemic of measles, the Whitmans and twelve other whites were killed at Waiilatpu by Cayuse who feared the influx of white settlers and suspected Dr. Whitman of using witchcraft to kill their children. Eliza Spalding's career as a missionary was somewhat more successful than Narcissa Whitman's, as Spalding had speedily learned the language of the Nez Perces, taught in the mission school, and benefited from the greater enthusiasm with which the Nez Perces greeted their arrival. However, by the mid-1840s, the Nez Perces, like the Cayuse, recognized the encroachment of whites on their lands and became increasingly hostile to the white missionaries. The Spaldings escaped death in 1847, but closed their mission and moved to the Willamette Valley.[10]

The woman given credit for founding the Catholic school system in the United States was also inspired by her faith. Elizabeth Bayley Seton left one male-dominated church to join another, but in quitting the Episcopal Church to adopt Roman Catholicism she chose a church with a centuries-old framework for women's achievement, the religious order. Seton grew up in New York and in 1794, at the age of nineteen, married William Seton. They had five children, but in 1803 he died in Italy, where they had traveled in hope of improving his health. In Italy, Elizabeth Seton became friends with two of her husband's business associates, Antonio and Filippo Filicchi, and their wives, Amabilia and Mary, and under their influence she became a Roman Catholic. In New York City she attempted to support her family by running a boarding school, but the number of boarders declined, and in 1808 she accepted an invitation to start a school in Baltimore for Catholic girls. The number of Roman Catholics in the United States was still small, but in Maryland, which had been colonized as a haven for English Catholics, the church had a firm foundation. Seton's school was located in a house on Paca Street adjacent to the Chapel of St. Mary's Seminary, which was maintained by the Society of St. Sulpice. The Federal-style brick house, with two-and-one-half stories, was newly built when Seton arrived and still exists. She was pleased with the quarters but soon faced disappointment when her school attracted few pupils.

Seton harbored a desire to establish a sisterhood, and several months after her arrival in Baltimore she made some headway toward that goal. A wealthy Philadelphian studying for the priesthood, Samuel Sutherland Cooper, offered her a site at Emmitsburg, Maryland, and Seton soon sought recruits for her order, named the Sisters of Charity of St. Joseph. Seton took her first vows on March 25, 1809, in the Chapel of St. Mary's Seminary, a building of Gothic lines that had been dedicated the previous year and has since remained in con-

Mother Seton House, Baltimore, Maryland. (Photograph courtesy of Mother Seton House)

tinuous use. In June 1809, Seton and her sisters-in-law, Cecilia and Harriet Seton, and several pupils, established their community at Emmitsburg in a four-room farmhouse. By 1810 they moved into a larger building, called the White House, and the community grew rapidly. St. Joseph's School, a boarding school for girls from affluent families, funded the order's other activities, including free education for girls who lived nearby.[11]

In 1818, Sister Rose Philippine Duchesne and four other nuns of the Society of the Sacred Heart left France for Missouri, where they established schools for Native American and French children, including the first free school for girls west of the Mississippi. In St. Ferdinand's Parish (now Florissant), the sisters taught boarding students from well-to-do families and local day students, first in a log cabin and then in the brick convent built in 1819. The convent is considered one of the best examples of Federal-style architecture in Missouri and is listed on the National Register of Historic Places. A brick church was erected adjoining the convent in 1821 and both are now known as Old St. Ferdinand's Shrine. Here Duchesne also ran the first school for Native American girls in the country. In 1841, at the age of 72, she left the parish to open a school for Potawatomie children in Kansas.[12]

During the nineteenth century, with the massive immigration of Irish and German Catholics, nuns established convents throughout the United States. Most nuns came from Europe and retained connections with their mother houses. Their purpose was to minister to the religious and temporal needs of the immigrants; they established schools and performed most charity work in their dioceses. As a nun, a woman could play a significant role in a religion whose hierarchy was dominated by men. By 1900 there were four times as many sisters as priests in the United States. Because the sisters answered to superiors within their religious orders (often located in Europe) and were governed by the constitutions of their sisterhoods, they could resist demands of uncooperative bishops. For the most part, however, nuns and priests worked together to meet the religious, educational, and corporal needs of the church.[13]

Presbyterian women who opened the first seminaries for women in areas of the West were part of the early nineteenth-century movement to provide higher education for young women. Among the best known individuals who were part of this movement were Emma Willard, Zilpah Grant, and Mary Lyon who founded, respectively, the Troy, Ipswich, and Mount Holyoke female seminaries. Mary Olver established Edgeworth Ladies' Seminary as a day school in her Pittsburgh, Pennsylvania, home in 1825, and a few years later transformed the school into a boarding school, moving to Braddock's Field, a few miles away. After 1836, when the seminary again relocated, this time at Sewickley on the Ohio River, Olver helped to establish a Presbyterian church in the town by holding worship services at the school. The three-year course at Edgeworth was especially strong in science and mathematics, including physiology, algebra, geometry, geology, chemistry, and astronomy, as well as humanities and religion. Another Presbyterian woman, Sophronia Crosby, a student of Zilpha Grant at Ipswich Seminary, founded the Hanover Female Academy in Indiana under the sponsorship of the Synod of Indiana. She modeled the four-year course on Ipswich's curriculum and instituted admissions requirements. She left Hanover after her marriage to James A. McKee, a Presbyterian minister, but continued to educate young women in the two Indiana towns in which they subsequently lived.[14]

Thus, early in the nineteenth century, Protestant, Jewish, and Catholic women pushed against former restraints to take an active part in helping the poor, settling missions, and founding schools. Religions that for a long time had successfully incorporated more extensive ideas of gender equality than the mainstream European denominations discussed above were Native American religions and the Society of Friends. The religious beliefs of Native Americans were the heart of their cultures and were equally diverse. As a group, however, they can be distinguished from European faiths in a number of ways. Among Native Americans no distinction existed between the secular and the sacred—spirits inhabited the earth and heavens and could be found in stars, rocks, plants, and animals. Humans were part of nature, not lords of it, and therefore not superior to other beings. Above all was the omnipotent Master Spirit or Creator, who knew everything and was the source of all that was good. In most Native American traditions, the Creator had female as well as male attributes. As members of a community whose secular and religious spheres were fused, women participated fully in rituals, songs and dances, feasts, and ceremonies. Male adolescents embarked more often than girls on solitary quests in the woods in search of a guardian spirit; and men were more often the shamans who performed many of the rituals and induced trances that allowed them to predict the future, influence the weather, interpret dreams, and cure illnesses. Nevertheless, Native American women were excluded from neither role.[15]

Before the late eighteenth century, if an American woman of European origins or ancestry wanted to preach or to have a formal role in the authority structure of her church, she had to join (or have parents who were members of) the Society of Friends. From the earliest years of Quakerism, when George Fox gathered followers from among the radical sects that flourished during the English Civil War, Quaker leaders included women. Elizabeth Hooten was Fox's first convert and an early missionary. Mary Dyer, Katherine Evans, Elizabeth Harris, and many other "public Friends" took their message to places as far away as North America, the eastern Mediterranean, and Venice. Of fifty-nine missionaries who went from England to America between 1656 and 1663, twenty-six were women.

Quakers believed in direct inspiration of each individual by the Light, lay ministry, and spiritual rebirth, all of which were important to the status of women in the religion. Like the Puritans, Quakers held that men and women were equal before God, but the Friends did not end equality there. They believed that the Bible was not the last word, that the Light could bring new understanding. Thus, the Light now told them that women should speak in meetings and as missionaries and should help to govern the church. Saint Paul, they contended, was trying to end a dispute in Corinth when he directed the women there to be quiet, not speaking of all women. Quakers also rejected any continuing meaning of the story of Adam and Eve, arguing that with spiritual re-birth, the equality of women and men returned. Fox explained that "man and woman were helps-meet in the image of God, and in righteousness and holi-ness, in the dominion, before they fell; but after the fall in the transgression, the man was to rule over his wife; but in the restoration by Christ, into the image of God, and his righteousness and holiness again, in that they are helps-meet, man and woman, as they were before the fall."[16]

In addition to preaching, Quaker women were active in governing meet-ings, especially in making disciplinary decisions concerning women and girls, approving marriages, and caring for the poor. Margaret Fell, who married Fox after her first husband died, was instrumental in incorporating women into the governance of the Society. The Friends set up separate business meetings for women and men. Many meetinghouses had partitions that could be opened and closed. During meetings for worship held on First-day (Sunday) and usu-ally one other day during the week, the men and boys sat on one side of the meetinghouse and the women and girls sat on the other, with partitions open. Once a month they held business meetings and women and men met separately with partitions closed. Once a year Quakers from a large area gathered for Yearly Meeting, at which the most respected Friends sat together to consider weighty questions that had come before their local meetings; again, women and men had separate meetings.

Thus, in the Society of Friends, women had considerable power. They preached, participated in approving marriages, provided assistance to poor families, and disciplined women and girls. They did not have complete equality, however, because most women's meetings were required to seek the permission of men before disowning anyone, while the men did not reciprocate. However, in the meetings that have been studied, the men always approved the women's decisions. In evaluating the authority of Quaker women in the church, it is im-portant to separate the concept of autonomy or independence from authority. In the meeting, women Friends had authority over young Quaker women, but they did not act independently of men (who were for the most part their hus-bands). Both the women and men worked together toward the chief goals of both meetings—keeping families within the Society of Friends and ensuring that members avoided sin.[17]

The spatial arrangement of both the meetings for worship and monthly business meetings was emblematic of gender relationships within the Society. At worship, ministers and elders of both sexes sat at the front facing the con-gregation. Men and women were divided by sex, but both—at least theoretically—had equal opportunity to preach and pray. The separate busi-ness meetings, held with partitions closed or sometimes in separate buildings, underscored the authority of esteemed Quaker women over the welfare and be-havior of women and girls. With separation came constraints, however, as women's meetings lacked formal involvement in many kinds of decisions, for example those concerning the construction and design of new meetinghouses.

Quaker Meeting House, Philadelphia, Pennsylvania. (Photograph courtesy of
Library of Congress Prints and Photographs Division)

The Arch Street Meeting House, at Fourth and Arch Streets, has been the
site of Philadelphia Yearly Meeting since the building was completed in 1805
and is the oldest Friends meetinghouse extant within the city's original boundaries. Impetus for its construction came from women Friends, who were forced
to convene their Yearly Meeting remote from the men; the women's Yearly
Meeting was the first to meet in the structure. Situated on land owned by
Friends since the founding of Pennsylvania and secluded behind a high wall,
the meetinghouse represented the Quakers' decision, in the mid-eighteenth century, to remove themselves from the center of political power in the commonwealth established by William Penn. In the early nineteenth century, despite
participation in organizations for social reform, Friends viewed themselves as a
separate people. The Arch Street Meeting House, a two-story brick edifice with
a thirteen-bay front, projecting central pavilion, and hipped roof with cross ga-
ble, is an example of Quaker plain style.[18]

Lucretia Mott, Quaker minister and the premiere female abolitionist
and woman's rights activist of the antebellum period, attended Yearly Meeting
at the Arch Street Meeting House until 1827, when Friends split over inter-

pretation of doctrines into the Hicksite and Orthodox factions. Mott sided with the followers of Elias Hicks who believed that Orthodox Friends had adopted unacceptable religious practices from their evangelical Protestant neighbors. By early 1828, the Philadelphia Hicksites quickly built a meeting-house at Fifth and Cherry streets. In 1856, however, at the urging of women Friends who needed a larger and more adequately ventilated space in which to meet, the Hicksites moved their headquarters to Fifteenth and Race streets, where the Race Street Meeting House still stands. Whatever the bitter differences between the branches, which reunited in 1955, the Race Street Meeting House remained within the Quaker architectural tradition and, like its Arch Street counterpart, was built at a distance from the street and enclosed by a fence.[19]

The Quakers preserved an expanded role for women as the religion moved from its early years of prophecy and evangelism to a more institutionalized form. African-American Baptist women also had substantial formal responsibility in their churches. They not only led revivals and were "expected to have as full an experience as each man; to recount it; to shout and have joy; to be baptized and to continue to witness," but also served as deaconesses, disciplined wayward women, and ran church societies.[20]

Methodist women, on the other hand, were much less successful in keeping a voice and authority within their church. During the eighteenth century, when Methodist preachers combed the Atlantic seaboard seeking converts among men and women, black and white, many women were attracted by the Wesleyan message that God speaks directly to each individual who, whether male or female, should then work to bring others into the fold. As in the case of religion more generally, women were drawn to Methodism in greater numbers than men. Two-thirds of the members of the New York society in 1791 were women, and in 1801, 64 percent of the Philadelphia society were women. Susanna Wesley, the mother of John, was the "original Methodist," holding prayer meetings in her Lincolnshire, England, household for as many as two hundred neighbors. In the colonies, women were active in setting up new societies and as class leaders. Elizabeth Piper Strawbridge fostered the growth of Methodism in Frederick County, Maryland, while her husband, Robert, sought converts in neighboring counties. Beginning in the late 1760s, Mary Thorn of Philadelphia served as leader of two classes, and from the 1770s to at least 1794, Mary Wilmer, of the same society, led a class in her home.

By the early nineteenth century, however, when the Methodist Church hierarchy was in place and churches had been built, the public role of women was more restricted. While female membership had grown considerably, the number of women class leaders did not. Women lost opportunities to preach and lead congregations when worship services moved from the fields and homes into churches that were built in the traditional Christian design with pulpit situated at the front. After 1800, among Methodists, women were prohibited from preaching in church, and evidence that they traveled as exhorters is scant.[21]

While the vast majority of religious American women have found fulfillment within the patriarchal Judeo-Christian tradition, either by acquiescence to gender limitations or by pursuing measured strategies to broaden women's realm, a few have defied denominational authority. Their rebellion has taken various forms, but in all cases it has emanated from religious conviction rather than from a feminist imperative to break down barriers against women. Cumulatively, however, their battles have resulted in widening opportunity, though sometimes, as in the case of Anne Hutchinson, few positive consequences were readily apparent. For some, extant historic sites give testimony of their achievements; for others, little authentic material evidence remains.

Anne Hutchinson arrived with her family and settled in Boston in September 1634, just four years after the founding of the Massachusetts Bay Colony. She was forty-three years old, the mother of eleven surviving children, and a follower of John Cotton, a Puritan minister who had emigrated the year before. As a nurse and a midwife, Hutchinson quickly came into contact with many women in Boston and started holding religious meetings in her house. She was concerned that many people in Boston accepted the Covenant of Works, the belief that a person could achieve salvation by living a good, moral life. Instead, Hutchinson argued that greater emphasis should be placed upon the Covenant of Grace, that salvation could not be earned but rather was bestowed upon the "elect" by the Holy Spirit. Hutchinson, like Cotton, emphasized the individual's direct communication with God. Her opponents placed more weight on the authority of ministers and magistrates.[22]

Hutchinson directly challenged the restrictions placed on Puritan women by holding meetings to which both women and men were invited. She criticized in public the Puritan fathers, who tolerated little diversity of religious belief. She was arrested in 1637 and brought to trial by the orthodox faction headed by Governor John Winthrop. She stood accused of defaming ministers and their ministry; nevertheless, she nearly escaped conviction until she horrified her judges by announcing that she had received a revelation from God that they would be destroyed. They pronounced her a heretic and banished her from the colony. She went to Rhode Island with her family. When the Puritan magistrates subsequently heard that she had had a miscarriage, they interpreted this "monstrous birth" as evidence of God's rebuke. Later, after the death of her husband, Hutchinson moved with her youngest children to New Netherland, where she was killed by Native Americans. A statue on the Massachusetts State House grounds memorializes Hutchinson's stand as a battle for "civil liberty and religious toleration," which it was not. Hutchinson wanted to convince others that her interpretation of Puritan theology was correct, not increase the variety of acceptable views. Equally unsatisfactory is a plaque at the corner of School and Washington streets in Boston that reads: "On this site stood the house of Anne Hutchinson, a religious leader, brilliant, fearless, unfortunate. Banished to Rhode Island 1637. Killed by Indians 1643."[23]

Other women in early New England similarly confronted the Puritan magistracy. Anne Eaton, the wife of Theophilus Eaton, governor of New Haven, was tried in 1644 and excommunicated for opposing infant baptism. Because she was the governor's wife, her opposition to the strict New Haven orthodoxy was especially provocative. Mary Dyer, a follower of Hutchinson and fellow exile to Rhode Island, joined the Society of Friends while on a visit to England in the 1650s. The Quaker teaching that the Light comes to each individual was similar to Hutchinson's emphasis on the Covenant of Grace. In 1657 Dyer traveled as a missionary to Boston, where she was quickly imprisoned and exiled. She returned to the Puritan commonwealth three more times, despite passage of a law in 1658 prescribing the death penalty for Quakers who defied their banishment. In 1659, Dyer and two English Quakers, William Robinson and Marmaduke Stephenson, deliberately challenged the law, returning to Boston a month after they had been banished, to "look [the] bloody laws in the face." Robinson and Stephenson were hanged, but Dyer received a last-minute reprieve. When she appeared in Boston again the next year, her purpose was to sacrifice her life to "desire the repeal of that wicked law against God's people." This time, on June 1, 1660, she was executed. A statue in her memory now stands on the grounds of the Massachusetts State House.[24] The hanging of Mary Dyer by the Puritan authorities created considerable revulsion both among New Englanders and within the home government in London toward the colony's policy of religious intolerance. No more Quaker missionaries were put to death, and over the decades that followed, dissenters such as Quakers and Baptists were able to establish meetings.

In 1774, more than a century after Mary Dyer's execution, Ann Lee arrived in New York from England with eight associates. Reared in the Church of England, she was one of the founders of the Shakers, or the United Society of Believers in Christ's Second Appearing. She had been jailed in England several times for violating the sabbath. The Shakers believed that God had both male and female elements, and that the first coming of Christ was followed by the second coming of Lee, who was called Mother of the New Creation. Until her death in 1784, Ann Lee traveled through eastern New York and New England with news that the millennium, or period of God's reign on earth, had begun. She and her disciples inspired followers to join together in colonies on the basis of celibacy, salvation by confession of sin, equality within the church irrespective of sex and race, opposition to slavery and war, and charity to the poor. Both men and women served as leaders. The Shakers established twenty-five perfectionist communities between 1780 and 1826 from Maine to Ohio. Those at Sabbathday Lake (Maine), Hancock (Massachusetts), and Mount Lebanon (New York) are National Historic Landmarks. The Shaker communities aspired to self-sufficiency, with agriculture and shops in which men followed such trades as cordwainery, furniture making, and coopering, and women spun

Shaker Community Dining Room. (Photograph courtesy of Library of Congress Prints and Photographs Division)

and wove cloth. The design of each community, its buildings and furnishings, represented the discipline with which followers were expected to lead their daily lives. Members cut their food square, sat on straight-backed chairs, kept to footpaths laid out in right angles, and maintained female and male spheres in their living quarters. In religious worship, however, they abandoned right angle order, as they danced, whirled, sang, and shouted. Their meeting room had no pulpit or pews but instead was a large open space. Worshippers entered the meeting room in two groups, women and men separately, and faced each other. The space between them was the altar. Thus, while Shakers held many beliefs that were different from the Quakers, both groups abandoned the traditional spatial form of Christian worship that centered attention on the pulpit and confirmed the dominance of male leadership.[25]

In the early nineteenth century, several African-American women resisted male dominance in the young African Methodist Episcopal (A.M.E.) Church in Philadelphia. The black Methodists, led by Richard Allen, in 1794 refused to accept segregated seating at St. George's Church. They founded the Bethel A.M.E. Church at Sixth and Lombard streets, but adhered to the Methodist discipline, which forbade women from preaching in the church. Around 1809, Jarena Lee first challenged this rule, petitioning Reverend Allen for permission to preach. He refused and relented only eight years later, when she spoke extemporaneously during worship. On that occasion, she said, she felt God call upon her to interrupt the sermon of the Reverend Richard Williams, whom she felt "lost the spirit" as he began to preach. Williams's text was Jonah 2:9, "Salvation is of the Lord," and Lee told the Bethel congregation that she "was like Jonah; for it had been then nearly eight years since the Lord had called me to preach his Gospel to the fallen sons and daughters of Adam's race, but that I had lingered like him, and delayed to go at the bidding of the Lord, and warn those who are as deeply guilty as were the people of Ninevah." Lee felt, "during the exhortation, God made manifest his power in a manner sufficient to show the world that I was called to labor according to my ability, and the grace given unto me, in the vineyard of the good husbandman." She demonstrated her spiritual gifts and preached occasionally at Bethel until the 1830s, when the successors of Richard Allen closed the pulpit to her. During the 1820s, 1830s, and 1840s she itinerated on A.M.E. circuits through Pennsylvania, Delaware, Maryland, New Jersey, New York, Ohio, and Ontario. The Bethel church building in which Jarena Lee preached no longer stands. Four structures, each larger than the previous one, have been built on the lot at Sixth and Lombard, which is thought to be the piece of real estate in longest possession of African Americans in the United States. The current and only extant building was finished in 1890 and has been designated a National Historic Landmark.[26]

Another Philadelphia woman who felt God's spirit directly was Rebecca Cox Jackson, also affiliated with the Bethel A.M.E. Church. She belonged to one of many "praying bands" started by religious women in Philadelphia, Baltimore, and elsewhere that would lead later in the nineteenth century to the Holiness movement. The purpose of the praying bands was to seek "sanctification," a higher stage than "justification," or conversion. At justification, the individual felt that her sins were forgiven; with sanctification she became incapable of committing intentional sins. Women met together each week in the homes of members and developed speaking skills and confidence in their spirituality among a small group of women friends. Many African-American Methodist women, like Jarena Lee and Rebecca Cox Jackson, left the confines of the bands to preach their gospel to the world outside.

Jackson experienced conversion in 1830 and was sanctified in 1831. She made a covenant with God to follow an inner voice explicitly and to do nothing without divine guidance. She fasted, prayed for long periods, went without sleep, and wept; and as a result, she believed, experienced visions and special powers. She was convinced that God commanded her to practice celibacy and so she separated from her husband. Jackson preached in Philadelphia and surrounding communities, attacking the established churches for "carnality," or failure to teach sexual abstinence. In 1837, two centuries after Anne Hutchinson's trial and banishment, Jackson was accused of heresy by church leaders and estranged from her family and the A.M.E. Church. She apparently continued to travel and to preach during the next several years, although this is unverified because of a gap in her writings. In 1842 and 1843 she visited the Watervliet, New York, community of Shakers, who shared her belief in the fundamental importance of celibacy.[27]

The Shakers welcomed African Americans into membership, so Rebecca

Cox Jackson and her companion, Rebecca Perot, at first felt unity with the largely white Watervliet community when they went to live there in 1847. Within four years, however, Jackson believed that she must take her message to her people in Philadelphia. She accepted Shaker doctrine without reservation, but was ill at ease with the community's isolationism. Thus, Jackson, with Perot's assistance, established a Shaker mission in Philadelphia that existed from 1858 until at least 1908. Little is known about the mission before Jackson's death in 1871, but records from the 1870s show that the group of women lived in a large house, described as "almost palatial" with modern plumbing, central heating, and a drawing room large enough to seat twenty people. They earned their support as seamstresses, laundresses, and domestic workers. Their religious beliefs and practices were a combination of Shakerism and the traditions of the Methodist praying bands.

Rebecca Cox Jackson, then, found the freedom to worship according to the leadings of her spirit only when she established a community of her own. In doing so, she also attained authority within an institutional framework. At Watervliet she was subject to the will of the white eldresses, and as an itinerant preacher her power was fleeting. In Philadelphia she became an eldress herself and had the autonomy to mold a religious community based on her beliefs in celibacy, sanctification, and the power of the spirit within the individual.[28]

The first woman who surmounted the formidable obstacles to become an ordained minister in the Conregational Church was Antoinette L. Brown. In 1846, with the help of her father, she entered Oberlin College; upon graduation from the literary course the next year, she announced her intention to study for the ministry. Brown encountered opposition from her parents and teachers but was admitted to Oberlin's theological course. She was refused institutional support in obtaining opportunities for student preaching, however, and after finishing the course in 1850, she and another woman student were denied the degree. Nevertheless, churches in Ohio and New York state had opened their pulpits to Brown and in 1853, after several years on the abolitionist and women's rights lecture circuit, she became the first woman to be ordained in a major denomination in the United States.

Brown retained her pastorate at the First Congregational Church in South Butler, New York, for less than a year, because she was increasingly uncomfortable with Calvinist doctrines. The building in which she was pastor still stands but has been converted into a barn. Brown became a Unitarian. With her marriage in 1856 to Samuel Blackwell, brother of doctors Elizabeth and Emily Blackwell, and the birth of seven children (of whom five daughters survived), she did not make public appearances again until 1878. Blackwell contributed articles to the *Woman's Journal*, the organ of the American Woman Suffrage Association, and published several books in which she grappled with religious and feminist issues raised by the writings of Darwin and Spencer. She helped establish All Souls' Unitarian Church in Elizabeth, New Jersey, and served as its pastor emeritus from 1908 until her death at age 96 in 1921. Blackwell preached until 1915, continued to support the movement for women's suffrage, and voted in the first election held after ratification of the suffrage amendment.[29]

In the nineteenth and early twentieth century, three American women organized new major denominations: Ellen Harmon White, Mary Baker Eddy, and Aimee Semple McPherson. Ellen Harmon, as a teenager in Portland, Maine, became involved in the movement that was later institutionalized in the Seventh-Day Adventist Church. With her family, who were Methodists, she accepted the teachings of William Miller, an itinerant preacher from western New York who in 1842 brought the message that Jesus Christ would return to earth "about 1843." After many other followers returned to their former churches when Miller's prophecy proved false, Ellen Harmon continued to believe that the Advent was at hand, though the exact date could not be known. In 1844 she experienced the first of approximately two thousand visions and set out on a traveling ministry that she sustained through her life. Two years later she married James Springer White, another Adventist preacher, and together they organized the scattered Millerites into the Seventh-Day Adventist Church, centered in Battle Creek, Michigan. Ellen White's interpretation of biblical passages and support for a seventh-day sabbath, her visions, and prohibitions of meat, alcoholic beverages, tea, coffee, and drugs shaped Adventist faith and practice. Her tireless travels and lecturing, including missionary work in Australia from 1891 to 1900, encouraged the denomination's growth. In 1901, concerned that centralization in Battle Creek made the church susceptible to takeover by outsiders, White called for dispersal of church functions. The headquarters moved to Takoma Park, Maryland, near Washington, D.C. White purchased Elmshaven, a comfortable house near St. Helena, California, and lived there until her death in 1915. The house is now a historic site operated by the Seventh-Day Adventist Church.[30]

Mary Baker Eddy, like Ann Lee and Rebecca Cox Jackson, found the religion of her childhood unresponsive to her spiritual insights and needs. Reared in the Congregational Church in New Hampshire, Eddy experienced chronic spinal problems, nervousness, and fevers through the first four decades of her life—until she met Dr. Phineas Parkhurst Quimby in 1862. Quimby taught that disease had psychic causes and could be cured psychically as well. He believed that he could make others well with telepathy, even over long distances. Eddy's ailments were relieved by Quimby; she accepted the essence of his teachings and later used them as the basis for Christian Science, which she founded in 1875 at a house on Broad Street in Lynn, Massachusetts. There, and at the more permanent headquarters on Columbus Avenue, Boston, she held services and taught students, most of whom were women, the elements of healing through Christian Science. Eddy withdrew from instruction and supervision of day-to-day activities after 1890, but she kept a firm hand on the church's governance, watched it grow, and ensured that it would be an enduring institution. And while she failed to attend the dedication of either the Mother Church in

Boston in 1895 or the massive Extension finished in 1906, she oversaw completion of both. The original stone edifice was ingeniously designed to make maximum use of a kite-shaped lot. With its bell tower and an imposing interior that was focused upon a raised speaking platform, the Mother Church was clearly influenced by traditional Christian church architecture. Even so, the building was overwhelmed by the huge domed Extension, a temple constructed of white granite and Bedford stone and characterized by a combination of Byzantine and classical features. Twenty to thirty thousand people attended the six identical services dedicating the Extension. The Christian Science Church operates interpretive programs about the life and work of Mary Baker Eddy at six house museums in Massachusetts and New Hampshire.[31]

The most famous woman evangelist of the early twentieth century was Aimee Semple McPherson, founder of the International Church of the Foursquare Gospel. Born in 1890 in Ontario, Canada, she was converted by Pentecostal evangelist Robert James Semple, who in 1908 became her first husband. After his death in 1910 and a subsequent unhappy marriage to Harold Stewart McPherson, a bookkeeper from Providence, Rhode Island, Aimee Semple McPherson in 1915 commenced her career as an evangelist. With two small children and aided by her mother, Mrs. "Minnie" Kennedy, who was an excellent manager, McPherson preached her message of personal salvation and individual reform from Maine to Florida. Her fundamentalist teachings were based on a literal interpretation of scripture and included premillennialism, acceptance of revelation through "speaking in tongues," and the possibility of healing by the laying on of hands. In 1918, McPherson headed west to Los Angeles, where she constructed her Angelus Temple, a pie-shaped hall of which the arc was composed of double-doors opening to the street and the focal point was the pulpit. She raised funds in part by selling seats for $25 each and obtaining donations for such features as the eight thirty-feet high stained-glass windows that she designed herself. The temple was dedicated on New Year's Day, 1923. During the mid-1920s, wearing a distinctive white dress and blue cape, McPherson preached each night and three times on Sunday to overflow crowds of five thousand followers. Her sermons were dramatized, complete with painted backdrops, special lighting, and costumed actors. The Church of the Foursquare Gospel was based on "the fourfold ministry of the Lord Jesus Christ" as savior, provider of holy baptism, healer, and "coming King of kings." It offered telephone counseling, hot meals to hungry people, an employment service, Sunday school, summer camps, conferences, a radio station, magazines, and a Bible College, which trained over three thousand evangelists and missionaries, of whom many were women. The college was located adjacent to Angelus Temple in the five-story Lighthouse of International Foursquare Evangelism.[32]

For over three centuries religion has played a prominent role in the lives of American women. Before the adoption of the women's suffrage amendment in

Angelus Temple, Los Angeles, California. (Photograph courtesy of Angelus Temple Archives)

1920, religion was, along with benevolent and reforming activities, women's chief avenue of public expression and influence. Despite the fact women increasingly dominated church membership after the mid-seventeenth century, however, they had little formal authority in major denominations. Male clergy and laity monopolized the pulpits and decision-making, though there is evidence that women applied pressure informally to influence church affairs. Membership in denominations such as the Presbyterian, Congregational, and Episcopalian churches provided women with the comfort that comes from religious faith, in some cases intellectual stimulation, and participation (though circumscribed) in activities outside the home. In the nineteenth century, women of major denominations in the Judeo-Christian tradition increased their formal role by forming committees to help the poor, distribute Bibles, and encourage moral reform; traveling west to serve as missionaries; and founding schools and female seminaries.

A few religions offered women greater freedom for expression, authority, and personal growth than the major denominations. Women had a central place in Native American religions and in some cases became shamans. In the Society of Friends, women served as ministers and elders and had separate meetings to supervise poor relief and the behavior of Quaker women. African-American Baptist women were preachers and deaconesses. In Methodism, women lost ground as the denomination became institutionalized, but Jarena Lee was able to use the power of her spiritual gifts to claim her right to preach in the African Methodist Episcopal Church. Antoinette Brown fought to become the first ordained female Congregational minister, but soon left that faith. Other women, including Ann Lee, Rebecca Cox Jackson, Ellen White, Mary Baker Eddy, and Aimee Semple McPherson abandoned the mainstream churches in order to follow their religious leadings. Like Anne Hutchinson and Mary Dyer centuries before, they left the established churches in order to find spiritual fulfillment according to the dictates of their individual consciences.

Further study of the design of historic places of worship should help us understand more completely the spiritual journeys of these women. Mary Dyer rejected the male-dominated, pulpit-centered Puritan church to join the Quaker meeting, in which both women and men sat on the facing benches and could rise to speak. Ann Lee escaped the formal ritual and patriarchal organization of the Church of England to establish a religion in which God had both male and female natures and both women and men participated fully. Women in Jewish, Catholic, Congregational, Presbyterian, Episcopal, Baptist, and Methodist denominations expanded the scope of their activities by the early nineteenth century, but rarely did they ascend a pulpit. While many established schools and asylums, held prayer meetings at home, and preached in the fields and streets, just a few, not entirely successfully, challenged the gendered spatial organization of their places of worship. Not until Ellen White, Mary Baker Eddy, and Aimee Semple McPherson founded new denominations did women control church hierarchies. Indeed McPherson, with the exaggerated focus on the pulpit in Angelus Temple, upended the ancient symbolism of male dominance in Judeo-Christian tradition.

NOTES

1. David Hackett Fischer, *Albion's Seed: Four British Folkways in America* (New York: Oxford University Press, 1989), 117–25, 332–40; Rhys Isaac, *The Transformation of Virginia, 1740–1790* (Chapel Hill: University of North Carolina Press, 1982), 58–65.

2. Mary Maples Dunn, "Saints and Sisters: Congregational and Quaker Women in the Early Colonial Period," in *Women in American Religion*, ed. Janet Wilson James (Philadelphia: University of Pennsylvania Press, 1980), 27–32.

3. Elaine Forman Crane, " 'The Sin of an Ungoverned Tongue': Women and the Church in Colonial New England" (paper presented at the annual meeting of the American Historical Association, 1985).

4. Dunn, "Saints and Sisters," in *Women in American Religion*, 35–40; Gerald F. Moran, " 'Sisters' in Christ: Women and the Church in Seventeenth-Century New England," in *Women in American Religion*, 47–53.

5. Laurel Thatcher Ulrich, *Good Wives: Image and Reality in the Lives of Women*

in Northern New England 1650–1750 (New York: Oxford University Press, 1982), 215–21.

6. Joan R. Gunderson, "The Non-Institutional Church: The Religious Role of Women in Eighteenth-Century Virginia," *Historical Magazine of the Protestant Episcopal Church* 51 (1982):347–50.

7. Nancy F. Cott, *The Bonds of Womanhood: "Woman's Sphere" in New England, 1780–1835* (New Haven: Yale University Press, 1977), 126–59; Suzanne Lebsock, *The Free Women of Petersburg: Status and Culture in a Southern Town, 1784–1860* (New York: W. W. Norton, 1984), 195–236.

8. Page Putnam Miller, *A Claim to New Roles* (Metuchen, N.J.: The American Theological Library Association and the Scarecrow Press, 1985), 9–29, 83–110.

9. Sydney E. Ahlstrom, *A Religious History of the American People* (New Haven: Yale University Press, 1972), 572–73, 578–82; Ann Braude, "The Jewish Woman's Encounter with American Culture," in *Women and Religion in America, Volume 1: The Nineteenth Century*, ed. Rosemary Radford Ruether and Rosemary Skinner Keller (San Francisco: Harper & Row, 1981), 150–59.

10. Thurman Wilkins, "Narcissa Prentiss Whitman," in *Notable American Women 1607–1950: A Biographical Dictionary [NAW]*, ed. Edward T. James et al. (Cambridge: Harvard University Press, Belknap Press, 1971), 3:595–97; Clifford M. Drury, "Eliza Hart Spalding," in *NAW*, 3:330–31.

11. Annabelle M. Melville, "Elizabeth Ann Bayley Seton," in *NAW*, 3:263–65.

12. "Mother Duchesne: Pioneer Educator," *Landmarks Association of St. Louis, Inc.* 23, no. 2 (1988); "Old St. Ferdinand's Convent," *Florissant Valley Quarterly* 5 (April 1988): 1–3.

13. Mary Ewens, "The Leadership of Nuns in Immigrant Catholicism," in *Women and Religion in America*, 1:101–107.

14. Miller, *Claim to New Roles*, 178–81.

15. James Axtell, *The Invasion Within: The Contest of Cultures in Colonial North America* (New York: Oxford University Press, 1985), 14–19; Jacqueline Peterson and Mary Druke, "American Indian Women and Religion," in *Women and Religion in America, Volume 2: The Colonial and Revolutionary Periods*, ed. Rosemary Radford Ruether and Rosemary Skinner Keller (San Francisco: Harper & Row, 1983), 1–8.

16. Mary Maples Dunn, "Women of Light," in *Women of America: A History*, ed. Carol Ruth Berkin and Mary Beth Norton (Boston: Houghton Mifflin, 1979), 114–36; Jean R. Soderlund, "Women's Authority in Pennsylvania and New Jersey Quaker Meetings, 1680–1760," *William and Mary Quarterly*, 3d ser., 44 (1987):722–49.

17. Soderlund, "Women's Authority."

18. George Vaux, "Early Friends' Meeting-Houses and Their Relation to the Building at Arch and Fourth Streets," in *The Friends' Meeting-House Fourth and Arch Streets Philadelphia* (Philadelphia: John C. Winston, [1904]), 30–34; Richard J. Webster, *Philadelphia Preserved: Catalog of the Historic American Buildings Survey*, 2d ed. (Philadelphia: Temple University Press, 1981), 60.

19. Margaret Hope Bacon, *Valiant Friend: The Life of Lucretia Mott* (New York: Walker, 1980), 45; Frances Williams Browin, *A Century of Race Street Meeting House, 1856–1956* (Philadelphia: Central Philadelphia Monthly Meeting of Friends, 1956), 7–19.

20. Mechal Sobel, *Trabelin' On: The Slave Journey to an Afro-Baptist Faith* (Westport, Conn.: Greenwood Press, 1979), 207, 233.

21. Doris Elisabett Andrews, "Popular Religion and the Revolution in the Middle Atlantic Ports: The Rise of the Methodists, 1770–1800" (Ph.D. diss., University of Pennsylvania, 1986), 164–217.

22. Emery Battis, "Anne Hutchinson," in *NAW*, 2:245–47.

23. Lyle Koehler, *A Search for Power: The "Weaker Sex" in Seventeenth-Century New England* (Urbana: University of Illinois Press, 1980), 216–37; Battis, "Hutchinson," in *NAW*, 2:246–47; Marion Tinling, *Women Remembered* (Westport, Conn.: Greenwood Press, 1986), 40.

24. Frederick B. Tolles, "Mary Dyer," in *NAW*, 1:536–37.

25. *Gifts of Power: The Writings of Rebecca Jackson, Black Visionary, Shaker Eldress*, edited and with an introduction by Jean McMahon Humez (Amherst: University of Massachusetts Press, 1981), 25–32; Edward Deming Andrews, *The People Called Shakers: A Search for the Perfect Society*, 2d ed. (New York: Dover, 1963), 47–69; Andrews, "Ann Lee," in *NAW*, 2:385–87; Dolores Hayden, *Seven American Utopias: The Architecture of Communitarian Socialism, 1790–1975* (Cambridge: MIT Press, 1976), 65–103.

26. *Gifts of Power*, 311–16, 321–27, 355; Webster, *Philadelphia Preserved*, 7.

27. *Gifts of Power*, 1–25, 311–16.

28. Ibid., 25–50.

29. *The Feminist Papers: From Adams to de Beauvoir*, ed. Alice S. Rossi (1973; reprint, Boston: Northeastern University Press, 1988), 340–46; Barbara M. Solomon, "Antoinette Louisa Brown Blackwell," in *NAW* 1:158–61; Elizabeth Cazden, *Antoinette Brown Blackwell: A Biography* (Old Westbury, N.Y.: The Feminist Press, 1983); Lynn Sherr and Jurate Kazickas, *The American Woman's Gazetteer* (New York: Bantam Books, 1976), 175–76.

30. C. C. Goen, "Ellen Gould Harmon White," in *NAW*, 3:585–88.

31. Sydney E. Ahlstrom, "Mary Baker Eddy," in *NAW*, 1:551–61; Joseph Armstrong and Margaret Williamson, *Building of the Mother Church* (Boston: Christian Science Publishing Society, 1980), 8–9, 78–83, 112–13, 144–47; Sibyl Wilbur, *The Life of Mary Baker Eddy* (Boston: Christian Science Publishing Society, 1907), 327–30, 334, 342.

32. William G. McLoughlin, "Aimee Semple McPherson: 'Your Sister in the King's Glad Service,' " *Journal of Popular Culture* 1 (1967):193–217; McLoughlin, "Aimee Semple McPherson," in *NAW*, 2:477–80; David L. Clark, "Miracles for a Dime: From Chautauqua Tent to Radio Station with Sister Aimee," *California History* 57 (1978–79):354–63.

8 ◆ Women and Work

LYNN Y. WEINER

Nothing short of a revolution has occurred in the history of women and work in the United States. The female labor force has more than tripled in size during the past century, yet for most of American history working women have been invisible—their labors undercounted by the census, ignored in standard histories, and distorted in popular culture. Recent scholarship has begun to piece together the complex picture of women's lives during the past three centuries. Scholars now recognize the experience not only of industrial laborers but also of housewives and domestic workers, western pioneers, office and sales clerks, farm women, entrepreneurs, and professionals in fields such as health care, aviation, social work, and education. Taking a closer look they note that segregation in the labor force exists not only by sex but by race, class, geographical location, and family status. There is not one story of working women in America, but many.

The rich and complex history of working women is captured in the stories of women told both collectively and individually. The interpretation of traditional historical sources such as census and government data, written documents, and oral history can be augmented by the study of tangible resources in the built environment which enhance our understanding of women's contributions to the family economy, to national production, and to the development of the professions. Such resources include southern plantations, factories, ranches in the West, and the buildings associated with such notable individuals as iron manufacturer Rebecca Lukens, pioneering nurse Clara Barton, astronomer Maria Mitchell, and Madame C. J. Walker, a black entrepreneur who was the first self-made woman millionaire in America. The preservation of these sites contributes to the collective memory in a powerful way.

Definitions of work shaped standard accounts of the numbers of wage-earning women during the past century. Employment considered "nonproductive" or difficult to assess was hidden in history. Housework, child care, agricultural labor, the keeping of boarders and lodgers, and industrial home work are among the activities missing from traditional labor histories. The pattern for visible wage-earning employment is one of steadily accelerating participation by women. In 1870, when records first became available on a national level, women represented less than one-fifth of the labor force. Only 14 percent of all women worked for wages, and the vast majority of them were young, single, and working temporarily until they married. A century later, in 1970, over one-third of all women worked, and the majority of women workers were married. By 1987, almost 60 percent of all women worked for wages, representing almost half of the American labor force. Today, married women, including mothers of young children, routinely seek employment.[1] Not only the size but the composition of the female labor force changed radically in a relatively short period of time.

The rapid entrance of women into the labor force stimulated various expressions of social change in America. Concerns with the morality and well-being of young working girls in the nineteenth century led to the establishment of boarding homes and clubs and the promotion of such pioneering labor legislation as maximum hour laws, safety and sanitary regulations, and the minimum wage. Unions attempted to improve work conditions for this new population of laborers. As more mothers sought employment after the mid-twentieth century, the need for day care and family legislation attracted public notice.

This chapter presents a broad survey of the history of women workers in the United States. The essay opens with a look at the experiences of women working through the colonial era, primarily in agriculture and household production. Next considered is the rise of industrial labor and factory work in the nineteenth and twentieth centuries. A survey of the entrance of women into the professions follows discussion of the participation of women in the settlement of the West and the growth of white-collar work. The essay concludes with a general discussion of women workers in American society. Throughout, reference is made to some of the historic sites in which these women lived and labored.

Agriculture has long been an important occupation for women, although their work in farm and field often has been undervalued. Since colonial times women labored on farms and plantations as producers for a family economy. The majority of Americans did not live in cities until 1920, so for much of our history, agriculture dominated the work experience of women as well as men.

The first women to work in America were the Native Americans. Little is known about the lives of Native American women, especially during the years before European settlement. Although there is evidence that some Native

American women were active as hunters, warriors, traders, sachems, and tribal leaders, most apparently worked to cultivate, gather, and process food, weave baskets and blankets, tan clothing and hides, and nurture their children.[2] Evidence of women as processors of food is reflected at Indian Grinding Rock State Park in California. There, a large sheet of granite is embedded with the marks of mortars, left by generations of Miwok women who ground acorns into flour, a task that was solely women's work. Despite their importance to the tribal economy, Native American women usually did not share the higher status of men, who achieved glory within their tribes through military and hunting achievements.

As Europeans colonized the continent in the seventeenth century and beyond, women participated in what historians call "household manufactures." Men and women were responsible for producing the food, goods, and services necessary for family survival in the new settlements. Women tended gardens and animals; pickled, canned, and preserved food; produced clothing, candles, soaps, and furniture; and in other ways contributed to the family economy. While this work was still defined by gender—men usually performed the outside work in fields and barns, and women did the inside tasks of house and garden—the work was nevertheless valued.[3] It was not until the onset of industrialism in the early nineteenth century and the subsequent separation of wage work from the home that a powerful ideology arose to define woman's place in society as strictly domestic and nonproductive.

Most colonial women worked at household or agricultural tasks. But there were exceptions, especially among widows and single women, who generally had more legal rights to make contracts and own property than did wives. There are records, for example, of women owning their own businesses and operating taverns, boardinghouses, sawmills, slaughterhouses, tanneries, upholstery shops, dry-goods stores, and barbershops. Mrs. Jose Glover of Cambridge, Massachusetts, owned the first printing press in the colonies, founded in 1638. Margaret Brent was a landowner, business agent, and executor for the governor of Maryland during the late 1640s. Margaret Philipse, of New Amsterdam, became a shipowner and merchant during the 1660s.[4] Unfortunately few structures remain standing to shed more light on the working and domestic environments of these women.

Far more typical work for women at this time was domestic service. About half of all women colonists came to America as indentured servants. They were generally young single women who contracted to work for four to seven years in return for passage from Europe to the New World. At first, these women were viewed as "help," as apprentices in the households in which they worked. But by the mid-nineteenth century, household workers were seen as servants, performing specialized work and acquiring a more distant and unequal relationship with their employers.[5]

During the antebellum era the rise of the domestic ideology, spread through new women's magazines such as *Godey's Ladies Book*, domestic novels, and sermons, defined the home as the middle-class woman's central place in society. Household maintenance, child rearing, and other domestic labors became woman's province alone; she was also to create a morally superior environment at home. If genteel poverty mandated employment, then teaching, dressmaking, or such home work as coloring fashion plates for magazines were considered acceptable occupations. Working-class women labored as seamstresses or in other employments without exciting much public concern.

From the outset, the experience of African American women diverged from whites. Black men and women were at first also indentured, implying a temporary period of servitude, but by the 1640s in Virginia they were considered to be slaves for life; by 1662 slavery was legalized in all the colonies. African American women were excluded from the domestic ideology. As one European visitor to the antebellum South noted, black women " . . . are not considered to belong to the weaker sex."[6]

Black women, brought to America as slaves, toiled in the fields and houses of their owners. Seven out of eight slaves worked in the South, on large and small plantations. Many extant properties, such as Mount Vernon and lesser-known structures, contain evidence of the slave quarters where these women lived. As agricultural laborers, black women plowed fields, picked cotton, laid fences, threshed wheat, harvested rice and sugar cane, pitched hay, and repaired roads. They worked up to fourteen hours a day under the hot sun alongside men. But the lives of these women were also burdened with additional demands. They were expected to produce more slaves—their children—for their owners. In the slave quarters, they tended gardens, prepared food and clothing, and performed the tasks needed for their own families and communities. In the North both slave and free black women worked as laundresses, cooks, dressmakers, hairdressers, and weavers and spinners. After slavery was outlawed in 1865, the majority of African American women continued to work as sharecroppers in the South and domestic servants in the North.[7]

During the antebellum era, a freedwoman named Marie Therese Coincoin achieved unusual fame as the operator of a successful plantation, known first as Yucca Plantation, then as Melrose. Born a slave in about 1742, Coincoin lived with a Frenchman named Claude Metoyer who purchased her freedom and deeded her substantial land holdings on the banks of the Cane River in Louisiana. There she successfully cultivated tobacco, corn, cattle, and cotton, exported wild bear grease to Europe, and was able with her profits to buy the freedom of her children and grandchildren. The buildings on the 13,000 acre estate, now a National Historic Landmark (NHL), are being restored. The plantation includes Yucca House, built of hand-hewn cypress, and African House, a unique structure built around 1800 with an umbrella-like roof; it is the only authentic Congolese architecture in America.[8]

The majority of women, black as well as white, who worked for wages in the years before 1940 usually toiled anonymously as domestic servants or in agriculture. Material reminders of the era when servants lived in private homes are the second staircases and the servants' quarters—extra rooms, often at the back or tops of houses—which separated the domestic lives of servant and employer. The Abraham Lincoln house in Springfield, Illinois, contains such a room. In the South the juxtaposition of slave quarters and the Big House on the plantations illustrates the more striking physical separation of master and slave.

At the turn of the century nearly half of American families still lived on farms, and farm women were active partners in their families' efforts to raise and sell crops and other products. In the Southwest through the twentieth century, Mexican-American women followed the harvest with their families and helped fill a migrant agricultural labor force. As wage work for women developed in the cities, however, the work of women in agriculture lost visibility in America.

The labor history of women entered a new stage when the first successful textile factory in the United States was organized in 1793 in Pawtucket, Rhode Island, by Samuel Slater and his associates. The Slater Mill Historic Site preserves the Old Slater Mill, restored to its 1835 appearance, with exhibits focusing on the evolution of the textile industry and the transition of hand to machine production. Other factories quickly sprang up on the banks of rivers throughout New England well into the early nineteenth century, making cloth manufacture, long a task performed by women in their homes, an occupation increasingly performed in the workplace. Hoping to avoid the "dark Satanic mills" of English industrial towns known for their population congestion and labor unrest, American factory owners at first recruited young unmarried farm women for their labor needs. These farmers' daughters, according to the manufacturers, would "avoid the sin of idleness" while working in the factories until they married, and would not only earn money to support themselves and their families but would benefit from the cultural programs and supervised housing provided by the mill owners. They were also cheaper to hire than men. By 1816, two out of three industrial workers in the United States were women. Through the 1840s, women factory operatives enjoyed an international reputation as an innovative and respectable labor force. Visitors from around the world included the New England mills on their tours of America.

These first factory workers were commonly known as Lowell mill girls, after the workers at the mills in Lowell, Massachusetts, built on the bank of the Merrimack River. Known as the "City of Spindles," Lowell contained at one time thirty-three mills and some five hundred boardinghouses. The mill complex is today an NHL and a unit of the National Park Service, preserving seven extant mill yards and their machinery, a company agent's residence, ten principal canals or feeders which were used to power the mills, and four red brick boardinghouses—the latter reflecting the paternalistic ideology of the mill owners who sought to supervise every aspect of the lives of their women workers. This site is considered one of the most historically significant aggregations of early-nineteenth-century industrial structures and artifacts in the United

Boott Cotton Mill, Boarding House Number 7, Lowell National Historic Park, Lowell, Massachusetts. (Photograph courtesy of the Lowell Historic Preservation Commission)

States, and it brings to life the environment in which thousands of female industrial workers in America lived and labored.

Seventy-five percent of the early Lowell mill workers were women, and they received about half of the wages offered to men. Typically they worked twelve to fourteen hours a day, for about two dollars a week, in mills grouped around a quadrangle of trees and flowers. They worked at a variety of tasks, including weaving, spinning, warping, and carding wool. Working conditions could be unbearable as the windows were kept closed to maintain humidity; in the winter months over 300 lamps burned and with as many as 150 operatives in one room the air would become thick with fumes.

Unmarried women workers were required to live in the company boarding-houses, which, like the extant Boott Mill Boarding House, contained rooms for a supervising landlady, communal dining and washing, and upper story dormitories housing four to eight women. The workers were expected to be in by curfew, not dance or act in an immoral fashion, obey the matrons, and attend church regularly. Remarkably, after the long day in the mills they also attended lectures, literary clubs, and language classes. In Lowell today, the Lucy Larcom Park, named for a textile operative known for her writings, is part of a tour of sites that includes a lyceum, boardinghouse, mill, labor association, and girls' club—the physical structures which defined this now lost world of women's factory labor.

The Lowell mill operatives published magazines such as the *Lowell Offering* and the *Voice of Industry*, indicating both gratitude for the experience of working and criticisms of the long hours and harsh conditions attending their work and efforts to unionize. These latter efforts, combined with waves of Irish and German immigration in the 1840s, resulted in change in the population of factory workers, as immigrants of both sexes replaced the native-born farm women. Subsequently the status of factory labor as an occupation for women declined.[9]

Slave women during this period also toiled in cotton and woolen mills under the direction of white supervisors, and manufactured sugar, tobacco, rice, and hemp. Seven-day work weeks were not uncommon, and health conditions were miserable. Women were believed to be more adept in some forms of factory work, although slave factory labor was generally believed to be less efficient than free labor in the North.[10]

By the late nineteenth century female factory work, now spread throughout the urban centers of the nation, had for the most part become the province of white immigrant women and their daughters. Women toiled in factories that produced items including shoes, hats, books, cigars, clothing, and boxes. Working conditions were abysmal. Hours were long, wages low, and sanitary and safety conditions nonexistent. Still, many urban young women preferred employment in factories to work as domestic servants, for if their hours were long and the tasks hard, at least they had the companionship of other women and the knowledge that time after the factory bell rang was their own.

In the South, textile factory owners often employed the family labor system, where men, women, and children were hired as a package, providing cheap labor at a lower cost. Work in the mills was segregated by sex. A typical factory experience for women occurred in Durham, North Carolina, at the Bull Durham Tobacco Factory, now a National Historic Landmark, first known as the Blackwell and Company Tobacco Factory. Thousands of women worked there from the mid-nineteenth century through the twentieth century. Their work was segregated by both gender and race. Black women processed dried tobacco, removing the stem and ribs of the leaf by hand. White women caught, weighed, and counted the finished cigarettes as they left the machines.[11]

In the North, factory workers were usually young, unmarried, white immigrant women or their daughters. These workers were employed in such industries as shirtwaist manufacture—about forty thousand operatives, four out of five of them women, were employed in this industry. The Triangle Shirtwaist Factory, located on the top floors of the Asch Building (now known as the Brown building) in New York City, was the largest of the many companies that produced shirtwaists—blouses worn with long dark skirts that were the conventional apparel of professional and white-collar women workers. Like other factories and sweatshops of its kind, conditions were intolerable. Sewing machines, dripping oil, rested on wooden tables jammed together amid piles of cloth and material. The air was heavy with flammable lint. Narrow staircases descended through drafty wells, doors opened inward, and the sound of clattering machines was deafening.

On March 25, 1911, fire erupted at the Triangle Shirtwaist Factory. The doors of the building were usually locked to keep workers in and labor organizers out. Because of the locked doors and the lack of sprinklers and fire escapes, 146 of the 500 workers perished in the flames or died after jumping from ninth-story windows.[12] Intense public outrage after the fire contributed to pioneering labor legislation which included factory inspection laws, reductions in working hours, an end to child labor, and the passage of fire safety measures. Although the interior of the Brown Building, which has been nominated for historic site status, now contains New York University classrooms, its importance as a symbol of women's labor history remains; yearly the International Ladies Garment Workers Union gathers outside the building to commemorate the lives lost in the Triangle Shirtwaist fire and recall the hard-won victories of the labor movement.

The profile of the woman factory worker changed dramatically during the 1940s, when the enormous demand for labor required by World War II caused employers for the first time to encourage married women and mothers to work outside the home. The military draft, combined with a dire need for wartime production, led to a severe labor shortage resolved by the employment of millions of women, many of whom had never before worked for wages. Government agencies such as the War Manpower Commission, supported by the active cooperation of the media, encouraged women to work. Soon "Rosie the Riveter" became the national symbol of the woman war worker, whose labor represented her patriotic duty not only to the nation but also to support her husband at war. Rosie the Riveter appeared as a housewife in overalls and factory goggles, who " . . . instead of cutting the lines of a dress, . . . cuts the pattern of aircraft parts."[13] The female labor force grew by 50 percent during the war years as some six million women, most of them married, took jobs for the first time to produce engines, guns, and tanks in war plants, and worked, as well, in some two million war-generated clerical jobs. Other women left poorer-paying jobs as domestic servants or textile operatives to find more lucrative work in the war industry. Factories such as the Kaiser Industries shipbuilding business in Oregon attempted to reduce absenteeism and meet the needs of these new workers with pioneering social services such as on-site day care, community kitchens, and the first health maintenance organizations. The Community Facilities Act, also known as the Lanham Act, provided over $50 million to support federal day-care centers for more than 1.5 million children of women war workers.[14]

But after the war, women, like men, were demobilized. Between 1945 and 1946, more than three million women left the labor force because of layoffs

Sidewalk scene of the Triangle Shirtwaist Factory fire in 1911, New York, New York. (Photograph courtesy of the Tamiment Institute Library, New York University)

Brown Building, New York, New York. From 1902 to 1911, the Triangle Shirtwaist Factory occupied the eighth, ninth, and tenth floors of this building. (Photograph by Andrew Dolkart)

and demotions. The federal day-care centers were closed, pay scales dropped, and public opinion favoring the employment of married women weakened. Ironically, while the popular notion of the postwar era is that women willingly returned home to be full-time housewives and icons of domesticity, it was during the 1950s that married women began to markedly increase their participation in the labor force.

Women have a long history of involvement in union activities, beginning in the New England textile mills in the 1820s and continuing through strikes of factory workers, seamstresses, and even domestic servants during the nineteenth century. The first "turnout" occurred in 1828 in Dover, New Hampshire, when hundreds of mill workers paraded with banners and flags to protest such rules as fines for lateness, mandatory church attendance, and bans against talking on the job. Lowell factory operatives, led by mill worker Sarah Bagley, formed the Female Labor Reform Association in 1845 and petitioned the state of Massachusetts for a ten-hour day. In 1881 the Knights of Labor opened membership to women and 192 women's assemblies were founded by 1886. Some fifty thousand "lady knights" participated in strikes of hatmakers, textile workers, and carpet weavers.[15]

In 1903, the National Women's Trade Union League opened its headquarters in Chicago, promoting the motto: "The eight-hour day; a living wage; to guard the home." Bringing together middle-class women reformers and working women, the League provided a forum for such prominent union activists as Rose Schneiderman, Leonora O'Reilly, Margaret Dreier Robins, and Mary Anderson, the shoeworker who went on to become the first director of the Women's Bureau of the U.S. Department of Labor.[16] The League supported a variety of labor movements, including the historic shirtwaist workers' strike in New York City during the winter of 1909–1910, which involved an estimated twenty thousand garment workers, including employees of the Triangle Shirtwaist Company.

Mary Harris Jones, known as "Mother Jones," was one of the most prominent labor activists of the early twentieth century. She is perhaps best known for her work organizing coal miners in West Virginia and Colorado, although she also organized railroad workers and lobbied against child labor. The imprisonment of Mother Jones during the historic 1912–1913 coal strikes brought nationwide attention to the labor situation in West Virginia; the house in Pratt, West Virginia, where she was confined for three months has been nominated for Historic Site status because her imprisonment there had a significant impact on coal miners and the coal industry nationally. At the Union Miners Cemetery in Mt. Olive, Illinois, a monument to Mother Jones includes a twenty-two-foot-high column flanked by bronze statues of miners; fifty thousand workers attended the ceremony dedicating the monument in 1936.[17]

In the West, another symbol of women's labor activism rests at the California Walnut Growers Association Building in Los Angeles. Workers in that industry were usually young, unmarried, immigrant women who shelled walnuts for low wages. Their unionizing efforts with the United Cannery, Agricultural, Packing and Allied Workers of America modeled a democratic, decentralized union that organized both men and women from a multiethnic workforce, and included Mexican-Americans and immigrants from Russia and other parts of Eastern Europe. The CWGA Building conveys both the power and resources of the agricultural industry; the building included offices, warehouse facilities, and walnut shelling operations, and represents as well the efforts of women to organize for better working conditions.[18]

On the whole, however, women did not benefit from unions to the same degree as men. Male-dominated unions, fearing that women would work for lower pay, long excluded women from their ranks, and working women themselves often viewed their employment as a temporary measure before marriage. Further, employers actively blocked the formation of unions. During World War I, an era of high union organization among male workers, less than 10 percent of women in manufacturing belonged to unions; in 1924, less than 5 percent of women workers were organized. By 1980, some 16 percent of employed women, compared to about 28 percent of working men, were union members.[19]

The contributions of women to the settling of the West are just recently being acknowledged. On the arduous migration west, they not only performed domestic chores but also drove teams of oxen and collected fuel and food. They were full partners in the establishment of homesteads, ranches, and farms. One observer suggested in 1886 that women held one-third of the land in the Dakotas. By the turn of the century, records show that almost 15 percent of all homesteaders in the West were women. In 1909, Elinore Pruitt, a widowed laundress from Denver, arrived in Wyoming to work as a housekeeper and soon filed her own homestead entry. She believed that homesteading was a better occupation for women than factory work. Although she married Clyde Stewart and eventually failed in her own efforts to homestead, she gained fame for her book *Letters of a Woman Homesteader*, which presents homesteading as a panacea for the poor woman with its potential for economic independence. Her homestead house, still standing in Wyoming's Burntfork Valley, is constructed of heavy, rough-hewn logs and typifies the characteristics of homestead construction.[20]

Ranch women, like farm women, worked alongside their husbands and when widowed, sometimes took over the management of the ranch and herds. Henrietta Chamberlain King, for example, inherited Santa Gertrudis, a National Historic Landmark now known as King Ranch, in Kingsville, Texas, when her husband died in 1885. At the time it was, at 500,000 acres, the biggest ranch in Texas, and burdened with debts of $500,000. For forty years King headed the ranch, leaving an estate of over $5 million and doubling the size of the property.[21]

The shortage of women in the West was often acute; in 1850, for example, only 8 percent of the residents of California were women. As a result of more liberal laws than in the East and unusual economic opportunities, women established saloons and restaurants, provided bakery and laundry services, invested in real estate, and in other ways tried to profit from frontier conditions. In Alaska during the 1920s, Rika Wallen, a Swedish immigrant, operated a roadhouse on the Richardson Trail, which exemplifies not only the transportation and communication networks of the period but also the common work of women as hotel and boardinghouse keepers, both in cities and on the frontier. Rika's log roadhouse, about ninety-five miles south of Fairbanks, is today on the National Register of Historic Places and is part of an Alaskan State Historical Park, which includes other pioneer log structures, a windmill, and a wrecked steamboat skeleton.[22]

Occasionally women turned to prostitution. While for some, prostitution was a matter of choice, for others, like the thousands of women who were kidnapped in China and sold in California, prostitution was slavery. Prostitution was, of course, not limited to the West, but had been long a feature of city life in the East, where public and religious officials had complained of sexual vice since the early eighteenth century. In the late nineteenth and early twentieth centuries cities often contained legally established red light districts to encompass brothels and taverns; Storyville in New Orleans, for example, numbered some 230 houses of prostitution during this era. In many working-class communities, prostitution was viewed as a consequence of poverty and lack of other options, rather than as a moral outrage.[23]

By the end of the nineteenth century, the development of new occupations opened opportunities that at first benefited young, single, native-born white women. This white-collar work was deemed more respectable than factory work, for it required a middle-class appearance and a modicum of education. The demand for this labor fit well with a growing supply of young, educated native-born white women who desired work without losing class status.

Women found employment as salesclerks in the new department stores built during the late nineteenth century by entrepreneurs like R. H. Macy in New York and Marshall Field in Chicago. In 1870, women salesclerks were "too few to count" by the census; within thirty years there were 142,000 of them. By the turn of the century, sales, which had once been a man's occupation, had become largely a profession for women. But where sales work for men was often an apprenticeship for eventual managerial or entrepreneurial status, sales work for women was seen by store owners as a short-term career before marriage. Women were in demand as salesclerks because they were believed to be more effective with women customers, more tractable as employees, and were paid less than men. From the workers' point of view, department-store sales offered opportunities for advancement, social status, and a sociability with co-workers unavailable in many other types of occupations.[24]

Similarly, office work became feminized during the last quarter of the nineteenth century. Clerical work was originally an occupation for young men, who learned the basics of business while keeping accounts and copying documents. The first women office workers were hired by the federal government during the labor shortage of the Civil War to clip and count currency for the Bureau of Printing and Engraving. During the 1870s and beyond, as bureaucracies and corporations grew and the commercial typewriter came into use, the nature of office work changed. Hierarchical structures of authority and an increasing division of labor lessened opportunities for advancement and decision making by individuals. At the same time, a rapid increase in the need for office workers merged with a ready pool of educated young workers available at lower wages than men. Women by the thousands found work as "typewriters," stenographers, copyists, and clerks. Advocates for women clerical workers suggested they would make better wives and mothers by learning how to be systematic, that their "higher moral caliber" would improve the office, and that typewriting was more suitable in any case for the "delicate" hands of women. By the 1890s, about half of all women high school graduates trained for jobs in offices. Within fifty years, office work replaced domestic service as the single most common occupation of women. African American women, too, increased their representation in clerical work. By the 1980s, about 30 percent of white and 26 percent of black women workers were employed as clerical workers in offices.[25]

By the early twentieth century the "pink collar" work of cosmetology offered another new avenue of employment for women. Beauty parlors and an interest in commercial preparations for hair and body care grew. In 1920, there were 5,000 beauty parlors in the United States; by 1925, the number had risen to 25,000.[26]

One pioneer in the business of beauty was Sarah Breedlove Walker, commonly known as Madame C. J. Walker. The first self-made woman millionaire in the United States, Sarah Breedlove began life as the daughter of former slaves. In mid-life she developed an enormously successful cosmetics company, based on her invention in 1905 of a hair formula and her later production of skin care items for African American consumers. The company was notable for its use of black women as sales agents and beauty culturists at a time when there were few employment outlets for black women outside of domestic service, manual labor, and agriculture. Some three thousand women, characteristically dressed in black skirts and white blouses, traveled throughout the United States, Central America, and the Caribbean introducing black women to the Walker hair and skin care systems. The national headquarters and manufacturing site for the company were housed in the four story Walker Building in Indianapolis beginning in 1910, a structure serving not only as a center for black female employment but also as a community cultural center including a theatre and ballroom. The restored building stands today as a tribute not only to Madame Walker and her philanthropies, but also as one of the few remaining examples of the Africanized architecture popularized in the 1920s and 1930s.[27]

The movement of women into the professions began in the nineteenth century, reflecting in part the increasing number of women receiving a higher education. The majority of women professionals worked in fields that could be construed as "nurturing" or "social housekeeping." These professions, which included nursing, teaching, library and social work, were believed to be extensions of women's domestic sphere. Women also made inroads into such traditionally male professions as medicine, law, and aviation. Still, the professions, like other areas of women's work, remained gender-divided. The entry of large numbers of women into a field typically drove down wages and led to the feminization of the profession. Moreover, men tended to dominate the more prestigious and administrative positions, even in fields that were highly feminized.

Nursing has long been considered a woman's profession. Before the mid-nineteenth century, nursing was akin to domestic service. Nurses not only cared for the ill, but cooked, cleaned, and laundered for their patients. During the Civil War some three thousand women on both sides of the conflict worked as nurses, often without pay. The U.S. Sanitary Commission, founded in 1861, raised money for medical supplies and recruited nurses for work on behalf of the Union. Dorothea Dix, already famous as a prison reformer, was appointed Superintendent of Army Nurses. When male physicians resisted the work of these nurses, arguing that women shouldn't care for strange men, the women responded that "the right of woman to her sphere, which includes housekeeping, cooking and nursing, has never been disputed." Training schools for nurses were established after the Civil War, and by 1890, there were thirty-five schools that contributed towards the standardization and professionalization of nursing practice. Clara Barton, who trained nurses during the Civil War and also collected provisions for the soldiers in the battlefields, founded the American Red Cross in 1882. Her thirty-six-room house in Glen Echo, Maryland, an NHL and unit of the National Park Service, reflects her pragmatism and ingenuity, for it was built partially from lumber salvaged from the disastrous Johnstown, Pennsylvania, flood of 1889 and was designed not just for her residence but also to store relief supplies and accommodate Red Cross workers. The house also served as the national headquarters of the Red Cross until 1904, when Barton resigned as head of the organization at the age of eighty-three.[28]

Midwifery, an occupation related to nursing, has followed a different historical path. Midwives, who were the usual attendants to birth in colonial America, had been pushed aside by obstetricians as the medical profession developed in the nineteenth century. Still, midwives continued to work, especially in rural areas. Mary Breckinridge, a public-health nurse, returned to the United States after studying midwifery in England to establish the Frontier Nursing Service and Mary Breckinridge Hospital in 1928, and the Frontier Graduate School of Midwifery in 1939. The Frontier Nursing Service sent nurse-midwives traveling on horseback to serve the widely scattered rural population of eastern Kentucky. Breckinridge's success in lowering the death rate in childbirth contributed to the acceptance of nurse-midwives as a means of delivering

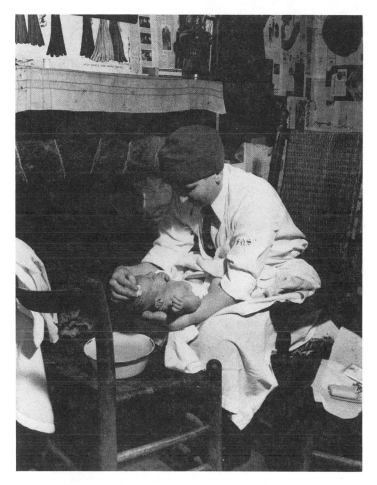

Nurse bathing an infant at Wendover, Frontier Nursing
Service Headquarters, Hyden, Kentucky. (Photograph
courtesy of Schlesinger Library, Radcliffe College)

health care at a manageable cost. One of her graduates set up a clinic in New
York in 1932, and midwifery education programs were established at other
sites during the 1950s. By 1976, there were approximately eighteen hundred
certified nurse-midwives in the United States.[29] Breckinridge built the Wendover Big House in 1925 to be the focal point of the Frontier Nursing Service;
this large two-and-a-half-story log building, located on a wooded hillside overlooking the Kentucky River about four miles outside of Hyden, Kentucky, has
been nominated for Historic Site status and still serves as a center for rural
health care.

Since the early nineteenth century teaching has also been an important profession for women. The founding of public schools during the 1820s created a new demand for teachers. School boards found they could pay women one-half to one-third the salaries of men, and so women educators became an economic imperative. By the end of the 1830s, one out of five native-born white women in Massachusetts had taught school for at least a short time. Reformers like Catharine Beecher promoted education as an appropriate task for women because of its domestic nature and involvement with children. The woman teacher, Beecher claimed, had a moral mission to contribute to the nation's advancement by teaching children "habits of neatness, order and thrift; opening the book of knowledge, inspiring the principles of morality, and awakening the hope of immortality."[30] By 1860, women made up 25 percent of the nation's teaching force; by 1880, 60 percent; and by 1910, 80 percent. Some of the schools which were established in the nineteenth century for training teachers later became women's colleges. After the Civil War, many African American women went south and found opportunities in teaching at freedman's schools. The nation's racially segregated school systems also created a demand for black teachers through the 1950s.[31]

Another profession to become feminized in the nineteenth century was librarianship. The first woman library clerk was hired at the Boston Public Library in 1852; by 1910 almost 80 percent of librarians were women. As public libraries proliferated during the last decades of the nineteenth century, women were welcomed into library work because they would work for relatively low salaries; because of the notion that women were preservers of culture, the work was considered suitable.[32]

Charity and social work were also identified as "social housekeeping" and therefore viewed as appropriate work for women. The field of social work has its roots in the social settlements that were established throughout the United States in the late nineteenth and early twentieth centuries. By 1900 nearly a hundred settlements, including Henry Street in New York (an NHL site) and Denison House in Boston, had been founded in poor immigrant neighborhoods, mostly by women. Typically settlement workers lived together in and used these houses as bases for social reform.

The most notable of these settlements was Hull House, founded by Jane Addams and Ellen Gates Starr in the west side of Chicago in 1889. Today the dining hall and main house—all that remain of the thirteen buildings which comprised the settlement in the early twentieth century—have NHL status and are visited by thousands yearly. Inside these now quiet red brick buildings, which front the modernistic campus of the University of Illinois at Chicago, are memorials which suggest the central role of the settlement to urban life a century ago when the surrounding neighborhood was a slum teeming with immigrants from around the world. In its heyday up to two thousand people visited the settlement daily, attending English language lessons, classes in Americanization and culture, and club meetings in a middle-class environment of walnut and mahogany furniture and fine art provided by the resident settlement workers. Although at this time women were still denied full participation in political life (they didn't receive the right to vote until 1920), they were able to shape social policy by working through the settlement houses on such issues as public sanitation, juvenile courts, playgrounds, and factory reform. The purpose of the social settlement was twofold. While providing important services for immigrants, the settlement house also provided an outlet for the energies of educated women. By 1920, nearly two-thirds of social and welfare workers were women.[33]

Women have been slower in making inroads into the professions of law, medicine, dentistry, and science. The first woman lawyer in the United States, Arabella Mansfield, was licensed by the Iowa bar in 1869 after studying with an established attorney. But many law schools still refused to admit women as students, one arguing that "women had not the mentality to study law." When Myra Bradwell was denied admission to the Illinois bar in 1870, she took her case to the U.S. Supreme Court, which ruled in 1873 that women's "delicacy and timidity" made them unfit "for many of the occupations of civil life." She was not admitted to the bar until 1890.[34] It would not be until the 1970s that the proportion of women as lawyers began to approach parity with men. As late as 1964, only 4 percent of first-year law students were women; by 1984, that proportion had increased tenfold.[35]

The field of medicine also resisted the participation of women. Elizabeth Blackwell, who in 1849 became the first woman to earn a medical degree, faced social ostracism and was at first barred from classroom demonstrations at Geneva Medical School, which had accepted her as a joke. Unable to secure a position after she graduated, she founded, with her sister Emily and Dr. Marie Zakrzewska, the New York Infirmary for Women and Children in 1857. In 1868, the Blackwell sisters established the Women's Medical College of New York, which they operated until Cornell University began to accept female medical students in 1899. Since that time, women have slowly increased their participation as doctors, growing to 17.6 percent of physicians by 1986.

Although the New York Infirmary is no longer standing, the New England Hospital for Women and Children, located in Roxbury, Massachusetts, and now known as the Dimock Community Health Center, serves as a reminder of the contributions of women to American medicine. Built at its present nine-acre site in 1872, the complex of eight major buildings is the oldest remaining example of the hospitals run by and for women during the late nineteenth and early twentieth centuries. These hospitals were founded by pioneering female physicians who, like Blackwell, encountered gender barriers in their profession and so chose to establish separate institutions for women where they could gain clinical experience and establish their careers. The New England Hospital reflects Marie Zakrzewska's desire to expand women's opportunities in medicine after her work with Blackwell in New York.[36]

One of the first woman dentists in the United States was Lucy Hobbs Taylor, who with her husband ran one of the largest dental practices in Kansas.

Refused admission to medical school, she was urged to pursue dentistry as a profession "more suitable to women." Denied admission to the Ohio College of Dental Surgery because of her sex, she nevertheless trained with a graduate of the college, and in 1865 reapplied and was admitted. When she was graduated the next year, Taylor became the first American woman to earn a dental degree. Moving to Lawrence, Kansas, she and her husband, James Taylor, for some twenty years resided in and practiced dentistry in what is now known as the Lucy Hobbs Taylor Building, listed on the National Register of Historic Places.[37]

Women fought hard to win acceptance in scientific careers. One nineteenth-century editor commented, "If an unfortunate female should happen to possess a lurking fondness for any special scientific pursuit she is careful (if of any social position) to hide it as she would some deformity."[38] But there were exceptions. One was Maria Mitchell, considered the first woman astronomer in the United States. For twenty years she worked at the Nantucket Atheneum and taught herself astronomy as she assisted her father in observing the night sky. On October 1, 1847, Mitchell discovered a new comet, which was named for her and won her worldwide fame. In 1850 she was elected to the American Academy of Arts and Sciences; it would be ninety-three years before another woman was so honored. In the early 1860s Mitchell joined the faculty of the new Vassar College and proved an excellent teacher, inspiring many of her students to follow in scientific careers. In 1873 Mitchell founded the Association for the Advancement of Women, supporting women in the professions, social service, and public life. Mitchell's home in Nantucket, Massachusetts, now a research center and museum, reveals much about her early life in a community which fostered independent women during the long periods when men were at sea. The Vassar College Observatory, built as a laboratory, classroom, and residence for Mitchell in 1865, has been nominated for landmark site status, for it represents her professional life as one of the nation's strongest advocates for the involvement of women in higher education and science.[39]

Aviation also has attracted women, although they were long discriminated against in this domain. The best-known aviator was Amelia Putnam Earhart, whose birthplace in Atchison, Kansas, is on the National Register of Historic Places in recognition of her accomplishments. In 1920 Earhart learned to fly with pioneer pilot Neta Snook and soon began to set women's records. In 1928, with two others, she crossed the Atlantic, achieving fame and the nickname "Lady Lindy." She became in 1929 the first president of the "Ninety-nines," an organization of women pilots. In 1932, Earhart became the first woman to fly the Atlantic alone and the first to make the crossing more than once. She was also the first person to fly nonstop across the continental United States. In 1937, Amelia Earhart attempted to fly around the world, but her plane was lost one hundred miles short of her destination. The Ninety-nines established near her childhood home an International Forest of Friendship,

Astronomy class with Maria Mitchell outside the Vassar College Observatory, Poughkeepsie, New York. (Photograph courtesy of Vassar College Archives)

planted with trees from around the United States and around the world, and including walking paths honoring contributions to aviation. In more recent years, women have participated in the American space program. In 1978, Sally Ride became the first American woman astronaut to leave earth's atmosphere; Kathryn Sullivan joined Ride on a *Challenger* mission in 1984 and then became the first woman to walk in space.[40]

Women were not officially part of the military until World War II. Before then, however, women participated in military life in a variety of ways. During the American Revolution women served as scouts, fundraisers, couriers, and cooks. One woman, Deborah Sampson, enlisted in the Continental Army under the name of Robert Shurtleff and was granted a war veteran's pension in 1792. During the Civil War, women participated as nurses, provisioners, and spies. At the time of World War I, some fifteen thousand women joined the Women's Land Army to provide farm labor for harvesting crops and tending livestock, and thousands more performed clerical and communications duties for the army in Europe. It was during the 1940s that women first achieved regular status in the military, as they participated in every activity short of combat. Over 350,000 women enlisted during World War II in the various branches of the American military, including the Women's Airforce Service Pilots, Women's Army Corps, and the WAVES of the Navy.[41]

We have seen that since colonial days individual women have succeeded as entrepreneurs. Despite social prejudice, these women—especially if they were widowed—found an alternative path for self-employment in the business world. In Coatesville, Pennsylvania, for example, Rebecca Pennock Lukens inherited upon the death of her husband in 1825 the struggling Brandywine Iron Works. Before a decade had passed she not only paid off the company's considerable debts but became the country's first woman ironmaster to turn a large profit. Lukens's belief that iron plate manufacturing was important on a national as well as local scale contributed to the building of railroads, ships, and factories during the nineteenth century. After her death, the company, now on the National Register of Historic Places, was renamed the Lukens Steel Company in her honor; by 1957 it was producing nearly six hundred thousand tons of steel annually.[42]

Another notable business leader was Maggie Lena Walker, daughter of a slave, who worked as a teacher, insurance agent, and leader of a fraternal organization before becoming the first American woman known to establish and head a bank. Her two-story, redbrick home in Richmond, Virginia, a National Historic Landmark and a unit of the National Park Service, contains historical

Interior of Brandywine Iron Works, ca. 1850s, Coatesville, Pennsylvania. Rebecca Lukens owned and managed the mill from 1825 to the early 1850s. (Photograph courtesy of Lukens Steel Company)

furnishings valuable to an understanding of the period during the first third of the century when she occupied the house. In 1903, Walker organized the Saint Luke Penny Savings Bank in Richmond, serving as president until 1930. She helped to reorganize it as the Consolidated Bank and Trust Company, the oldest continuously existing African American bank in the United States.[43] In recent years the number of women in business has accelerated rapidly. Between 1974 and 1984, the rate of self-employed women grew by 74 percent; by 1984 women owned about 20 percent of the small businesses in the United States.[44]

Although housework usually is not treated as employment for women, it is nevertheless a form of labor contributing to the economy. The role and status of the housewife has changed during the past three centuries, from the household manufacturer of colonial days to the domestic and maternal ideal of the nineteenth century and later. By the middle of the nineteenth century, writers attempted to redeem the image of housewifery by arguing that it was like a profession; the housewife, to succeed in her role, required knowledge of such sciences as hygiene, architecture, and economics. By the early twentieth century, a movement to elevate housework was reflected in the home economics movement, pioneered by women like Ellen Swallow Richards, first president of the Home Economics Association. Home economists suggested that the running of a successful home and even motherhood itself were scientific endeavors requiring study and the mastery of new techniques dictated by experts. New technologies and services, including gas, electricity, ready-made clothing, and various home appliances, lessened the burden of daily tasks and led to an emphasis on mothering and consumption as key dimensions of housewifery. One reflection of the social and economic value of housework is the tendency of contemporary working wives and mothers to purchase services that they no longer have time to perform themselves, such as cleaning, child care, and cooking. The changing domestic architecture of kitchens and other physical areas of the American house reflects these ideological shifts about the values and functions of housewifery.[45]

The movement of women into the paid labor force has been difficult. During the nineteenth century, a deep concern with the morality and living conditions of working girls was fed by an underlying anxiety about their fitness as future mothers and led to the establishment of supervised boarding homes by YWCAs, church groups, and other institutions, following the earlier model provided by the owners of the Lowell mills. Hundreds of thousands of young working women lived in these homes, which were meant to provide a substitute family environment conducive to their moral protection and the maintenance of social status. Many of these boardinghouses remain standing today, testimonies to social change. Additionally, efforts at unionization and such labor legislation as the minimum wage and maximum hour statutes passed before 1920 were fueled by a recognition that working conditions were not beneficial for women. This labor legislation materially improved conditions for many women workers but at the same time created restrictions and unequal treatment for others.

The needs of working mothers were not widely acknowledged until their numbers grew in the mid-twentieth century, and then day care and other policies, including part-time work, flexible hours, and home-based work, were seen as important consequences of women's employment. As mothers of very young children have gone to work, family policy issues have arisen on the federal and state levels and in the private business sector. Future historians may well find that building sites that include day-care centers reflect this trend in women's labor history.

Certain characteristics of the female labor force have persisted over time. First, the vast majority of women have historically worked in occupations where the proportion of workers who were women was much higher than in the general population. For example, in 1986, women comprised more than 95 percent of all child-care workers, dental assistants, and nurses, while they represented under 5 percent of airline pilots, carpenters, and dentists. Women have also been disproportionately represented in the fields of clerical work, elementary school teaching, librarianship, and social work—all occupations that became feminized in the nineteenth century. From 1900 through 1960, between 60 and 73 percent of employed women were in occupations where the majority of workers were female; up to half of these workers were in fields which were 80 percent or more female. By 1973, about half of all women workers were in clerical and service work, and more than half of all women professionals were teachers and nurses.[46]

Secondly, women have historically earned less than men in identical and comparable occupations, although the ratio of earnings has varied depending on year, region, and occupation. Occupations dominated by women have been the lowest paying. Generally, since 1963, women have earned about 60 percent of men's earnings. Before that time, the income gap was even greater.[47] Finally, most women have worked because they had to support themselves or their families, despite widely accepted assumptions that women worked for "pin money," which was nonessential for family maintenance.

Scholars now agree that the history of women is inextricably intertwined with the history of American labor. Historians are exploring new topics such as the work culture of women, the intersections between family life and employment, and the nature of work for women in various ethnic and racial groups. The interpretation of such tangible resources as work sites and residences can capture another dimension of women's labor history and reflect the richness and diversity of women's experiences. The understanding of America's past in general is enhanced by recognizing the complex and dynamic history of the American woman worker, for it is a history with profound and continuing consequences for all of American society.

NOTES

1. Sarah E. Rix, ed., *The American Woman, 1988–89: A Status Report* (New York: W. W. Norton, 1988), 338–39; Lynn Y. Weiner, *From Working Girl to Working Mother: The Female Labor Force in the United States, 1820–1980* (Chapel Hill: University of North Carolina Press, 1985), 4.

2. Sara M. Evans, *Born for Liberty: A History of Women in America* (New York: The Free Press, 1989), 7–20; Barbara Mayer Wertheimer, *We Were There: The Story of Working Women in America* (New York: Pantheon Books, 1977), 4–5.

3. Alice Kessler-Harris, *Out to Work: A History of Wage-Earning Women in the United States* (New York: Oxford University Press, 1982), 7. See also Laurel Thatcher Ulrich, *Good Wives: Image and Reality in the Lives of Women in Northern New England, 1650–1750* (New York: Alfred A. Knopf, 1982).

4. Wertheimer, *We Were There*, 13–18; Edward James, ed., *Notable American Women* (Cambridge: Harvard University Press, 1971), vol. 3, 61–62; vol. 1, 236–37.

5. On domestic service see Faye E. Dudden, *Serving Women: Household Service in Nineteenth-Century America* (Middletown, Conn.; Wesleyan University Press, 1983), and David Katzman, *Seven Days a Week: Domestic Service in Industrializing America* (New York: Oxford University Press, 1978).

6. Cited in Deborah Gray White, *Ar'n't I a Woman? Female Slaves in the Plantation South* (New York: W. W. Norton, 1985), 120.

7. Ibid. Jacqueline Jones, *Labor of Love, Labor of Sorrow: Black Women, Work, and the Family, from Slavery to the Present* (New York: Vintage Books, 1985).

8. Marian Tinling, *Women Remembered: A Guide to Landmarks of Women's History in the United States* (New York: Greenwood Press, 1986), 173–74; Charles Reagan Wilson and William Ferris, eds., *Encyclopedia of Southern Culture* (Chapel Hill: University of North Carolina Press, 1989), 142.

9. On the Lowell mill girls, see Thomas Dublin, *Women at Work: The Transformation of Work and Community in Lowell, Massachusetts, 1826–1860* (New York: Columbia University Press, 1979); Evans, *Born for Liberty*, 82–84.

10. Wertheimer, *We Were There*, 118–19.

11. Dolores E. Janiewski, *Sisterhood Denied: Race, Gender and Class in a New South Community* (Philadelphia: Temple University Press, 1985), 100–101; Jacqueline Dowd Hall et al., *Like a Family: The Making of a Southern Cotton Mill World* (Chapel Hill: University of North Carolina Press, 1987), 52.

12. Wertheimer, *We Were There*, 309–15; Corinne J. Naden, *The Triangle Shirtwaist Fire, March 25, 1911: The Blaze That Changed an Industry* (New York: Franklin Watts, 1971), 8–9.

13. Ruth Milkman, *Gender at Work: The Dynamics of Job Segregation by Sex during World War II* (Urbana: University of Illinois Press, 1987), 61.

14. Susan M. Hartmann, *The Home Front and Beyond: American Women in the 1940s* (Boston: Twayne Publishers, 1982), chaps. 4–5; Weiner, *From Working Girl to Working Mother*, 135.

15. Wertheimer, *We Were There*, 67, 182–91.

16. Ibid., 274–81; Kessler-Harris, *Out to Work*, chap. 6.

17. Wertheimer, *We Were There*, 342–51.

18. See Vicki Ruiz, *Cannery Women, Cannery Lives: Mexican Women, Unionization, and the California Food Processing Industry, 1930–1950* (Albuquerque: University of New Mexico Press, 1987).

19. Weiner, *From Working Girl to Working Mother*, 67; Rix, *The American Woman, 1987–88*, 233; Ruth Milkman, "Women Workers, Feminism, and the Labor

Movement since the 1960s," in Ruth Milkman, ed., *Women, Work and Protest: A Century of U.S. Women's Labor History* (Boston: Routledge & Kegan Paul, 1985), 301.

20. Elinore Pruitt Stewart, *Letters of a Woman Homesteader* (Lincoln: University of Nebraska Press, 1961); Lillian Schlissel, *Women's Diaries of the Westward Journey* (New York: Schocken Books, 1982), 156; Sandra L. Myres, *Westering Women and the Frontier Experience 1800–1915* (Albuquerque: University of New Mexico Press, 1982), 258.

21. Tinling, *Women Remembered*, 272.

22. Kathryn Koutsky Cohen, "Rika's—An Historic Roadhouse Park on the Richardson Trail," in *Transportation in Alaska's Past* (Alaska Historical Society, 1982), 140–57; Myres, *Westering Women*, 243–45, 259–61.

23. Evans, *Born for Liberty*, 106; Barbara Meil Hobson, *Uneasy Virtue: The Politics of Prostitution and the American Reform Tradition* (New York: Basic Books, 1987), 26; *Encyclopedia of Southern Culture*, 225–26.

24. Susan Porter Benson, *Counter Cultures: Saleswomen, Managers, and Customers in American Department Stores, 1890–1940* (Urbana: University of Illinois Press, 1986), chap. 1.

25. Cindy Sondik Aron, *Ladies and Gentlemen of the Civil Service: Middle-Class Workers in Victorian America* (New York: Oxford University Press, 1987); Margery W. Davies, *Woman's Place Is at the Typewriter: Office Work and Office Workers, 1870–1930* (Philadelphia: Temple University Press); Rix, *The American Woman, 1987–88*, 309.

26. Lois Banner, *American Beauty* (New York: Knopf, 1983), 271.

27. James, *Notable American Women*, vol. 3, 533–35; A'Lelia Perry Bundles, "Madame C. J. Walker: Cosmetics Tycoon," *Ms.* (July 1983): 91–94; Tinling, *Women Remembered*, 493.

28. Susan Reverby, *Ordered to Care: The Dilemma of American Nursing, 1850–1945* (New York: Cambridge University Press, 1988); Barbara Melosh, *The Physicians Hand: Work Culture and Conflict in American Nursing* (Philadelphia: Temple University Press, 1982); Evans, *Born for Liberty*, 141–42; Tinling, *Women Remembered*, 351.

29. Barbara Katz Rothman, *In Labor: Women and Power in the Birthplace* (New York: W. W. Norton, 1982), chap. 2; *Encyclopedia of Southern Culture*, 1364–65; Mary Breckinridge, *Wide Neighborhoods, A Story of the Frontier Nursing Service* (New York: Harper and Brothers, 1972).

30. Kathryn Kish Sklar, *Catharine Beecher: A Study in American Domesticity* (New Haven: Yale University Press, 1973), 174; Sklar, "The Founding of Mount Holyoke College," in Carol Berkin and Mary Beth Norton, eds., *Women of America: A History* (Boston: Houghton Mifflin, 1979), 181.

31. Glenda Riley, *Inventing the American Woman* (Arlington Heights, Ill.: Harlan Davidson, 1986), vol. 1, 130. See also Dorothy Sterling, ed., *We Are Your Sisters: Black Women in the Nineteenth Century* (New York: W. W. Norton, 1984), chap. 16.

32. Dee Garrison, "The Tender Technicians: The Feminization of Public Librarianship, 1876–1905," in Mary Hartman and Lois Banner, eds., *Clio's Consciousness Raised: New Perspectives on the History of Women* (New York: Harper and Row, 1974), 158–78.

33. Kathryn Kish Sklar, "Hull House in the 1890s: A Community of Women Reformers," *Signs* 10, no. 41 (1985): 658–77; Sheila Rothman, *Woman's Proper Place: A History of Changing Ideals and Practices, 1870 to the Present* (New York: Basic Books, 1978), 112–20; Kessler-Harris, *Out to Work*, 116. For a rare description of a settlement

house by one of its patrons, see Hilda Satt Polacheck, *I Came a Stranger: The Story of a Hull-House Girl*, ed., Dena J. Polacheck Epstein (Urbana: University of Illinois Press, 1989), part III.

34. Lois Banner, *Women in Modern America* (New York: Harcourt, Brace, Jovanovich, 1974), 35; Nancy Woloch, *Women and the American Experience* (New York: Alfred Knopf, 1984), 284.

35. Rix, *The American Woman, 1988–89*, 61.

36. Ibid.; Mary Roth Walsh, *Doctors Wanted: No Women Need Apply* (New Haven: Yale University Press, 1977); James, *Notable American Women*, vol. 1, 161–65; see also Gail Lee Dubrow's interpretation of the site on the National Park Service registration form for the New England Hospital for Women and Children (April 1990).

37. James, *Notable American Women*, vol. 3, 433–34.

38. Cited in Riley, *Inventing the American Woman*, vol. 1, 133.

39. Ibid. See also Margaret W. Rossiter, *Women Scientists in America: Struggles and Strategies to 1940* (Baltimore: Johns Hopkins University Press, 1982); Tinling, *Women Remembered*, 61–62.

40. Judith Lomax, *Women of the Air* (New York: Ivy Books, 1987); Tinling, *Women Remembered*, 511–12.

41. Hartmann, *The Home Front and Beyond*, chap. 3; Rix, *The American Woman, 1987–88*, 202; Riley, *Inventing the American Woman*, vol. 1, 41.

42. Riley, *Inventing the American Woman*, vol. 1, 70; James, *Notable American Women*, vol. 2, 442–43.

43. James, *Notable American Women*, vol. 3, 530–31; *Encyclopedia of Southern Culture*, 1588–89.

44. Rix, *The American Woman, 1987–88*, 197–201.

45. On the history of housework, see Susan Strasser, *Never Done: A History of American Housework* (New York: Pantheon Books, 1982), and Glenna Matthews, *'Just a Housewife': The Rise and Fall of Domesticity in America* (New York: Oxford University Press, 1987).

46. Evans, *Born for Liberty*, 303; Valerie Kincade Oppenheimer, *The Female Labor Force in the United States* (Berkeley: University of California Press, 1970), 70.

47. Rix, *The American Woman, 1988–89*, 382; Rix, *The American Woman, 1987–88*, 124–25.

CONTRIBUTORS

GAIL LEE DUBROW is Assistant Professor of Urban Design and Planning and Director of the Historic Preservation Planning and Design Program at the University of Washington. Her dissertation, "Preserving Her Heritage: American Landmarks of Women's History," which focused on integrating new scholarship in women's history into historic preservation planning, won the Mary Wollstonecraft Prize from UCLA's Center for Research on Women.

JOAN HOFF, Professor of History at Indiana University, is former Executive Secretary of the Organization of American Historians. Her work focuses on twentieth-century U.S. foreign policy and politics and the legal status of U.S. women. She is the author of books and articles on Herbert Hoover, Eleanor Roosevelt, and Richard Nixon. Her most recent work is *Law, Gender, and Injustice: A Legal History of U.S. Women.*

HELEN LEFKOWITZ HOROWITZ is Professor of History and American Studies at Smith College. The author of *Culture and the City, Alma Mater,* and *Campus Life,* she is completing a biography of M. Carey Thomas, college president and feminist.

BARBARA J. HOWE is an Associate Professor of History at West Virginia University, where she directs the public history program and teaches American women's history. She has been active in several women's history projects in West Virginia and has published work on women's organizations and women in historic preservation. She is the coeditor of *Public History: An Introduction.*

BARBARA MELOSH, Associate Professor of English and American Studies at George Mason University, has also been curator of Medical Sciences at the National Museum of American History, Smithsonian Institution. Her recent publications include "Speaking of Women: Museums' Representations of Women's History," in *History Museums in the United States,* and *Engendering Culture: Manhood and Womanhood in New Deal Public Art and Theater.*

PAGE PUTNAM MILLER is the director of the National Coordinating Committee for the Promotion of History, a national advocacy office supported by fifty historical and archival organizations. In addition to writing regularly on legislative issues for several historical association publications, Miller testifies frequently before congressional committees on federal information policy, access to federal records of historical value, and preservation and interpretation of cultural resources.

JEAN R. SODERLUND, Associate Professor of History at the University of Maryland, is the author of *Quakers and Slavery: A Divided Spirit* and coauthor of *Freedom by Degrees: Emancipation in Pennsylvania and Its Aftermath.*

LYNN Y. WEINER, Associate Professor of History at Roosevelt University, is the author of *From Working Girl to Working Mother: The Female Labor Force in the United States, 1820–1980.* Her current project is a study of working mothers and the changing culture of family life in the twentieth-century United States.

INDEX